Gender

transitions

General Editor: Julian Wolfreys

Published Titles

BATAILLE Fred Botting and Scott Wilson
NEW HISTORICISM AND CULTURAL MATERIALISM John Brannigan
GENDER Claire Colebrook
POSTMODERN NARRATIVE THEORY Mark Currie
FORMALIST CRITICISM AND READER-RESPONSE THEORY
    Todd F. Davis and Kenneth Womack
IDEOLOGY James M. Decker
QUEER THEORIES Donald E. Hall
MARXIST LITERARY AND CULTURAL THEORIES Moyra Haslett
LOUIS ALTHUSSER Warren Montag
RACE Brian Niro
JACQUES LACAN Jean-Michel Rabaté
LITERARY FEMINISMS Ruth Robbins
DECONSTRUCTION•DERRIDA Julian Wolfreys
ORWELL TO THE PRESENT: LITERATURE IN ENGLAND, 1945–2000
    John Brannigan
FROM CHAUCER TO SHAKESPEARE, 1337–1580 SunHee Kim Gertz
MODERNISM, 1910–1945 Jane Goldman
POPE TO BURNEY, 1714–1779 Moyra Haslett
PATER TO FORSTER, 1873–1924 Ruth Robbins
BURKE TO BYRON, BARBAULD TO BAILLIE, 1790–1830 Jane Stabler
FROM MILTON TO POPE, 1650–1720 Kay Gilliland Stevenson
SIDNEY TO MILTON, 1580–1660 Marion Wynne-Davies

Forthcoming Titles

TERRY EAGLETON David Alderson
JULIA KRISTEVA AND LITERARY THEORY Megan Becker-Leckrone
NATIONAL IDENTITY John Brannigan
HÉLÈNE CIXOUS: WRITING AND SEXUAL DIFFERENCE Abigail Bray
HOMI BHABHA Eleanor Byrne
POSTMODERNISM•POSTMODERNITY Martin McQuillan
ROLAND BARTHES Martin McQuillan
PSYCHOANALYSIS AND LITERATURE Nicholas Rand
SUBJECTIVITY Ruth Robbins
POSTCOLONIAL THEORY Malini Johan Schueller
TRANSGRESSION Julian Wolfreys
DICKENS TO HARDY, 1837–1884 Julian Wolfreys

**Transitions
Series Standing Order
ISBN 0–333–73684–6**
(*outside North America only*)

You can receive future titles in this series as they are published by
placing a standing order. Please contact your bookseller or, in case of
difficulty, write to us at the address below with your name and address,
the title of the series and the ISBN quoted above.

Customer Services Department, Palgrave Distribution Ltd
Houndmills, Basingstoke, Hampshire RG21 6XS, England

transitions

Gender

Claire Colebrook

palgrave
macmillan

First published 2004 by
PALGRAVE MACMILLAN
Houndmills, Basingstoke, Hampshire RG21 6XS and
175 Fifth Avenue, New York, N.Y. 10010
Companies and representatives throughout the world

PALGRAVE MACMILLAN is the global academic imprint of the Palgrave
Macmillan division of St. Martin's Press, LLC and of Palgrave Macmillan Ltd.
Macmillan® is a registered trademark in the United States, United Kingdom
and other countries. Palgrave is a registered trademark in the European
Union and other countries.

ISBN 0–333–99457–4 hardback
ISBN 0–333–99458–2 paperback

This book is printed on paper suitable for recycling and made from fully
managed and sustained forest sources.

A catalogue record for this book is available from the British Library.

Library of Congress Cataloging-in-Publication Data
Colebrook, Claire.
   Gender / Claire Colebrook.
      p.   cm. — (Transitions)
   Includes bibliographical references and index.
   ISBN 0–333–99457–4 (cloth) — ISBN 0–333–99458–2 (pbk.)
   1. Feminist theory.   2. Gender identity.   3. Sex—Philosophy.   4. Sexual
   orientation.   5. Gender identity in literature.   I. Title.   II. Transitions
   (Palgrave Macmillan (Firm))

   HQ1190.C653 2004
   305.42'01—dc21

                                                             2003054922

10   9   8   7   6   5   4   3   2   1
13   12   11   10   09   08   07   06   05   04

Printed in China

Contents

General Editor's Preface   vii
Acknowledgements   ix

1. Gender before Modernity   1
   * Gender and polarity   4
   * Nature/culture: Sex/gender   9
   * What sort of difference is gender difference?   11
   * Essence and gender   15
   * The gender of souls   18
   * Matter and the realisation of gender   24
   * Gender without sex   26
   * *A Midsummer Night's Dream*   29

2. Gender as Form and the Masculinity of Reason   40
   * The gender of form and reason   50
   * Deconstruction   54
   * Binaries of reason and gender: Genevieve Lloyd   58
   * *Paradise Lost*   62

3. Modernity and the Materiality of Gender   76
   * Sex and matter: Modern empiricism and liberalism   76
   * Third-wave feminism: Reality and essence   82
   * Subjectivity, ideas and experience   88
   * Man and modern subjectivity   93
   * Modern science and mathematics   97
   * Patriarchy   104
   * Patriarchy and the sexual contract: Carole Pateman   109

4. Sex without Gender   117
   * First-wave feminism and the sex/gender distinction   117
   * Enlightenment feminism   119
   * Marriage and gender harmony   123

- Second-wave feminism and difference   126
- Psychoanalytic feminism   135
- The Oedipal production of gender   137

5. Beyond Sex and Gender   145
   - Third-wave feminism   145
   - Difference before sex and gender   147
   - Lacan and the subject of signification   152
   - Levi-Strauss and the exchange of women   160

6. Sexual Difference and Embodiment   192
   - Lacan, negativity and desire   192
   - The body   194
   - Luce Irigaray and the positive feminine   198

7. Sexuality and Queer Theory   206
   - Michel Foucault and the history of sexuality   206
   - Performativity   211
   - Volatile bodies   215
   - Queer theory and the critique of gender: Butler,
     Sedgwick, Edelman and Bersani   228
   - Moira Gatens and the critique of gender   234

Conclusion: Reading Gender   239
   - *Frankenstein*   239
   - First-wave feminist and humanist reading   239
   - Second-wave or radical feminist readings   240
   - Third-wave feminist readings   241
   - Reading gender   243

Annotated Bibliography   253
Bibliography   258
Index   272

General Editor's Preface

Transitions: *transition-em*, n. of action. 1. A passing or passage from one condition, action or (rarely) place, to another. 2. Passage in thought, speech, or writing, from one subject to another. 3. **a**. The passing from one note to another **b**. The passing from one key to another, modulation. 4. The passage from an earlier to a later stage of development or formation…change from an earlier style to a later; a style of intermediate or mixed character…the historical passage of language from one well-defined stage to another.

The aim of *Transitions* is to explore passages and movements in critical thought, and in the development of literary and cultural interpretation. This series also seeks to examine the possibilities for reading, analysis, and other critical engagements which the very idea of transition makes possible. The writers in this series unfold the movements and modulations of critical thinking over the last generation, from the first emergences of what is now recognised as literary theory. They examine as well how the transitional nature of theoretical and critical thinking is still very much in operation, guaranteed by the hybridity and heterogeneity of the field of literary studies. The authors in the series share the common understanding that, now more than ever, critical thought is both in a state of transition and can best be defined by developing for the student reader an understanding of this protean quality.

This series desires, then, to enable the reader to transform her/his own reading and writing transactions by comprehending past developments. Each book in the series offers a guide to the poetics and politics of interpretative paradigms, schools, and bodies of thought, while transforming these, if not into tools or methodologies, then into conduits for directing and channelling thought. As well as transforming the critical past by interpreting it from the perspective of the present day, each study enacts transitional readings of a number of well-known literary texts, all of which are themselves conceivable as having been transitional texts at the moments of their first appearance. The readings offered in these books seek, through close critical reading and theoretical engagement, to demonstrate certain possibilities in critical reading and theoretical engagement, to demonstrate certain possibilities in critical thinking to the student reader.

It is hoped that the student will find this series liberating because rigid methodologies are not being put into place. As all the dictionary definitions of the idea of transition above suggest, what is important is the action, the passage: of thought, of analysis, of critical response. Rather than seeking to help you locate yourself in relation to any particular school or discipline, this series aims to put you into action, as readers and writers, travellers between positions, where the movement between poles comes to be seen as of more importance than the locations themselves.

Julian Wolfreys

Acknowledgements

I would like to thank Julian Wolfreys for his encouragement and thoughtful suggestions. I am also extremely grateful to Jane Goldman for her comments, advice and intelligent feedback.

1 Gender before Modernity

We might think that a concern with gender is a peculiarly modern and Western phenomenon – that it is only with the advent of feminism and the demand for equal rights that we start to think about gender, sexual difference or the relation between male and female. Popular books such as *Men are from Mars Women are from Venus* (Gray 1992) seem to announce gender difference as a revolutionary discovery: unified humanism is declared to be a myth, for there are basically two kinds of humans. But nothing could be further from the truth than the idea that gender is a new and revolutionary preoccupation. The earliest myths of Western and other cultures usually concern the interaction of male and female genders (Bourdieu 2001). We say *gender* here and not 'sex' because the primary contrary in mythic accounts is not that between a male and female body, but between two polarities, tendencies or principles – two *kinds* or modes. The interaction and dynamism from which creation emerges is figured in terms of male and female (King 1994), with men's and women's bodies being the outcome of an original relation of contraries. From the pre-Socratics and Plato to Freud and New Age philosophy the concept of gender has been inextricably intertwined with questions regarding the generation or genesis of the universe. The opposition between masculine and feminine extends far beyond the relation between men and women. Life, in general, is frequently explained through the interaction of two principles – male and female – with actual men and women being expressions of an underlying, universal and cosmic harmony.

Gender is, therefore, one of the most common figures for thinking the basic differences or difference from which all life emerges. In both contemporary and ancient cultures the image of marriage or copulation is often used to describe processes of creation and social harmony. The English Romantic poet, William Wordsworth, described the writing of poetry as 'spousal'; the poet's mind marries nature in order to create verse as a form of divine offspring or 'great consummation' (Wordsworth [1814] 1969, 590). Many generation stories present a formless female matter impregnated by an active male power. In the Christian creation myth it is God as word, light and form who is male, giving life to darkness and chaos. In most creation stories this passive darkness and chaos is presented as feminine and is clearly opposed to the masculine power of light and form. Even when the metaphor of marriage is not used, or is not explicit, social, political and cosmic harmonies are frequently depicted as a relation between male and female. William Blake ended his great prophecy *Jerusalem* with the reunification of the male spirit with his female emanation (Blake 1988, 258), while twentieth-century feminists frequently argued that the retrieval of female qualities would be crucial for the salvation of humanity. Gender, or the very notion of distinct male and female kinds has a long and complicated history, ranging well beyond relations between men and women. In fact, it is the modern understanding of two biological *sexes* which tends to reduce the complexity of the concept of gender to the relation between men and women.

The concept of maleness and femaleness as primarily sexual and biological is a relatively modern notion. Indeed, the very concept of 'biology,' as a body of brute matter without form or spirit only occurred with the development of science and medicine. According to Jean-Pierre Vernant, the ancient Greeks did not have a distinct word for 'body' as we know it today; the word 'soma' could only refer to a corpse, not a living body (Vernant 1990). Not only was there no sense of a separate body or sexuality before culture, the image of gender was charged with a cosmological significance. Male and female principles were used to explain the ultimate forces of the cosmos, with the very generation of the universe often being explained as a result of the encounter between masculine and feminine forces. Today, we think of male and female as qualities determined by physical aspects, such as genes, whereas pre-moderns thought of gender as two opposing principles or modes. Gender was not so much physical and material, as *formal* – to do with the way something interacts, relates and positions itself. Masculinity, in general was active and life-giving, while femininity was passive and receptive. Gender could, therefore, be used to explain and describe creative processes well beyond human bodies – everything from the interaction of life forces, to nature and politics. Before modern science defined the genetic and anatomical differences between sexes, Western thought had defined some of its most basic notions – including being and non-being – through the image of gender.

According to the twentieth-century French feminist, Simone de Beauvoir, *the* most basic category of human thought is the relation between self and other; without a notion of an otherness *against which* the self is defined, there could be no experience, no sense of distinct selfhood. And for Beauvoir and many other feminists, it is woman who has always been used to represent the Other (Beauvoir 1972, 29). While other historically formed categories also take on this function – Beauvoir cites anti-Semitism, racism and class antagonisms that produce various Others – woman is the exemplary Other: not a self so much as an inert being against which active selfhood is defined (19). Beauvoir's criticism of the traditional understanding of woman as the Other raises a fundamental question in the consideration of gender: to what extent has the distinction between man and woman been used to explain fundamental and transcendental structures of thinking? Beauvoir draws attention to the ways in which the myth and ideal of femininity has been essential to a certain understanding of life. For Beauvoir, one can only begin to think about women's rights and the political situation of women, once one has addressed the ideals of gender that underpin our thinking – the ways in which we think of the subject in opposition to Otherness. We will return to de Beauvoir's radical form of feminism later. What needs to be noted here is the *metaphysical* status of gender. The opposition between male and female goes beyond the politics of women's rights and concerns just how we understand what it is to be a self, and what it is to *be*.

Beauvoir argued that human beings, in contrast to animal life, were defined by their capacity to be self-creating and active. Whereas everything that is not human simply 'is' in itself, humans have the capacity to create what they are, or to exist *for themselves*. But if this is so, if this is what it means to *be*, then women have been deprived of being. For women, traditionally, are seen as physical objects of beauty, as bearers of children and as domestic labourers who live their lives not through their own self-created ideals, but through the man who represents active humanity for them. Women are therefore Other than human; they are associated with that fixed and bodily being against which male subjects define themselves. Beauvoir's story of woman as the Other lies at the end of a long tradition that contrasts an active masculine creativity with a passive feminine receptivity. Beauvoir assumes the classic opposition between active male subjectivity and passive female materiality, and she accepts that men and women do, indeed, fall into this opposition. Unlike those before her, though, Beauvoir suggests that we challenge this *myth* of gender. What makes Beauvoir typically modern is her parcelling out of male activity and female passivity between the bodies of men and women. It is men, Beauvoir argues, who have the opportunity to exist for, and define, themselves; women's biological conditions of childbirth, menstruation and physical subjection preclude them from active self-formation. Like most contemporary feminists, Beauvoir explains the relation of male and female – and our intuition of radical otherness – from men's and women's bodies. Beauvoir does not assume that there is something like maleness or femaleness prior to the existence and relation of concrete men and women.

Gender and polarity

Whereas contemporary feminists and political theorists explain sexual politics from the capacities of men's and women's bodies, in premodern cultures the distinction between active and passive masculine and feminine principles was understood in a far more general way: both as a way of understanding life in general and as a way of explaining the process of life within each human body. Plato's *Timaeus* likened the active forming power of the world to the father and the formless passive receptacle to the mother (Plato 1963, 1177 [50d–f]). The *Timaeus* was a 'poetic' explanation of the universe, which made explicit its reliance on metaphors and figures. Plato insists that the abstract processes of creation and origination can only be understood by analogy, through concrete figures. But it was this very distinction – between pure intellect and the material figures or metaphors – that was itself made possible through the idea of gender. Only with the image or figure of male and female principles was it possible to describe or explain the opposition between mind and matter, or concept and figure. Mind was always thought of as the disembodied, universal, conceptual and intellectual side of a binary, with the contrary side of particularity, materiality, and embodiment being associated with a feminine and secondary dependency. In ancient Greek thought, it was the intellect that was associated with a pure, active, disembodied, masculine and form-giving power. Body or matter was the material and female stuff, which the intellectual power *used* in order to actualise or give form to itself. Plato's dialogues frequently make a contrast between the creations of reason, which are disembodied, eternal and self-sufficient, and the creations of bodies, which are temporal, corruptible and dependent. Plato described the sensual world we experience as a secondary copy of the eternal world of forms, and he used the metaphor of gender to make this distinction. Forms are like the father – a principle that gives shape and existence – while matter is like the mother, a body that receives the power of creation from outside, and cannot produce without this infusion of life.

For Plato, and Aristotle after him, what has true reality are the forms or kinds, the distinct existences that allow each thing to have a specific identity; matter is merely the vehicle or passive recipient of form. While Plato and Aristotle privileged form over matter, they did so through a hierarchical relation between two kinds or genders: the distinction between active male form and receptive female matter. For Aristotle, matter strives towards the form it ought to have 'as the female desires the male' (Aristotle 1995, 328 [*Physics* 192a 23]). We could say then that the very theory of distinct forms and kinds – the theory of the true being of forms over against the mere matter in which they are instantiated – already relied on a distinction between male and female. For the very nature of the universe was explained according to a fundamental opposition and hierarchy: form gives being to matter, and form is the active and masculine fathering principle, which gives life to the inert material and maternal body. In the long history of science that stretches from ancient Greece to the twentieth century, the basic structure of the universe was defined according to abstract principles of attraction and repulsion, or positive and negative (Lloyd 1966, 38). Science has drawn upon a series of binary opposites that have, more often than not, been likened to the relation between male and female. Recent attempts to escape such a binary or dualist way of thinking in science have, today, often tried to do so through a reconfiguration of gender. How would science look if we abandoned the fundamental male–female binary that opposes form to matter, active to passive or solid to fluid (Hayles 1993; Shulman 1996, 442)? Whether such a project is desirable or possible is one of the key questions in the concept of gender: is thought necessarily structured by oppositions? And to what extent is the opposition of gender – the difference between male and female – an opposition that structures all other oppositions? By looking at the ways in which the male–female binary has underpinned some of the most fundamental arguments of metaphysics we can see both how historically persistent the gender binary is, and how the meaning of this binary has also shifted radically.

One of the main differences in the understanding of genders between our own biologically oriented understanding and that of the past lies in the primacy given to kinds or forms. For both Aristotle and Plato, the world we see and live in is one of change and generation, but the kinds or forms taken on by that world are unchanging. Kinds or identities neither evolve, nor do they pass away or come into being. The world just has the number of complete kinds that it has (Owen 1986, 159). Indeed, the cosmos is a balanced and unified whole, where each kind has its determined relation to other kinds. Sexual activity or generation was merely the way in which forms came into being. And everything that is going through change is either achieving a form that it lacks but ought to have, or it is falling away from or corrupting the form that makes it what it is and ought to be (Aristotle 1995, 322 [*Physics* 188b 20]). Aristotle explained the world as a unity of forms achieved through production and privation, with the sexual difference of specific bodies – the distinction between male and female – as a means for maintaining permanent kinds (Bostock 1982, 183). We see a world of change and becoming, with bodies coming into being and dying. But the forms or kinds of the world remain the same, and remain harmoniously balanced (Cooper 1982, 202). Sexual reproduction allows the world to remain the same – to be populated with the same kinds despite the birth and death of particular bodies. Behind sexual difference, then, was a harmonious order of being. All becoming for Aristotle could be reduced to a relation between form and privation, between something positively taking on a quality and something not having that quality. Form and privation were, in turn, likened to maleness and femaleness: the male is that which gives form and allows something to be, the female is that which lacks form, must take on form, and must come to be. Maleness and femaleness could therefore be considered literally – as the sexual difference of bodies in generation – and figuratively – as two principles, principles that were *metaphysical* or capable of explaining the physical.

By making gender a metaphysical principle Plato and Aristotle were both reacting against and extending a tendency of early Greek thought. Most, if not all, cultures, as anthropologists have noted, explain the world through opposing principles of maleness and femaleness (Bourdieu 2001; Ortner 1974). Such principles are *metaphysical* because they do not refer to male and female physical bodies, but to opposing tendencies. Plato and Aristotle were themselves drawing on an earlier tradition of thinking that was mythic rather than logical. Rather than form and privation – abstract principles which were *likened* to male and female – earlier thinkers had defined the universe as the production of opposing natural forces, such as heat and cold, high and low, male and female, dry and moist. With Plato and Aristotle, however, there was an attempt to free thought from myth and explain categories logically, without relying on already existing images or bodies. By grounding the world on a logical order Plato established the priority of form and reason. The world was not a natural plane of competing forces, likened to or analogous to male and female, the world expressed a law or logic of pure principles which could be *compared* to male and female. As Martin Heidegger has noted, this primacy of logic allows actual bodies and experience to be grounded on some prior and always present order (Heidegger 1998, 213). Luce Irigaray, following Heidegger, extends this observation to note that the supposed primacy of form and logic and its elevation above actual bodies, itself reflects a gendered opposition (Irigaray 1985, 182). Western reason defines itself as other than any natural, physical or finite body, and in so doing devalues the process of natural and maternal birth. Maternal generation is seen as dependent upon and expressive of an eternal and rational order. Gender becomes a metaphor, figure or image to explain a purely logical process. Plato and Aristotle – in insisting that the forming of the world was only *like* the male creative body – sought to find a universal, disembodied and scientific position from which differences could be explained.

Like later scientists who tried to explain the makeup of the world through the attraction and repulsion of forces, the ancient Greek attempt to explain the genesis of the world through a pure and abstract opposition set itself against any understanding of the world as literally made up of male and female contraries. Indeed, Western philosophy begins with a rejection of mythic oppositions and tries to establish *what is* – the basic substance that exists and remains present before all opposition. All the oppositions and kinds that make up the world should not simply be accepted, but should be explained from some grounding principle (Solmsen 1950). On the one hand, then, Western metaphysics began with the refusal of a mythic story of generation and asked the question of being: what does it mean for something to be? What exists as the fundamental and self-sufficient presence before all difference and becoming? On the other hand, this rejection of myths of cosmic generation from male and female force itself had to use gender as a metaphor. Philosophy must be about what exists in itself; it must not rely on received figures distinctions, metaphors and borrowed images. Philosophy must be self-fathering, active, purely intellectual and disembodied (Derrida 1981, 76). It must reject the dependent, the changing, the material and all imposed or received ideas. In this process of self-justification or reason, philosophy must account for the genesis of the world, and it must do so by explaining – rather than just accepting – the differentiated world. Both Plato and Aristotle therefore set themselves a task that has dominated the history of gender: how does the difference of gender emerge? What is the basis or origin of difference? What is the substance or being that underlies the change and opposition of genders? Instead of accepting the myth or image of gender – the world as composed of oppositions and polarities – philosophers from Plato onwards have aimed to account for the emergence of gender. How is it that we see a world of different kinds? And why are these differences oppositional and frequently explained as male and female?

What Plato and Aristotle did *not* consider was a world that was form-less, and that then received forms or differences by the acts of human language and culture. Until relatively recently – at least until the seventeenth century – our knowledge of the world was seen to lie in the grasping of distinct essences or forms. The world of change and differ-ence was underpinned by essential distinctions and differences, which perception and knowledge could grasp with varying degrees of accur-acy. The human knower was situated in a world with its own order, and it was the essence of human reason to be able to discern the forms or essences that structured the world (Foucault 1970, 37). All this changes in modernity with the separation of the subject. In the eight-eenth century Bishop George Berkeley, for example, argued that colours we perceive are only real for our perception; the world itself is not coloured (Berkeley [1710] 1965). Much more recently, structural-ists, pragmatists and social constructivists have insisted that the world itself has no truth or logic; meanings and differences are imposed upon the world by experience. The idea of the human self as a *subject* who, to use Beauvoir's terminology, creates the meaning of their world by actively deciding their own existence, could have no place in a pre-modern world where forms or kinds were the only stable reality.

The idea that forms or differences are *imposed* on the world, or that social forms such as gender are constructed, is a modern notion. It depends upon us reversing the respective reality of form and matter (Adorno 2000, 61). Today, we think of matter as the ultimate stuff of the universe – the brute and real nature before all culture – and we tend to think of kinds, meanings and ordered distinctions as less real, as having no basis in the ultimate hard facts of the world. We think of nature on the one hand as a domain of facts, and culture on the other as a domain of values; the former is what is fixed and determined, the latter is open to dispute. We have also, since late in the twentieth century, divided sex from gender – our biological and bodily being, from the meanings and values we give to that being in the gender system (Oakley 1985, 16).

Nature/culture: Sex/gender

There are today, in general, two competing accounts of gender. The first is the explanation from sexuality. There are two types of biological body – male and female – that are then socialised and represented through certain stereotypes or images: gender is the social construction of sex:

> 'Sex' is a word that refers to the biological differences between male and female: the visible difference in genitalia, the related difference in procreative function. 'Gender', however, is a matter of culture: it refers to the social classification into 'masculine' and 'feminine'.
>
> (Oakley 1985, 16)

The second account is the explanation from culture. There are, in fact, no essential differences, but societies order the world into male and female oppositions. Sexuality is meaningless, complex and bears none of the binary simplicity that characterises gender. It is gender – or cultural differentiation into kinds – that allows us to think of distinctly different bodies (Delphy 1993). Current debates about sex and gender therefore dispute whether gender is natural and essential or cultural and constructed. What such debates tend to assume, therefore, is an opposition between nature and culture. Sex is natural – the genetic or reproductive givenness of the human body – while gender is cultural. We can argue around this assumed distinction: to what extent does our sexual difference – our genetic and bodily make-up – determine gender difference? But in all cases we assume and trouble ourselves over the boundary between our biology and our social identity. Some of the most heated debates today concern whether certain characteristics, such as homosexuality, or even a greater competence in mathematical thinking, have their basis in genetics or cultural prejudice (Hamer and Copeland 1994; Levay 1993). For every scientific claim regarding sexual determination there are counter-claims insisting on the construction and contingency of gender opposites (Fausto-Sterling 2000).

The contemporary emphasis on the opposition between nature and culture makes it difficult to understand the difference and significance of gender in pre-modern and non-Western modes of thought. To make a distinction between sex and gender is to already assume that there is a domain of human, malleable and constructed cultural difference distinct from a supposedly timeless and unchangeable matter. By opposing determined biological sex to social and constructed gender, we present nature as radically pre-social, and the social as an arbitrary overlay. If we insist that gender is *merely* cultural then we have a great deal of difficulty explaining its pervasiveness, for many anthropologists insist that the opposition between male and female is universal and that it has always referred beyond men's and women's bodies to cosmic principles or contrary tendencies in nature as a whole. But if we go on to argue that the opposition is natural, caused by the physical make-up of bodies and sexual reproduction, we have to ignore all the ways in which gender extends beyond bodies. Why has the supposedly biological fact of maleness and femaleness taken on such mythic, poetic and cultural significance? Why has the polarity of gender been represented as incontrovertible and rigidly dualist, when physical sexuality is more often than not far from dichotomous? Even before the twentieth-century acceptance of trans-sexuality, trans-gendering, cross-dressing, drag, hermaphroditism and other disruptions of supposedly natural sexual boundaries, there has been a long history of sexual confusion and ambiguity. Even so, despite the existence of bodies that cross gender boundaries, those boundaries have remained in place. Why has this ideal boundary – despite its constant actual confusions and transgressions – taken on such metaphysical, mythic and explanatory force?

Before considering the contemporary debates about gender and sexuality we will therefore consider the various ways in which the concept of gender – the concept of differences in kind – has been approached and accounted for in the Western literary and philosophical tradition. Some anthropologists and historians of science have argued that while all cultures oppose male to female, and privilege the former over the latter, the Western scientific tradition is marked by a tendency to ground that opposition in some fundamental principle which is itself not gendered. That is, we could say that other cultures might be able to entertain the possibility that the male and female principles might interact, contaminate and confuse each other (Shulman 1996). From Plato onwards, however, gender difference has been explained by a logic or reason which is itself not gendered. This underlying genderless 'substance' is the basis of all difference. According to Luce Irigaray, the very notion of that which is neutral, ungendered or prior to all opposition and becoming is itself a myth of gender, for it has always been the prerogative of male reason to be the basis of all becoming and difference, and to understand itself as unsexed (Irigaray 1985). Women, by contrast, are sexed – different from the neutral and sexless norm of 'man.' This raises what will be the key question of this book: what type of opposition is the opposition of gender? Is it just a metaphor or figure – a mythic way of explaining the opposition of physical forces that could also be explained scientific-ally – or, is this notion of a genderless, non-mythic and purely rational science dependent on a myth of gender? Can there be a genderless reason, a non-sexed account of the emergence or genesis of difference? Or is the ideal of sexlessness an inherently totalising (and masculine) refusal of difference and otherness?

What sort of difference is gender difference?

We could imagine that there have always been competing definitions of what defines humanity – competing definitions of reason that are more or less inclusive. From Plato and Aristotle onwards the power to reason has been considered as essentially human. Despite these defin-itions of an essential and single humanity there have also, in the same writings that assert the universality of reason, been exclusions of women. One way to approach this seeming contradiction is through the idea of gender. Reason may be an essential feature of humanity, but could be expressed in varying degrees depending on the kind or gender of human being in question. In its broadest sense, 'gender' refers to kinds or types – so that there could be one humanity that then presented itself in two different kinds, male and female. Genders or kinds allow us to think of different ways in which the same substance might be specified. We certainly do not think of men and women as belonging to different species, but we nevertheless make huge claims about essential differences between genders. The history of ideas evidences a constant tension between the insistence on a common humanity on the one hand, and an emphasis on insurmountable and fundamental gender difference on the other. Gender seems sometimes to function as an essence, as a crucial property that makes something what it is, and at other times to function as accidental: one is basically human, with one's gender being irrelevant to what one ultimately is. If gender were essential then we would say that there was not one essence – humanity – that then presented itself in two different kinds, but two distinct essences – maleness and femaleness. These two essences might also extend beyond humanity; we could talk of male and female animals, male and female qualities, male and female emotions. If this were so then there would be some essence of femaleness that was shared by humans, plants, animals and other entities deemed feminine.

While gender refers to kinds it did not, originally, refer to *sexual* kinds; we could have different genders in the sense of different kinds of all sorts of phenomena – not just organisms but principles and mechanisms. Languages, for example, have different genders that have nothing to do with sex, reproduction or biology. Two questions, then, need to be held together when thinking about gender. First, how is it that we think of gender today as *sexual* gender, as human and embodied maleness and femaleness? How did this difference in kind come to take on such importance, and when did the difference of sex – male and female – become the model of all difference? Second, what sort of division or kind – what sort of gender – is the gender of male and female? Is it a biological difference, a cultural difference or a metaphysical difference, expressing two essentially different principles? If the difference of gender were essential then male and female would not be different kinds of anything; there would just be distinct and self-sufficient substances of maleness and femaleness. The idea of a common humanity would be an illusion.

Understanding gender, then, involves more than looking at the various ways in which maleness and femaleness have been, and are, divided in science, history and everyday life. It involves deep and far-reaching questions about ontology, or what it is for something to be. How is it that something has the identity or being that it does? In order to make this clear, we can take two extreme examples. Consider the theory of the 'social construction of reality' which, until relatively recently, dominated the understanding of sexual identity in the humanities and the social sciences (Hacking 1999). Here, the identity or being of a thing – what it is – is constructed through language or culture. There are no essences strictly speaking, for an essence defines what something is *before* all relations. For the social constructivist, what something is is determined by cultural expectations, divisions, relations, discourse, perception and embedded beliefs (Berger and Luckmann 1966). Maleness and femaleness, then, would simply be one way in which we represented human life, one way in which we divided up a world or life that, in itself, had no meaning or essence. For the social constructivist there are no essences: no intrinsic properties that have being regardless of how or whether they are perceived. Gender or the opposition between male and female would, like all other kinds or differences, be produced through systems of relations. Maleness and femaleness would be differences created through language and culture. We could, therefore, imagine a culture without the division of male and female. One popular form of feminism in the twentieth century adopted the ideal of androgyny, where the self could participate in both maleness and femaleness (Heilbrun 1973). Other forms of feminism have sought to go beyond maleness and femaleness altogether in order to imagine sexual difference beyond binaries, either through the dissolution of gender (Delphy 1993) or through the multiplication of sexualities beyond the male–female dyad. For social constructivists, in order to think and speak we have to divide the world up into *some* sort of system. But such differences are arbitrary and contingent, socially and culturally relative, rather than essential. Nothing is meaningful in itself; what something is can only be determined through reference to a cultural whole. What any individual sees or experiences depends on structures beyond the existence of that individual. We see human beings as male or female because of the language we speak and the beliefs we inhabit.

At the other extreme from social constructivism, the essentialist insists that maleness and femaleness are not just categories or representations imposed upon the world. The world consists of essences, or what something intrinsically is. We may only know those essences through language, perception, culture or representation, but what something is remains the same regardless of our knowledge and perception. Our language and culture are the way they are because the world has certain essential features. Different cultures and epochs may represent the world differently, attributing different meanings to essences, but those essences would remain unchanged and might also allow for points of translation and comparison. Some forms of feminism have therefore seen power relations as being caused by the nature of bodies, so that patriarchy is the effect of men's sexually violent domination of women (Dworkin 1981). It would be possible, therefore, to retrieve and articulate a feminine voice and language outside the expressions of male power (Daly 1979). Even if we accept essentialism, though, this still leaves us with problems about gender. Is gender an essence or one of the ways in which the essential world is represented? Bodies may have an essence – their intrinsic genetic make-up – but does this have anything to do with cultural maleness and femaleness? There may be some intrinsic property that under-lies, say, all the female bodies that we know and experience, but we still only experience these bodies as culturally mediated. Whatever the essence of something may be, we only know it in its cultural form. We may accept that there are essences, but deny that talk of essences is appropriate when looking at human life. Because human beings have language, culture and history they have no essential being; what they are is what they become, and they become according to decisions and chosen situations. Language allows humans to create their own world and identity, to become – in Simone de Beauvoir's terms – self-transcending. How we relate to or speak about a sub-atomic particle may not change how that particle behaves, but referring and relating to a person in a certain way undoubtedly determines that person's being. A person is not an essence but a relation, an existence. Even if there were some essential sexual quality, such as femaleness, it could neither exhaust nor determine what it is to be a woman.

Any rejection of essence in favour of existence, construction or self-creation raises the following problem. If we reject the idea of a human essence and insist that humans are self-creating, historical or self-constructing, are we not relying on another essence? It is our essence not to be reduced to our bodies, to create, construct and transcend ourselves. And what if this essence of self-transcendence had a gender? What if, as Beauvoir suggests, men's bodies were more conducive to self-transcendence and self-definition? Women have less capacity to act, exist and be self-transcending both because they have been enslaved to men and because their capacity to bear children impedes their subjectivity; a woman bearing a child is neither subject nor object, neither fully herself, nor a relation to a distinct other. If we were to accept, then, that the very idea of human beings as pure subjects without essence – as defined by self-creation – were actually a definition of the *male* human being, then we see the question of sexual essence as itself gender-biased. Women have often been deemed to be essentially sexed, incapable of transcending their nature, while men are the agents of history, art and production. We might ask then whether the very idea of gender as nothing more than a social production or political relation is not already an image of the male gender, an image of the self who is nothing more than his political and active being. And we might also ask whether the notion of gender as essential, as grounded in something pre-social or pre-relational is not an image of the feminine? The question of gender – whether it is relational or essential, grounded in human decisions or the natural body – is already a political and gendered question, for it concerns just what we take the political to be. Are political wholes or social bodies produced from the nature or essence of bodies, or do bodies only have a nature or gender because of political relations?

Essence and gender

This question of the status of gender – essential or conventional, grounded in the world or produced through culture – is not just a question that has various answers historically; it is also a historically specific question. To ask whether there is an *essential sexuality* is a predominantly modern question. The idea that one's body, the matter from which one is composed, might have an essence relies on two modern presuppositions. First, it requires the existence of the body as matter distinct from mind and culture. This distinction, as many feminists have noted, has its clearest early expression in René Descartes who divided the world into two substances, thinking stuff (*res cogitans*) and extended stuff (*res extensa*) (Descartes [1637] 1968). Second, the idea that this extended stuff might have an essence, or that the essence of something or someone might have to do with the matter from which it is composed, is also distinctly modern. Sexuality, as one's biological essence, relies on locating one's essential sex either in genetic predisposition or in reproductive and hormonal specificity; on this picture what something *is* would be determined by the matter from which it is composed. Prior to modernity, however, the essence of something was its *form* – not the basic stuff from which it was composed but the *way* in which something is, its behaviour, its purpose or those capacities that identified it as being the kind of being it was. The essence of human life, for example, was considered to be the power to reason, and if women on this picture were 'essentially' different from men this was because they were less capable of realising the proper form of humanity, the form of reason. Before going on to look at the (modern) question of whether sexual difference is or is not an essential difference we need to understand how it is that *essence* changed its meaning historically.

It would have made no sense, in Aristotle's day, to ask whether being a woman was an essential or cultural determination. It would have made no sense to ask how much of one's bodily identity was natural and essential and how much was cultural and contingent. Today, when we talk of an essential sexual identity we attribute essential properties to matter or the body. While one's body is what one essentially is – the unchanging or brute fact – one's social gender is subject to change and history. We locate gender in a domain of culture, ideology, stereotyping or society and see this as added on to what something is naturally or essentially. Not only have we shifted essence from something's form (its mode of being and position in the cosmos) to its matter or physical basis, we have also assumed a divide between what something is naturally, before all culture, and what something comes to be in society or in relation to others. But such a nature–culture divide is not pertinent to a pre-modern way of thinking (Daston 1998, 154). For Aristotle, a human being was *essentially* political; it made no sense to speak of maleness, femaleness or humanity before cultural life. Nature is not brute matter but has a proper form, a tendency to realise its own end or good. There is not brute nature as matter on the one hand and a political order on the other. For Aristotle matter is *hyle*, indeterminate stuff, but nature is *physis*, and *physis* has a *proper nature*, in the way that, today, we refer to 'human nature,' or the 'nature of politics.' 'Nature' is what something becomes in relation to an order of ends and purposes.

The pre-modern conception of nature was certainly not defined as prior to or opposed to culture; nor was culture the imposition or construction of meaning on an otherwise meaningless matter. Nature was teleological, or directed towards specific and proper ends. Politics was the proper and natural development of human life, not an order imposed upon life. On this picture, then, it would make no sense to talk of one's essential sexuality – the genetic, biological or hormonal determinants of one's being. Essences did not lie at the level of brute physicality but in the position a body occupied in a system of relations. Questions that today are thought of in *sexual* terms – 'Is homosexuality natural?' – were, in ancient times, thought of in ethical terms: with whom should one have sexual relations?; how can one maintain sexual activity, without falling into weakness, passivity, or disorder? The debate, today, over whether homosexuality is essential or socially constructed is a biological or genetic question, where we interrogate the extent to which the self is determined by the body. Is there something in our bodies, our genetic make-up, which predisposes us to act and relate in certain ways? Are we essentially female, homosexual or polymorphous? Is there some determination that occurs at the bodily and material level that cannot be done away with no matter how much we change our language, legislation or behaviour? If, today, we approach the question of essential sex and constructed gender from this point of view we do so because we assume that what is ultimately real (or essential and unchanging) is matter, while our concepts, categories or forms are imposed or arbitrary.

Now this is a specifically modern understanding of essence. We could also say that it is a specifically modern understanding of gender in general, a specifically modern way of thinking about *kinds* or differences in being. The modern notion of sexuality makes, as we have said, two significant assumptions that were virtually unthinkable on a pre-modern understanding. First, the very idea of sexuality or one's body causing one's being assumes that it is the matter or physicality of the world that produces distinct kinds; only if we assume this can we ask whether our gender is essential – determined by biology – or arbitrary – imposed by culture. Second, the concept of one's sexual being as one's ultimate or true being, also assumes that our bodies or material selves have substance and reality, whereas the form that body takes is less real, merely conceptual, and possibly a result of culture, ideology or stereotypes. These two assumptions are so taken for granted today that they hardly seem like assumptions. How on earth could we think of our material bodies as having less reality than the concepts we employ to think about those bodies? How could we think of our biological nature as *inessential*? But this is just how most philosophers, scientists and theologians prior to the seventeenth century did think. One's body was inessential dross, chaotic matter without form; what was real was our immaterial being: the soul that gave form to the body.

The gender of souls

The main contrast between modern notions of sexuality and pre-modern understandings of genders lies in the status of difference. The contemporary distinction between sex and gender assumes that however the world is in itself, we know the world through the differences created by language and culture. On a pre-modern ontology, genders and kinds were not differences imposed upon the world; they were not just ways in which the world was known or represented. Human life and language reflected, rather than created, the world's system of differences. These distinctions were not overlaid categories but fixed forms underlying the perceived world of change. The order of the world, its organisation into identities, resemblances, differences, analogies and hierarchies derived from some transcendent or external principle (Foucault 1970, 37). Gender, or the kind of thing something was, was determined by an ordering power that was not bound up with the changes of the world. If men were different from women this was because the creation of the world dictated various kinds, with each kind bearing its specific and proper relation to the whole.

For Plato the order of the world was dictated by an eternal and other-worldly realm of forms, an eternal realm which this temporal and changing world merely imitated (Plato 1963, 1510 [*Laws* 965b]). Our reason, therefore, was a mirror or likeness of an eternal reason or *logos*. Understanding what is right, true and proper required looking beyond oneself to an order that transcends human decisions and will. Self-reflection was not about discovering one's specific and personal identity, but had to do with the cultivation of an eternal soul, a soul that allowed one to discern truths that derived from a source beyond human cognition (Plato 1963, 48 [*Phaedo* 65c]). One looked into oneself to discover what was true eternally, but this activity of *theoria* or contemplation was only open to those who had the luxury to be liberated from the needs of life. For Plato the existence of reason in all souls meant that women *could* be capable of the higher activities of theory and contemplation, but this would require detachment from the domestic duties of mere life. In the *Republic*, Plato entertains the possibility of women cultivating their reason, even though his image of the contemplative life was, in actual fact, not available to the slaves and women who were bound to bodily work and life (Plato 1963, 695 [*Republic* 456a–460d]). Hierarchies of gender could also, however, be justified in Plato's image of the good polity. Because the state ought to reflect a divine harmony – with reason governing the passions, and the philosophical and contemplative elite governing those caught up in labour – the actual subordination of women derived from, and could be justified by, the eternal priority and elevation of reason. Until women were able to cultivate reason they ought to remain subordinate to the men of reason.

For Aristotle, even though there was not an eternal and otherworldly realm of distinct forms, the world itself was composed of distinct kinds or genera, which remained unchanging. The matter of the world tends towards and realises itself in these forms or genera. Each kind had its place in an order of being, and that order was determined by an ultimate principle: the prime mover or self-causing cause. Even without the Christian notion of a single God as author and moral judge of the world, the ancient Greeks could locate the proper behaviour of each being in the appropriate realisation of what it was *meant to be*. For Aristotle all life tends towards its own good or form, with the highest form being reason, and with reason itself being the recognition and consummation of natural hierarchy and harmony (Aristotle 1995, 1798–1799 [*Ethics* VI.2]).

From the Christian point of view, which in its systematised and theological writings relied heavily on ancient Greek metaphysics, God created the world of beings, each with their own preordained position in the whole. The world expressed an ultimate *logos* or reason. Any divinely created world would have to be a logically ordered, harmonious, productive, full and *good* world – where goodness referred to the ability of each being to recognise its end. Evil, by contrast, was the perversion or lack of form, the failure of something to realise what it ought to be, the failure of something to fulfil or actualise itself. It was in the fifth century that Saint Augustine defined the tendency to evil, not in the body's corruption so much as the body's failure to go beyond itself:

> It is not by having flesh, which the devil does not have, but by living according to his own self, that is according to man, that man has become like the devil. For the devil too chose to live according to his own self when he did not adhere to the truth, and thus the falsehood that he told had its source not in God but in himself.
>
> (Augustine 1966, 271–273)

What the self was – the form, kind or genus of human life – was determined by one's position in a created and ordered totality. Human reason could, and should, read or intuit this order by studying nature and the heavens; but the order was independent of human observation. Knowledge of the world did not *impose categories*, it recognised distinct kinds, and submitted to a logic of which it could only know a finite part. Kinds were, therefore, independent of human knowledge. What something was – its being or essence – could be determined by referring to some transcendent order.

In the case of gender, for example, we could say that there was a rational or divine hierarchy that placed maleness above femaleness. At the top of the chain of being or order would be pure reason: God in the Christian ontology, or simply the rational order or *logos* in the ancient Greek cosmos – pure thought thinking itself. Both men and women had a position in the cosmology, with men often deemed to be in greater possession of reason. If men were elevated above women in the divine cosmology or eternal order of things this had little to do with their bodies – for on this schema bodies, materiality or brute physical being was itself positioned at the bottom of the hierarchy. It was the soul – *psyche* – that was divine and disembodied; the soul was that part of the self that was closer to God or divine order, while one's body was mere matter.

It was frequently argued that women were more inclined towards the bodily aspects of their nature, while men were more inclined towards reason. Women and slaves, in the ancient Greek polis, for example, were not included in political affairs. Such differences were, however, given a *political* rather than biological justification; some group needed to tend to the affairs of the home (women), while others had lost their freedom simply by being incapable of reason (slaves). In such cases, the difference between men and women was determined by a political order, the shape human relations should take as a whole (Aristotle 1984, 2006 [*Politics* II.5]). It had little to do with one's body, although Aristotle also describes physical tendencies of male superiority due to a greater possession of 'heat' (Aristotle 1984, 1199 [775a]). If there were differences of gender that went beyond the social and political position of women, if there were *reasons* why women were given the role of domestic labour while men were concerned with political and rational affairs, this was not because of a difference in one's bodily sex, but because of a difference in soul, the form or direction one's being took. Soul was the animating principle, the ineffable and immaterial life that determined each being's position in the cosmos. Women's souls, it was often argued, were less refined than men's, less capable of clear and distinct reason. Women had a greater tendency to move 'downwards,' to be affected by bodily drives and passions (Aristotle 1984, 1999 [1260a]). Many writers, such as Plato, did not see any reason why women could not be as rational as men. The human soul is rational; human *psyche* is endowed with reason, and reason is the power to see the forms or essences (*eidos*) that give the world its order. All human souls have reason, so all humans have the capacity to see beyond the flux of appearances and become truly rational – including women. For Plato, however, the realisation of women's potential for reason would require radical political reform. In *The Republic* Plato suggested that only collective child rearing, where no child was tied to any particular set of parents, would allow for all human beings to realise their proper form – the exercise of reason (Plato 1963, 699 [*Republic* 460d]). Plato was, therefore, the first of many writers who suggested that the realisation of human potential would require a reform in the division of sexual labour *and* that such reform would not just be liberating for women, but would create a more rational world in general. For Plato, it is only through philosophy and contemplation (*theoria*) that one develops one's reason, liberates oneself from the body and recognises what is eternally or essentially true. The body itself, therefore, was inessential – capable of corrupting the recognition and attainment of what is true eternally. On the one hand, then, Plato recognised the rationality of women and their potential inclusion in the republic of reason. On the other hand, he intensified an association between reason and freedom from the bodily constraints, such as childbirth, that were attributed to women.

Writers who followed Plato, including Aristotle and the Christian tradition, could place women's souls closer to animal natures, more drawn towards the chaos of bodies. In so doing, however, they did not give women's *bodies* a separate *essence*. Essences were not material, and they transcended specific individuals. All human bodies, for example, could participate to a greater or lesser extent in reason – and it was reason, not physicality, that was essentially human. One's *soul* or *form* was what determined one's being. Differences in gender, therefore, were produced by differences in the realisation of reason, with women being subordinate because their bodies were less capable of realising a reason that was essentially distinct from sex and embodiment. One could not argue that sexuality or embodiment itself determined what one was. Matter, itself, always required some form or proper end, but matter was merely *the potential* for *form*. Form was the realisation, actualisation or achievement of what matter *should be*

(Williams 1958, 510). Aristotle, famously, rejected the notion of essences or forms that existed in some eternal realm beyond this world. But he nevertheless saw each body as directed towards an essential end or form, which that body *ought* to achieve. For Aristotle, what something is – its form or its true being – was what something became, its *telos* or the end towards which it strove. Human life was defined by its end of 'living well.' And living well was defined as exercising one's highest capacity – wisdom – in order to form one's life into a stable and coherent whole (Aristotle 1984, 1738 [*Ethics* 1101a]). What was *essentially* human for Aristotle, what made something the kind of being it was, was its proper activity. Like Plato, then, there was nothing to stop women from realising this proper human life, and again like Plato, this life was best achieved through *theoria* or contemplation, where one is not determined by one's body but reflects upon the truth of life in general. For writers who followed Plato and Aristotle, one could debate about the extent to which women were capable of realising reason, but both men's and women's bodies were just that – bodies – and what determined one's true being was one's soul. One could argue that women's souls, like those of animals and lesser beings, tended more towards the body, but one did not think of sex: some bodily quality that determined what one was.

When Plato and Aristotle were taken up by Christian theologians this hierarchical and immaterial way of thinking about gender was given a moral inflection. It was possible to see the body not just as lower down on the scale of being, but as corrupt, fallen – possibly evil. Some Christian writers explained the presence of evil in the world through the corruption of the body. Our divine souls are pure and intact, capable of realising God's will, but we are dragged down by our bodies, by those mortal, decaying and disruptive forces that God expelled from paradise. Other Christian writers – notably Saint Augustine – refused to see the body itself as fallen. Because it was part of God's creation the body could not be dismissed as an evil. What resulted from the fall was not a corrupt body but a loss of harmony; the once ordered and obedient body was now capable of disrupting reason. The body has its own legitimate role to play in life when it is ruled by reason. It is the relation between reason and the body that is fallen, not the body itself (Augustine 1966, 273). This disruptive relation is more evident in women, whose weaker wills and stronger sense of the own bodies allow reason to be led astray. The concept of will allows Augustine to explain the relative weakness of women, and to justify the presence of evil in a world created by God. In an unfallen world, all power and life reflects and expresses divine power. An evil will, however, turns against creation and its own true being (Hundert 1992, 89). Rather than direct-ing itself to what is greater than itself and the source of all life, the evil will remains unproductively within itself, concerned with nothing other than itself. The fallen *will* of human pride takes greater pleasure in its own being than in the divine forms of this world and is, therefore, drawn towards the body. Such a will does not realise its form or become what it should be; it is drawn towards mere physical being rather than allowing its physical being to be ordered by reason. Again, this had consequences both for the understanding of genders and the relation between genders.

Many Christian writers warned against the excessive allure of the female body, the power of this body to deflect reason from its ascendance to God. If both men and women were created by God, then both needed to be capable of redemption; it would not do to see either the body or women as essentially fallen. But it was nevertheless possible to see women, by virtue of the attractiveness of their bodies, and their weaker wills (their weaker capacity to develop reason) as drawing male reason away from its spiritual goal. On this understanding, gender still does not lie at the level of the body. Like the Platonic and Aristotelian conceptions, body is inessential; one's soul is one's real being. There may be varying degrees of refinement or realisation of the soul, but even those with a greater tendency to the body – women – would still have reason as their proper form (Matthews 1990). One could think of a difference in gender, or a difference between masculinity and femininity, as a difference of degree, with varying degrees of rationality or spiritualisation being possible. But there could not be two distinct and essential *bodies* on this picture. The Christian narrative of the fall *could* provide one way of think-ing a more distinct relation between male and female, tracing the fall back to Eve. But one could not argue that women were essentially fallen, or essentially different and irrational, for this would suggest that God had created some essentially corrupt kinds of being. Genders, or kinds, would need to be seen as expressions or embodiments of reason, and not essen-tially different kinds of reason – for reason has neither sex nor body. If women were to be subordinate to men in a divine cosmology this would be because their will, or their capacity to arrive at their true rational and spiritual nature, was less capable than that of men. Only through the guidance of the right reason of men – those whose wills were less drawn to the body – could women also realise their reason.

Matter and the realisation of gender

We have already seen that for most writers up until the eighteenth century the real being of a thing was not determined by its matter or physical existence, but by its soul, and that soul is the *form* of a thing – what a thing tends or *ought* to be. This 'ought' is dictated either by God (on a Christian schema) or the harmony and rationality of the universe. The second point that needs to be made is that the pre-modern ontology reverses our modern understanding of what is real, and this in turn effects how we understand gender. Today, we think of substance as matter or physical existence. Substance can be defined as what has being or existence in itself, requiring nothing else in order to be. Substance is what is ultimately real. On a contemporary understanding we might think of our physical bodies as substantial, as having true being, while our gender, personality or social types are dependent or less real. We might also think of the ultimate substance of the universe as 'matter' with the various forms that matter takes – how we perceive, order and define that matter – as not being truly real. Sex, on this picture, would be real and immutable, with gender being an imposed ideology, stereotype or contestable representation. On a pre-modern understanding, however, the reverse is the case (Adorno 2000, 61). What is substantial, what exists in itself before all relations, what requires nothing else in order to be are the forms. Essences are immaterial and possess the only, or at least the higher, reality. Matter or physicality is mere stuff. It is form that is substantial, that can be known, and that allows something to *be*. Substances are not the physical things that we perceive, feel, encounter and towards which we bear a relation. Substances are the underlying realities, which we only perceive through various qualities – such as colour, shape, weight or duration. To know what something really is is not to know its physical or bodily being, but its ground – that which determines what it is. This determining ground or ultimate reality is its substance.

Now it was the definition of substance that greatly altered in the move towards science in the seventeenth century, and which also changed the way of thinking about genders or kinds. Substance, or what was ultimately real, was redefined as the physical ground of the universe, with various accidents, predicates or qualities being the way in which those substances are known or experienced. The essence of substance was not its form or what it *ought* to be, but its intrinsic properties – say, an intrinsic property which caused us to see it as coloured, while substance in itself was colourless (Lewis and Langton 1998). In terms of gender, this meant that kinds could, in the modern world, be thought of as being determined by the underlying physicality of the world, rather than the form or position of kinds in a preordained whole. One's body could be what one essentially was, while the division into male and female, master and slave, or king and servant could now be explained through relations and human actions. The position or essence of a body was not determined by some transcendent order; rather, order was produced from the relations of bodies. It was the underlying physical forces of life – the power that each thing has – that could determine its position in a hierarchy: one became a slave because one was weaker; women were seen as subordinate because of their lesser power.

Aristotle had thought that the reverse was the case: there were not struggles of power that then produced relations; relations were determined by the type of being one was. Slaves and women were subordinate by nature. One was a slave, servant or woman because of one's soul, and no relations among bodies – no mere struggle of forces – could alter those hierarchies (Aristotle 1984, 1987–1990 [*Politics* 1252b1–1255a1]). Up until the seventeenth century, true being or reality – what was substantial – was the form of something or its proper position in the order of things. The matter from which things were composed had being only in a secondary sense. There was, on this pre-modern picture, a hierarchy of substances, a way of considering varying degrees of reality. If God was the ultimate reality or one true substance, then the various kinds of the world could be ordered according to the degree to which they realised or expressed that true reality (Heidegger 1967, 80–81). We will look at the modern shift in the status of substance in greater detail in a later section. What needs to be emphasised here is that understandings of gender have always been based on some distinction between what is ultimately real, and what is subsequently differentiated by human relations. The politics of gender concerns the distinction between legitimate and real differences, as opposed to differences that are subsequently imposed or derived. Is the distinction between male and female *substantial*: is it based in the very being of the world, or is it just the way in which that world has been represented?

As we have already noted, from a pre-modern point of view – where substance or the ultimately real is not matter but the form matter takes – it would make no sense to talk about essential sexuality, or that one's real being might be determined by one's body. One's real being was one's proper form, the *idea* that gave matter its proper end and order. This had two consequences for gender. First, one could see different forms or kinds play themselves out in bodies. Maleness and femaleness might be two distinct forms, but this would not fully determine one's body. One's body could participate variously in maleness and femaleness, and one's body could also waver from its proper form, fail to realise its gender – and this because the body did *not* have an essence, but had to realise or take on its essential or proper being. There were both medical and theatrical texts of the Renaissance that explored the ways in which bodies wavered from their gender – an excess of heat rendering women masculine, or a failure of strength and development allowing male bodies to 'regress' to effeminacy (Greenblatt 1986; Laqueur 1990, 141). Second, if gender did not have its determining cause in the body's matter, then it was possible to establish a relation between maleness and femaleness that was moral rather than physical. A man, for example, could be rendered 'effeminate' – and hence corrupt – through a weakness of reason or an excess of bodily lust (Orgel 1989). Each body, therefore, ought to be dominated by the male, rational or form-giving power and should guard against 'effeminacy.' Not only were men and women organised politically by a hierarchy of form and reason over matter and the body, bodies themselves needed to be well-ordered and saved from an excessive effeminacy. We will consider these two strands of gender – the relation between men and women, and the relation of maleness and femaleness within men's and women's bodies – in turn.

Gender without sex

First, to say that bodies themselves were not sexually distinct is not to suggest that there was a world where men and women were equal, or where genders did not have political, moral, religious, social and literary significance. Difference was not located in bodies, but it did play itself out at the level of the body. According to Thomas Laqueur, whose highly influential work on the history of sex demonstrates the fluidity and fungibility of pre-modern gender differences, bodies of men and women were not radically distinct. Indeed, the male and female genitals were described and depicted as versions of each other, with the vagina as an infolded penis, and with female bodies emitting a weaker or formless form of seed. Sexual difference was not a question of each body bearing its own essence or sexual specificity. Rather, there was one matter, one flesh, which was then distributed according to different gendered principles or types. Gender was the form one's fleshy matter took; it did not lie at the level of what today we would refer to as 'biology' (Laqueur 1990, 61). It was often argued, for example, that the female orgasm was required for procreation because both bodies needed to contribute their seed (Laqueur 1990, 43). The very possibility that female pleasure or 'heating' was deemed to be important indicated that both men and women were seen to play *analogous* roles in production – not two distinct sexual bodies, but varying kinds of body. Gender differences, or the male and female roles in creation were therefore mirror images of each other. Instead of a division between male matter (or sperm) and female matter (or ova), the reproductive process was likened to a distinction between a forming power and a receptive power.

Reproduction was not seen in terms of two distinct *types of matter* contributing to the creation of life. Rather, women's bodies contributed the material element, a seed that was mere stuff, while male seed was pure form or creative power. The male body in creation plays the role of God-like artificer, shaping matter, giving it life and force. Female bodies contributed the passive and meaningless stuff, which would be endowed with life in the act of procreation. Sexual difference was not biologically determined so much as decided through the role each body played: the male being a principle of form, the female occupying the position of formless, inessential matter. On this picture, there could be female men, and male women. There could be bodies that, though over-exertion or heat, could shift genders to become masculine, or who through excessive passivity could be effeminated. We could conclude then by saying, as Laqueur insists, that our notion of a 'real' sexuality underlying social roles, types and divisions would have had no meaning. Matter was meaningless, and the body was capable of tending towards either the forming power of masculinity or the formless passivity of femininity. Matter would have to take on its gendered form, and all physical human matter – all bodies – would have both male and female tendencies (Laqueur 1990, 61–62).

Women, therefore, were subordinated politically, socially and culturally, but this had less to do with the nature of their bodies than it did with a theory subordinating embodiment and physicality to form and reason (Laqueur 1990, 59). Social hierarchies were made sense of through cosmic principles – ways of organising gender – that cannot be understood in today's strict division of the cultural from the bio-logical. If women were regarded as lesser beings because they were less endowed with the forming, disembodied, creative and active power of reason, so were slaves, effeminate men, and those men who allowed their reason to stray. Such men were, therefore, frequently described as 'effeminate' or 'effeminated.' This was not a world of two distinct bio-logical beings with men holding power over women due to their clear liberation from the sexual predicament of child rearing or procreation. This was a world where reason, or the male form-giving power, was distributed in varying degrees, and where bodies had to struggle or work towards achieving their form. One's gender – the proper form of one's body – was precisely what inessential matter needed to acquire. This proper movement of matter towards its real form, this proper realisation of substance where beings must come to be what they really and eternally are, created a political hierarchy of levels and resemblances: women must be to men what men are to God. Just as men strive to achieve a position of pure reason and active self-determination, and do so in reference to a divine creative reason, so women need to defer to male reason – not because women are essen-tially irrational but because the essence of human life – reason – is exemplified in men. We could say, then, following Laqueur's argument, that this was a world where gender or form governs sex; one's body or matter must take on or realise one's true being (Laqueur 1990, 62).

Nowhere is this more evident than in Renaissance drama where one's physical being – far from determining one's gender – disrupts and perverts one's true self. But this is not to say that gender was seen as purely conventional. One does have a proper or 'real' gender role, and this is one's role in a social and cosmic whole. Indeed, many of Shakespeare's comedies play on the tension between the *natural* order – where men rule over women, where men are active and women are passive, where bodies and desires conform to their recognised and collectively harmonious role – and the *material* order where bodies are chaotic, physically and chemically anarchic, and at odds with one's identity. Nature as harmony and rational order is *not* chaotic matter, for it is the disruption of anarchic bodily life that is monstrous, inessential and *un*natural. Whereas today we would oppose nature to culture, it would have made more sense prior to the seventeenth century to oppose nature to the monstrous, unnatural, supernatural or preternatural (Daston 1998).

A Midsummer Night's Dream

One traditional reading of *A Midsummer Night's Dream* sees the comedy as a resolution and harmonisation of temporary, playful and illusory disruptions to social harmony. The happy marriages that conclude the play represent the renewal of the social bond and the correct coupling of male and female partners in the political contract (Olson 1957). Shakespeare was a playwright who, as part of the Elizabethan world order, presented the world as a hierarchically ordered chain of being, with both his comedies and tragedies presenting the natural order of law (Lovejoy 1936). Whereas the tragedies demonstrate that the transgression of nature – say, Macbeth's murder of Duncan – will lead to social chaos, the comedies show that any disruption of nature – say, in the magic of the fairies or the chaos of love not bound to its proper object – can only be happily resolved in the final hierarchy and submission of marriage. On such a picture there would also be a natural hierarchy of gender, the disruption of which would lead to the tragic annihilation of life, as in Lady Macbeth's assertion of manly ambition which brings about the demise of both Macbeth and social harmony. Alternatively, the comic play with sex roles that is ultimately restored by love would provide a brief respite from the otherwise fixed norms of gender.

It is just this image of a natural hierarchy, and a natural gender order that new historicist readings of Shakespeare have set out to challenge. According to the new historicist reading, there are no natural hierarchies, nor do Shakespeare's plays simply assert that there are. Gender is achieved through performance. Further, the plays are self-conscious about the performance of power, and the capacity for power to produce the selves it supposedly governs (Greenblatt 1980). Instead of assuming that there is a social order which the play represents, new historicism makes two claims. Following on from Michel Foucault's conception of power as positive, new historicists do not accept that there are male and female genders that power comes along to repress or organise. On the contrary, power produces bodies as gendered through performance. Bodies become gendered through their presentation, performance and enactment of themselves as either male or female. Second, not only do plays and other modes of performance, including public displays of royal power, *produce* power relations; Shakespeare's plays reflect upon the performance of power, and demonstrate the power *of performance*. His comic plots, for example, exploit the ways in which sexual identities can be transformed through disguise. In *A Midsummer Night's Dream* we see masculine power produce itself through effective performance. What new historicist readings want to reject is that there simply is a natural order that art presents, or that political power either manages or represses. Art is as much an action as it is a reflection, and gender is as much a performance as it is an expression. Further, the performance of power is always addressed to, and dependent upon, a specific historical context. According to Louis Montrose *A Midsummer Night's Dream* negotiates the tension between the body of Elizabeth I, sexed as female, and her public position of power – a position occupied by men. The play was also aware of its role in producing and sustaining the gender roles it presented (Montrose 1983, 86).

Such a mode of reading aims to overturn the idea that pre-modern or Elizabethan culture was unquestioningly bound to a 'great chain of being.' Rather, such images of natural hierarchy needed to be created and performed. There were also tensions and contradictions in the affirmation of hierarchy, and works of art frequently negotiated and managed such tensions. According to Montrose *A Midsummer Night's Dream* is haunted by images of an unmanageable female power. On the one hand, women were deemed to be politically subservient individuals; on the other, Queen Elizabeth presented herself as a figure of fatherly authority, possessing the body of a woman but the spirit of a man. Elizabeth's female body is at odds with her position as ruler; her might and authority threaten the containment of female sexuality within the private sphere of the family. Central to the force of the play, according to Montrose, is the anxiety that must have been generated by the female body and sex of the queen, coupled with her legitimate masculine power: how could Elizabeth have the body or sex of a woman and the mind or gender of a king? The play must therefore show women being brought into line, women's bodies being properly subordinated and ruled. The play shows Oberon retrieving a changeling from Titania, the fairy queen; Hermia, whose desire is initially at odds with her father's will, is eventually incorporated into social harmony; and the framing marriage of Theseus to Hippolyta presents the conquering of female power by political order. In order to resolve the social tension and anxiety of Elizabeth's royal body – a virginal body that had shunned the sexual hierarchy of marriage – the play must also present the object of that anxiety in its process of being tamed. The play does this through a reinforcing of gender roles; men are seen to manage the bodies of women, and in so doing the play re-inscribes the border between male and female that Elizabeth's royal body threatens to undermine. In this re-inscription, however, the play demonstrates that power relations, including relations of gender, are nothing more than acts of creation – that gender has no reality outside its political performance: '*A Midsummer Night's Dream* is, then, in a double sense, a *creation* of Elizabethan culture: for it also creates the culture by which it is created, shapes the fantasies by which it is shaped, begets that by which it is begotten' (Montrose 1983, 86).

If we accept this mode of reading then we assume that the current notion of sex and gender, where biological sex underlies social gender, applies to all modes of thought. Gender is a social and political construction, and was always recognised as such. Historical contexts differ only in the roles they accord to gender, not in the distinction between sex and gender. Montrose assumes that there must have been a contradiction and tension between the sexed body of Elizabeth and her position as ruler. To assume that gender is a social role imposed on *male and female bodies* reinforces a peculiarly modern notion of power and social relations. It assumes that *kinds or genders are produced through relations of power*, and that the opposition between male and female is achieved by male bodies ordering female bodies. We may want to contest the idea that there simply is a gender hierarchy that art reflects and supports, but we might also want to read the specific ways in which historical texts negotiate the problem of gender, and whether differences in the very mode of gender might also tell us something about different understandings of power. We can summarise this by offering a schematic reading of *A Midsummer Night's Dream*, which we will flesh out below. Shakespeare's play rejects both the notion of a natural and immutable order *and* the idea that power is simply imposed or performed, and he does this through the relation between sexuality and gender. Sexuality or nature is not yet ordered into kinds and relations, but there is a natural tendency to produce relations. Good political power, power that produces the right balance between order and disorder, is the direction or cultivation of these natural propensities. Gender is an exemplary model of hierarchy, for it has a natural basis but requires political management in order to be realised. A power that merely strives to impose itself on nature, or a power that presents itself as nothing more than nature will ultimately fail. These points can be expanded as follows.

First, a constant theme in Shakespeare's plays is the disjunction between political order and nature. Those rulers, such as Richard II, Macbeth, or Julius Caesar, who believe that nature, blood or necessity will guarantee their rule are ultimately brought down by those who can engage in performance, political negotiation or effective rhetoric. Without the active intervention in politics, without the negotiation, management and development of the social body, power regresses into mere chaos. *A Midsummer Night's Dream* opens with Egeus's invocation of 'ancient privilege', that *because* he is Hermia's father and she is his property he can declare who she will marry, and can totally appropriate her will and sexuality: 'As she is mine, I may dispose of her' (1.1.42). Theseus, who is in agreement with Egeus, does however acknowledge both that Hermia's own choice is intrinsically appropriate – Lysander is suitable if one ignores social worth – and that Egeus's power is not that of ancient privilege and ownership but resides in a father's analogy to a forming power. Theseus's representation of authority is not based on received power and property but on the difference in mode of male and female power, a difference between form and matter:

> *Theseus*: To you your father should be as a god:
> One that compos'd your beauties, yea, and one
> To whom you are but as a form in wax
> By him imprinted, and within his power
> To leave the figure, or disfigure it.
> Demetrius is a worthy gentleman
> *Hermia*: So is Lysander
> *Theseus*: In himself he is;
> But in this kind, wanting your father's voice
>   (1.1.47–54)

Whereas being a father, according to Egeus, is a sufficient basis of power, Theseus attributes the authority of fathers to an *analogy* they bear to the law in general. The father has authority because he represents the law; the law is not reducible to the mere body of the father, his ownership or precedence. The desire of the father could – and will – be overturned if it is not in accord with what *ought to be*. The rest of the play will therefore oppose an authority achieved by force, precedence and property to an authority based on form, order and harmony.

Egeus exercises his power arbitrarily and not for any offered reason other than his role as father. Further, Egeus takes his role of father literally and biologically; he rules and has power *because* he is Hermia's father, and he appeals to the king to reinforce this right. This is a rule of control through literal ties of blood, where the rule of patriarchy does not represent the law as a transcendent father to the social body, but where power acts directly on bodies through sexuality and the family. Similarly, this power that operates by imposing its will as quantitative force is echoed in Oberon's rule over Titania. The fairy world of nature is certainly not an image of divine and preordained order. This natural world is dominated by caprice, contingency and arbitrary will. While Oberon and Titania are at war the supposedly natural cycles of harmony are disrupted: 'And this same progeny of evils comes / From our debate, from our dissension; / We are their parents and original' (2.1.115–117). The fairies inhabit a nature that is at odds with human order (2.1.32–55). Any attempt to read these events of natural disruption as omens or signs of intent would be to attribute a reason to this supernatural world, which is in actual fact dominated by chance. This is a world without gender, where Oberon's power over Titania is simply the power of one body over another, and where all relations are produced from strife, contrary wills and competing forces. Oberon wants Titania's boy as his 'henchman,' and seizes the boy by virtue of the essential fluidity of desire, and the power of natural poisons to mobilise desire. His 'herb' will cause Titania to shift her attention to 'the next thing then she waking looks upon' (1.1.179). Oberon's power is achieved through illusion and forceful submission. He *seizes* the changeling boy who has deflected Titania's desire, and who Titania herself has taken from a world without gender; for she has received the boy from a woman who is a member of Titania's 'order.' Titania recalls how she and the 'votress' looked laughingly on male enterprise mimicking female fecundity: 'When we have laughed to see the sails conceive / And grow big-bellied with the wanton wind' (2.1.128–129). Titania and Oberon's relation is one of warring contraries: of a female order attached to its own naturally produced offspring, set against Oberon's appropriating but unreliable arts of deception. Oberon's power, like Prospero's power in *The Tempest*, is nothing other than performance, illusion and deceit. Just as Prospero gives away his magic and allure in order to return to the right reason of the polity, so Oberon's rule that is based on appearance and manipulation of bodies and desire eventually gives way to the law of Athens.

Unlike Oberon's world where illusion produces reality, where there is nothing outside his manipulative will, Theseus's rule claims to bring bodies, nature and reality to what they *ought to be* – their proper form – but what they are not yet. Indeed, it is not Thesues's *will* that results in the play's harmony; rather, he oversees and manages the restoration from the night's 'accidents' to its final 'amends' (5.1.424). Oberon's fairy world is one of sexuality and excessive desire: warring and competing bodily forces, flows of love with no proper or stable object, mere material causes and effects. And so power can be nothing more than wilful performance and imposition, a series of 'misprisions' which may or may not result in order (3.2.90). Love is presented as a distortion of right seeing, while Oberon himself refers to his own power as producing 'hateful imperfection' (4.1.62), 'accidents' (4.1.67) and 'error' (3.2.368). Shakespeare presents the hyperbolic and subjective rhetoric of love as that which knows no borders or proper bounds: 'For you, in my respect, are all the world' (2.1.224). And, as the lovers' interchanges show, there is no *reason* to love; the more one declares one's love the less is one loved (2.2.88), with love producing its whims as reason: 'The will of man is by his reason sway'd / And reason says you are the worthier maid' (2.2.114–115).

Athens, by contrast, is a site of gender, where each body takes on its proper form, and where this form is conducive to overall harmony and natural tendencies, but is determined neither immediately by nature nor by the whim of Theseus's will. The 'power' that produces the final 'gentle concord' where the lovers conveniently align their wills with the will of law appears as a mystery both to Theseus and those involved. Demetrius declares that he is restored to the 'virtue' of his heart but, 'I wot not by what power – But by some power it is' (4.1.163–164). When the lovers return to Athens they adopt a distanced attitude to powers and desires. No longer caught up immediately in the forces that take hold of them, they are capable of seeing the difference between powers and their effects and between the force of illusion and its creations. The Athenians can view the play performed by the rude mechanicals and laugh or distance themselves from the idea that they might be seduced by the mere appearance of tragic effects. Athens deploys illusion and performance to master reality. Indeed the power and elevation of Theseus is displayed in his capacity to allow the illusions and distortions of the players, who believe all too readily in their capacity to perform and take on any appearance: 'Our sport shall be to take what they mistake' (5.1.90). Theseus can read the players' illusion *as illusion*, and therefore has an imagination capable of reading the real passion through its presentation. His right reason separates image from reality, the performed play from its sense. Theseus's Athens is a world where appearance refers to, but does not produce, reality, and where real forms underlie presentations:

> I read as much as from the rattling tongue
> Of saucy and audacious eloquence.
> Love, therefore, and tongue-tied simplicity
> In least speak most, to my capacity
>   (5.1.102–105)

When the play opens, Theseus admits that he has wooed Hippolyta 'with my sword' (1.1.16). By the end of the play 'another key' has been adopted and we see power and marriage relations not in terms of force and the competing wills of bodies but as a harmony that transcends the wills of the participants, and which follows the potential virtues of nature. Both Athenian art and politics operate by acknowledging the difference between force or power on the one hand, and the law or order that power ought to serve and uphold. The Athens that concludes the play is neither a world of immediate and immutable natural order, nor an arbitrary imposition in a world without natural tendencies. The only lover's will to have changed is Demetrius, who regards the change as a restoration of health (4.1.178). Good law or good political performance negotiates natural tendencies, and brings natural forces or the tendency to sociality to completion. Whereas the play opens with Theseus' relation to Hippolyta being one of a love won by 'doing injuries,' their pre-nuptial state is one of gentle negotiation. Theseus *persuades* Hippolyta that they may view the clumsy play, not because the players will pay them any duty in offering them a good performance, but because Theseus himself will appear as the better ruler in graciously receiving that which has no value. Hippolyta is brought into line here, not by force, but by a lesson in what counts as good management. They will, Theseus points out, be rulers of *merit* not *might*, a merit achieved not by exerting their power but by allowing the players' incompetent efforts:

> The kinder we, to give them thanks for nothing.
> Our sport shall be to take what they mistake:
> And what poor duty cannot do, noble respect
> Takes it in might, not merit
>   (5.1.89–92)

It is in this framing of the play within a play that the due hierarchy of gender is established. Theseus allows the players to believe in their capacity to capture reality so convincingly that the players voice disclaimers about the 'reality' of their play (5.1.215–220). In allowing their naïve beliefs in verisimilitude Theseus distances himself from the confusion between appearance and reality that has provided all the comedy and distortion of the previous acts. He also appears as a figure of reason, persuasion and right seeing in relation to Hippolyta whose sensibilities he will protect: 'Why, gentle sweet, you shall see no such thing' (5.1.87). Like Oberon, Theseus masters appearances, but unlike Oberon he does so by insisting on his power to differentiate appearance from the real feeling that subtends performance. Theseus now leads Hippolyta by reason and persuasion, and this reason is just the power to discern the difference between the artful and the artless:

> Where I have come, great clerks have purposes
> To greet me with premeditated welcomes;
> Here I have seen them shiver and look pale,
> Make periods in the midst of sentences,
> Throttle their practis'd accent in their fears,
> And, in conclusion, dumbly have broke off,
> Not paying me a welcome. Trust me, sweet,
> Out of this silence yet I pic'd a welcome,
> And in the modesty of fearful duty
> I read as much as from the rattling tongue
> Of saucy and audacious eloquence.
>
> (5.1.93–103)

A *Midsummer Night's Dream* subverts the simple matter/appearance or bodies/culture opposition that underpins our modern understanding of gender. The fairy world can be read as an allegory of nature, where nature is neither formless matter, nor ordained law. Nature is a site of conflict and contraries, with tendencies and potentials that need to be managed and ordered by an art or politics that works with its given material, that brings out the implicit law of nature. If one were to believe in a natural lawfulness one would simply see bodies as having an already constituted essence, as having no nature or being outside their expression of proper kinds: this is certainly how Egeus sees Hermia (and how Prospero sees Caliban in *The Tempest*). Such characters see nature, the body, sex or race as causing social and political relations; it is as though nature has a law in itself that politics need only read or express. But good political management is like good art; it works with the form implicit in bodies and nature, bringing out their virtues or tendencies to excellence. Gender – the right relation between male and female – is not located in the body, for the body can always be manipulated, effected, transformed and distorted by physical force. Nor is gender simply imposed or performed. The rude mechanicals, who perform the tragedy of Pyramus and Thisbe believe that their performance will be taken as real, failing to see the obvious disjunction between their bodies and the roles they adopt. Not only do Shakespeare's comedies play on the absurdity of disguised and cross-dressed bodies, acknowledging a disjunction between performed role and performing body, they also present harmony and resolution as the fulfilled virtue of bodies. Bodies themselves are natural with the capacity to be at odds with their form or gender. Gender is social and political, not because it is an imposed overlay, but because it is the fulfilled and proper form, the correct art, of the body whose potential it realises.

By referring to the Elizabethan 'gender system' Montrose assumes both that there must have been a cultural tension and anxiety surrounding the occupation of masculine power – the position of ruler – by a female body, a body sexed as weak, submissive, passionate and unruly. One could argue, however, that far from being a cultural contradiction, the disjunction between Elizabeth's body and her social function was only possible because Renaissance thought had not yet established a sexuality or physicality that could dictate one's social being. A female body could take on another form or gender, and this was because there was no sex/gender system. One's sex did not cause or dictate one's gender or social role. All bodies needed to take on their proper form through art and performance, but this would always be an art or performance in tune with the natural forces *awaiting order*. The forms of gender determine, and are not determined by, bodies, desire and sexual relations.

Even though the play's conclusion overturns the father's will, this is not to assert the rights of the daughter so much as the rights of law: Theseus the king allows the marriage to Lysander for the sake of social equilibrium. The play's triumph is that of reasoned law – a law based on order, hierarchy and proper form – over a law that is mere will, force or the chaos of whim and passion. Sexuality is threateningly mutable; the lovers have a *tendency* to good object choice, for the lovers' preferred partners, as the end of the play makes clear, are also in accord with the order of law. The play demonstrates, not the triumph of free sexual love over the rule of law, but the development of sexuality toward its proper goal and immanent form. Magic may have intervened to redirect Demetrius's object-choice, but magic is presented in two forms: the unruly caprice of Puck that plays havoc with forms for the sake of pleasure and delight, and the redirecting magic of Oberon that ultimately restores proper hierarchies and ownership, but does so only in its deference to Athens and the lovers' imminent return to Athens. Sexual tendency needs to be given proper form and direction, guided by right reason and right vision.

The play's theme of the fluid boundary between appearance and reality has often been seen as potentially subversive, as though the real world of Athens, law, right reason and proper judgment were just as much of a fiction and performance as the fairy world of spectacle, illusion and deliberate distortion. But the play emphasises the fluidity, unreliability and threateningly intrusive world of seduction and distortion only to indicate the degree to which nature must be mastered and formed. The dream world and the illusions of art may at first appear to be at odds with the strict realm of law and right reason but, as the play's development makes clear, the adjustment that law makes to nature, the performance and art of law, are in some ways perfectly natural. Nature comes to perfection through art, performance and manipulation. Nature itself is neither a blank and unformed matter, nor an already determined hierarchy. Nature requires the gentle force of law.

There are always two modes of law, two modes of artifice and two modes of submission. These opposing modes do not so much divide along masculine and feminine lines as they oppose gender to sexuality. In its legitimate form, law is the proper relation of distinct kinds; artifice directs real or brute nature to what it ought to be, and submission is a free acceptance of authority as conducive to the stability of the self. The second mode of law is one of force and natural tyranny, where Oberon rules by virtue of superior power, where the body's tendencies are not directed to any transcendent end or order, and where relations are determined by mutual conflict and reaction, rather than being harmoniously directed. Sexuality, like nature, in Shakespeare's plays is neither the biological matter of modern 'sex' – a biology that causes one's being – nor is it a social construction, a mere role, performance or stereotype. There can only be genders, or the ordered relations among bodies because human life is *essentially artful*, it must actively bring itself to its imminent potential. There is a sexual politics in Shakespeare's plays that cannot be made sense of in the modern understanding of a natural sex or cultural gender. Nature has a tendency towards kinds, and can realise itself only in an artful and managed nature, a performed and continually rehearsed hierarchy. The world of gender – the world of male and female relations – can be undone by sexual desire, by the chaotic and fungible forces of a nature that is not brute matter but that demands direction. There is an essential human tendency to artifice, to create itself as it ought to be.

As we will see in later chapters, recent work on the body has challenged the notion of a gender that is nothing more than artifice and has done so by challenging the modern distinction between nature as matter and culture as art. Nature is itself art, the creation of forms; and such forms are neither automatically determined by what nature is, nor purely arbitrary and imposed. Rather, nature forms itself *politically* – in relation to other bodies, through the negotiation of per-ceived bodies, and in the perception of its own body. Whereas modern thought has tended to see the mind as distinct from the body, as a sub-ject that manages the body as its object, pre-modern thought saw mind (and the ideas we have of ourselves) as part of nature, a nature which itself comes to its form, and can always be deflected from that form. If we see matter as tending towards forms, with these forms themselves adapting to other bodies in political relations, then we can also see gender as exemplary of political formation. How do natural bodies come to represent themselves as being of a certain kind, as hav-ing a certain natural political place?

2   Gender as Form and the Masculinity of Reason

In *A Midsummer Night's Dream* bodies have a potential gender – what they ought to be – but the matter of bodies can stray from and disrupt this proper end. While the status of matter and its relation to gender changes in modernity, it is still the case that the very concept of gender relies on a form–matter distinction. In the contemporary debate about the relation between sex and gender, sex is understood as the unchanging matter upon which social forms of gender are laid. But it is not only the case that the modern concept of gender depends on the form–matter distinction; the very distinction between form and matter is more often than not explained and described in terms which are implicitly gendered. Form is the active, disembodied, knowable and bounded power which gives being, sense and order to an otherwise chaotic, passive, undifferentiated and inessential matter – a matter which has only potential being. The distinction between form and matter was described and detailed through the figures and metaphors of gender: form is the fathering, stronger and dominating force that gives being to a feminine, passive and acquiescent matter.

> And we may liken the receiving principle to a mother, and the source or spring to a father, and the intermediate nature to a child, and may remark further that if the model is to take every variety of form, then the matter in which the model is fashioned will not be duly prepared unless it is formless and free from the impress of any of those shapes which it is hereafter to receive from without.…Wherefore that which is to receive all forms should have no form…Wherefore the mother and receptacle of all created and visible and in any way sensible things is not to be termed earth or air or fire or water, or any of their compounds, or any of the elements from which these are derived, but is an invisible and formless being which receives all these things and in some mysterious way partakes of the intelligible, and is most incomprehensible.
>
> (Plato 1963, 1177–1178 [*Timaeus* 50d–51c])

The distinction between form and matter has been continually represented through a heavily gendered series of metaphors: form impregnates matter; chaotic stuff requires the active insemination of form; the light of form penetrates material darkness; the diffuse material receptacle is partitioned and made real by the active artificer. Form was the male, creative, active and bounding principle, while matter was the female, receptive, passive and amorphous stuff. Such images were crucial to philosophy, which presented reason as a self-fathering power giving birth to eternal truths in opposition to the creations of matter (Derrida 1981, 80). These sexual metaphors that divided form and matter also underpinned the discourses of early medicine and science. Each domain borrowed from the other: reason was likened to an inseminating body, but semen was described as a purely rational or form-giving force (Laqueur 1990, 59). Reason was likened to a fathering principle, but fathers or men were also figured using the image of the pure disembodied light of reason. In ancient thought the discourses of reason and the body were mutually constitutive; there was no separate discourse of biology or the body (Vernant 1990), for the body itself was described through metaphysical language. Laqueur noted that male semen was not physical stuff so much as a pure power, a capacity to form. Indeed, most of the ways in which the form–matter distinction was described, employed metaphors of gender (Laqueur 1990, 61). But most of the ways of thinking about gender were also metaphysical: maleness was form; femaleness was form-receiving matter.

Now there are two ways of dealing with this gendered picture of Western thought's most fundamental distinction, and we will deal with these in turn. Before doing so, however, we need to note a problem that we will take up in more detail later, and which is crucial to the politics of gender today. The matter–form distinction can be aligned with the nature–culture distinction. Whereas ancient or pre-modern thought differentiated genders through a matter–form binary; modern thought more frequently defines gender according to a nature–culture distinction. Sex is the natural unchanging basis upon which culture imposes various social types, roles, forms or genders. The matter–form distinction in ancient thought was a way of describing gender as that which enables difference and distinction: there is one bodily matter that is then gendered by taking on the form of maleness or femaleness. So matter was, in general, formless or genderless. This is what allows Plato to place the ultimate 'nurse' or receptacle of generation

(Plato 1963, 1176 [*Timaeus* 48e–49b]) before the distinction between fathering form and maternal substance, before the difference between what exists eternally and what changes and passes away:

> Wherefore we must also acknowledge that one kind of being is the form which is always the same, uncreated and indestructible, never receiving anything into itself from without nor itself going out to any other, but invisible and imperceptible by any sense, and of which the contemplation is granted to intelligence only. And there is another nature of the same name with it, and like to it, perceived by sense, created, always in motion, becoming in place and again vanishing out of place, which is apprehended by opinion jointly with sense. And there is a third nature, which is space and is eternal, and admits not of destruction and provides a home for all created things, and is apprehended, when all sense is absent, by a kind of spurious reason, and is hardly real – which we, beholding as in a dream, say of all exist-ence that it must of necessity be in some place and occupy a space, but that what is neither in heaven nor in earth has no existence.
> (Plato 1963, 1178–1179 [*Timaeus* 51e–52c])

Not only does Plato *liken* form to a fathering principle and the gen-eration of time and change to the mother who receives forms, he also places this difference of genders within some ultimately ungendered space. There is then an ambivalence in the status of gender in Plato's thought which is typical of all later attempts to understand the duality of terms. Is the ultimate difference of the universe gendered: do we think of reality through a difference between male form and female matter? Or does the opposition between male and female have as its prior ground some unsexed and undifferentiated ground? In contem-porary terms we can ask the question in the following way: is there some ultimate matter that in itself has no qualities, but comes to be sexed and gendered through the process of life and generation? Questions such as these expose the difficulty of thinking of gender as a purely cultural or conceptual problem, for it may well be the case that the concept of culture – some formal and intelligible overlay to an other-wise uniform matter – has always been thought of in gendered terms. Whether we think of matter, as Plato did, as a receiving principle with the potential for form or, as we do today, as pre-cultural meaningless stuff that may or may not cause genders, we tend to think of culture and gender as immaterial. In all cases, the underlying term of bodily nature is made sense of or known through the forming, active and conceptual power of culture. Nature can be likened to matter, and culture can be likened to form because – as in the ancient understanding of matter – nature is that undifferentiated blank stuff requiring the differentiating and meaning-giving power of culture.

Just as the form–matter distinction was explained through gendered metaphors, the modern nature–culture distinction is also tied up with figures of gender. Nature is feminised while culture is described using masculine imagery. In addition to the clichés of mother nature or nature as the nurse, home and origin of our being, there are also more subtle associations. Culture divides, orders, penetrates and illuminates an otherwise inert nature. But while matter–form and nature–culture seem to be analogous there is also an important difference. Today we think of culture as what is open to change, with nature as the ultimately real substance upon which culture is overlaid. We even think of our sexuality, our inner, biologically, genetically, psychologically or hormonally determined being as *real*, while our social and cultural roles can be criticised as mere stereotypes. Our body is the basis or substrate underlying social roles. We think of gender as a construction, and of sex as real. Often, feminist politics takes the form of refusing the social construction of gender in favour of our real sexuality: either by aiming to remove stereotypes or by striving for authentic representation of women. By contrast, the pre-modern distinction between form and matter considered our material and bodily being as inessential, while the form of being was essential. Our real being was not located in our bodies, with the essence of human life more often than not being defined as a capacity to transcend the body, through language, sociality, politics or reason. Essentialism in contemporary gender politics is often associated with biologism; to make a claim for an essential femininity or essential homosexuality usually means enlisting the support of fixed hormonal or genetic determinants – the female brain or the gay gene. The criticism of essentialism proceeds by demonstrating the absence of any link between biology and social behaviour, and thus still posits a distinct real body which is deemed to be irrelevant to our chosen, specific and lived identity (Fausto-Sterling 2000). There is a bodily nature before culture, which is the site upon which gender-political debates are located.

On the ancient picture, nature (or *physis*) was not only matter (*hyle*); nature was the process by which matter came to form. Nature was a principle, a tendency or – as in Aristotle – a teleological process of achieving ends. We could say then that 'nature' was once located on the immaterial or formal side of the binary. Nature was the order or form-dictating power of the cosmos. In *A Midsummer Night's Dream* we can see an ambivalence surrounding the status of nature. Nature is certainly not meaningless or mechanically caused matter, for nature produces prodigies and disruptions. Human culture is a second nature, a necessary supplement that will order the tendencies of a nature that would otherwise fail to complete itself. Nature is neither strict cause nor immutable order, for human nature *as political* still has to be achieved. On a modern conception if nature is deemed to be the site of essences this is because essences are now located in the physical stuff of the world, in biology, genes or the material substrate that are then made meaningful and related to through culture.

Nature has, and has always had, a double meaning. On the one hand, as in ancient thought, nature can be thought of as what is proper, ordered, meant to be; this is the sense nature takes on in the phrase 'human nature.' This nature is neither radically pre-cultural, nor is it opposed to form. And to say that genders were *natural* on this picture would not be to say that they were strictly biologically determined, but that genders were bound up with the order of things. On the other hand, there is another sense of 'nature' as that which is meaningless and pre-cultural. Nature is the domain of chaos, brute need, biological determinism and necessity, while culture is the capacity to defer, order, civilise and temper the violence of need. There is, then, a nature that (as in the ancient conception) includes a matter that tends towards its proper form, and can be opposed to what is corrupt, monstrous or out of order. There is also a nature that is other than order, other than culture, and which can be likened more to the chaotic formless matter of ancient thought. We can think of these two natures in gendered terms: the first is a nature that orders itself, propels itself towards reason, gives birth to itself and produces form itself – a self-fathering nature. The second is a nature that is the passive basis of form: that which must be ordered, rendered meaningful, bounded and determined – a nature that is the womb of reason. For this reason, the nature–culture binary can sometimes be presented as a male–female binary, and at other times as a female–male binary. Woman may appear as the natural, biological and embodied origin of being, or she can be associated with surface, display artifice and fashion.

Anthropologists have often argued that woman is associated with nature, with the bodily, reproductive and material life against which culture must act. In an influential essay, 'Is Female to Male as Nature is to Culture?,' Sherry Ortner goes so far as to argue that, 'The secondary status of women in society is one of the true universals, a pan-cultural fact' (Ortner 1996, 21). Ortner explains this by arguing that culture must – if it is to be *culture* – work against that which is given immediately and precedes meaning (Ortner 1996, 25). Here, nature is taken in the sense of mere matter, as that which must be formed, ordered and structured by culture. While the feminine is often associated with the nature side of the nature–culture binary, where nature is the devalued term, there are also senses in which culture is regarded as secondary and supplemental to an original nature. And here, as Jacques Derrida has pointed out, 'man' can be defined as the proper, living and self-governing subject who defines himself against technology (Derrida 1981). Masculinity can be seen as natural in the earlier or pre-modern sense, where nature is the intrinsic form and proper order of the world: man is the rational centre of the cosmos, the essential human form. Woman, by contrast, can be associated with culture in its derivative, supplementary or secondary sense. Women are associated with distortion and corruption, with the deflection of nature from its rational end. Such associations occur in contemporary discourse in the linking of women with fashion, popular culture, artifice, surface appearance (Felski 1995), while men are associated with the useful, ordering, universal and logical domains of life. Whereas the male body is naturally governed by reason, good sense and its own proper form, the female body is disruptive, unruly and capable of subverting the true relation between mind and body.

In this complex web of gendered associations the nature–culture binary sometimes mirrors the traditional form–matter binary – with nature being the feminine ground that must be given form, order and realisation through culture. But this is not always the case, and the 'natural' can also be associated with order, propriety and reason – opposed to the demonic, corrupting and irrational workings of technology and artifice. One needs to be wary then of certain anthropologists, such as Claude Levi-Strauss, who claim that the universal position of women as objects rather than subjects can be explained by the universality of the nature–culture opposition. For Levi-Strauss, it is the distance from, and prohibition of, the mother as first natural object of desire that established the system of social and cultural exchange among men (Levi-Strauss 1969, 481). But it would be a mistake, and unsustainable, to think of nature–culture as either a fundamental and necessary opposition, and even more of a mistake to think that it was always gendered in one particular way. Sometimes nature is feminine and opposed to reason; on other occasions, reason is natural and masculine, while the feminine is the unnatural corruption of reason. What does seem to be a constant, however, is *some* structuring binary that is organised and represented through complex and contradictory gender oppositions. Furthermore, the very concept of gender, as that which differentiates kinds, is itself bound up with a defining and fundamental binary: either gender is the division of an otherwise neutral ground, or gender is the reflection, expression or realisation of prior intrinsic differences. It may be that the concept of gender is inherently metaphysical and dualist, for the very notion of kinds implies that there are kinds *of* some prior ground. To ask questions about the reality of gender – whether gender is based in sex difference or whether gender is an idea or concept that differentiates nature – presupposes something like a real nature whose cultural representation and sense can then be debated.

For many anthropologists it is the universality of the nature–culture distinction, or this type of distinction, which also explains the universality of gender (Young and Harris 1976). Some distinction needs to be made between the world as it is and the form it takes on, and the usual way for thinking about this distinction is through a female nature/matter and a male culture/form (Ortner 1996). Whatever value the binary between nature and culture or matter and form takes, it needs to be noted that it is a peculiarly forceful opposition. Whereas other values vary historically and culturally, and while we have already noted the differences in the form–matter distinction in ancient and modern texts, it is nevertheless the case that a binary way of thinking characterises most, if not all, cultures. One of the crucial questions for the politics of gender is whether binary thinking is essential, and whether such binaries need necessarily be figured through male and female opposites.

On the one hand, one could argue that some minimal binary is necessary to the very activity of thinking: without the distinction between what is and what is not one could not say anything at all, for to assert that something *is*, is at least to reject its opposite. Such an insistence on the necessity of a distinction between being and non-being or presence and absence has been maintained since Plato. But does such a distinction or difference need to be thought through a hierarchy, and a gender hierarchy at that? And is this *logical* binary at all relevant to the binaries of nature and culture, or matter and form? According to Vicki Kirby there is still a 'rampant culturalism' and 'inadvertent Cartesianism' in contemporary theory which maintains the distinction between nature and culture' (Kirby 1997, 151–152). In the final chapters of this book we will return to recent attempts to think difference beyond the hierarchical nature–culture binary. But even if we concede that such a binary has been assumed, and is not necessary, it remains the case that binarism is intertwined with the very concepts through which the gender debate is undertaken. Jacques Derrida has argued that the concept of the sign, and the 'concept of the concept,' will necessarily constitute a hierarchical distinction between presence or being, and that which signifies or refers to being (Derrida 1978, 280–281). Indeed, the very structure of language, as signifying or making sense, presupposes some distinction between the presented or spoken sign and the subtending meaning. If our very idea of communication is dualist, how do we negotiate the imaginary way in which we think such dualisms, and why has gender been so crucial to what Michele LeDoeuff has referred to as the philosophical imaginary (LeDoeuff 1989, 23)?

With these questions we are brought up against the circular problem of the concept of gender. On the one hand, we could say that the gender system is merely a cultural construct, having no real or natural being. On the other, we could say that this distinction between nature and culture, between the real and the ideal or between matter and its form is itself only thinkable through gendered metaphors. Without the notion of a passive feminine stuff that is there to take on active and rational form we could not imagine 'mere' nature, nor could we imagine a form or culture capable of redefining or recreating itself. For this reason, many feminists have tackled the problem of gender by targeting an entire structure of binaries; for they insist that one cannot detach one pair – say, male and female – from all the others. Our thought is located in a structure of differences and oppositions, all involved and intertwined with each other (Shulman 1996, 432). According to Monique Wittig, this structure of oppositions goes back to Plato and Aristotle, and only by understanding the ways in which our values have emerged from supposedly metaphysical foundations will we be able to rethink the valence of gender: 'For Being is being good, male, straight, one, in other words, godlike, while non-Being is being anything else (many), female: it means discord, unrest, dark, and bad' (Wittig 1990). The most famous example of this presentation of the binary structure of Western thought is given by the contemporary French feminist writer and dramatist Hélene Cixous:

> Activity/Passivity,
> Sun/Moon,
> Culture/Nature,
> Day/Night,
> Father/Mother,
> Head/heart,
> Intelligible/sensitive,
> Logos/Pathos,
> Form, convex, step, advance, seed, progress.
> Matter, concave, ground – which supports the step, receptacle.
> Man
> ——
> Woman
>
> (Cixous 1981, 90)

What Cixous's table seems to suggest is that gender is part of a whole series of oppositions, and that one cannot think the opposition between nature and culture, or reason and the body *innocently*, for these distinctions are already associated with maleness and femaleness and a host of other values. In many ways this position can be aligned with a much broader tradition of anthropology and sociology influenced by structuralism. Here, gender is a way of ordering the world, and even though the values attached to each gender may vary, *some* binary structure is operative. Gender is intertwined with some of the most basic categories, such as nature and culture, and so tackling gender requires tackling an entire conceptual apparatus. Two questions emerge here, both of which will be dealt with in far greater detail in later chapters when we look at the contemporary debates surrounding the status of gender and its relation to sex. First, is gender just one opposition among others – part of a mutually defining series where no single opposition can be considered primary, or is the male–female opposition that which grounds all others? Second, is some form of dualism necessary? It may, for example, be possible to do away with an opposition between male and female, possibly even between mind and body, but surely *some* oppositions – such as truth and falsity, presence and absence, or being and non-being are *necessary*? For without these logical oppositions one could not even argue. And do we need to think these necessary logical opposites through some concrete opposition, such as male and female? What would the relation be between logically necessary distinctions – the true and the false, the present and the absent – and the figural oppositions that we lay over those basic distinctions? We could say that being and non-being, presence and absence, or truth and falsity, are *necessary* and logical, while the representation of these distinctions and their association with gender is *arbitrary* or cultural. We would then have the logical and the necessary opposed to the cultural and the arbitrary.

Once again, we would be brought back to *some* type of original distinction, and it is just this type of distinction that has always been gender-inflected. Man is associated with logic, reason, necessity and judgement, while woman has been associated with mere seeming, vague passions, the ephemeral and surface appearance. Can the *logical* categories that we use to discuss gender, such as the distinction between the real and the constructed, or the necessary and the contingent, be detached from a history of gendered metaphors and associations? Until relatively recently debates around gender were also debates about nature and culture: to what extent is gender the result of natural sexual differences, or are these supposedly natural differences themselves imagined because of social genders? The concept of gender, today, as one's social or cultural role or type, can only with difficulty be detached from the distinction between nature and culture, and the distinction between nature and culture – what something is naturally and intrinsically, versus its interpretation – plays back into fundamental distinctions between being and non-being.

Anthropologists and psychoanalysts have argued that in order to think these abstract and metaphysical oppositions – between presence and absence, the essential and the arbitrary – most cultures and individuals have to have some figural or imaginary scheme, some concrete or embodied way of thinking these basic oppositions. More often than not, the very difference that is required in order to establish civilisation – that difference between nature as it is, and culture as the form and order that nature may take on – has been imagined through the opposition of feminine and masculine. Gender may not be an essential or logical category, but it is the way we think and imagine such categories: a Mother Nature on the one hand and the father figure of the law on the other. According to Pierre Bourdieu, we should neither ignore the force of images of gender binaries, nor should we accept such hierarchies as universal.

Masculine domination, Bourdieu argues, is *the* structuring principle
that helps organise and structure social spaces, which have differed
historically and culturally (Bourdieu 2001, 108). And this is because
whatever cultural 'habitus,' or organisation of relations and values we
inhabit, such relations always begin from the relation of bodies:

> The *biological* difference between the *sexes*, i.e. between the male and
> female bodies, and, in particular, *the anatomical* difference between
> the sex organs, can thus appear as the natural justification of the
> socially constructed difference between the *genders*, and in particular
> of the social division of labour. The body and its movements, matrices
> of universals that are subject to work of social construction, are
> neither completely determined in their significance, especially their
> sexual significance, nor completely undetermined, so that the sym-
> bolism that is attached to them is both conventional and 'motivated',
> and therefore perceived as quasi-natural. Because the social principle
> of vision constructs the anatomical difference and because this
> socially constructed difference becomes the basis and apparently
> natural justification of the social vision which founds it, there is thus
> a relationship of circular causality which confines thought within the
> self-evidence of relations of domination inscribed both in objectivity,
> in the form of objective divisions, and in subjectivity, in the form of
> cognitive schemes which being organized in accordance with these
> divisions, organize the perception of these objective divisions.
>
> (Bourdieu 2001, 11–12)

Bourdieu's 'circularity' of the relationship between biology and gender
insists that one can neither see gender differences as merely imposed,
nor see them as directly caused. Rather, a biological difference that
leads to masculine domination is both justified by, and used to
represent, social relations. Even in Bourdieu's highly reflective and
non-reductive approach to gender, an approach that stresses the
importance of dynamic social relations, there is nevertheless a clearly
marked difference between biology/anatomy and the social field.

The gender of form and reason

As the contemporary debate about sexual essentialism versus gender
construction demonstrates, the relation between what being in itself *is*
as opposed to its perceived form or representation, plays out one more

version of the matter–form distinction. The modern position, which we will examine in the next chapter, that insists that it is matter that is real and that we merely impose our categories upon it, nevertheless relies on a distinction between what is truly real and what is merely apparent or secondary. Bourdieu, for example, insists that as long as we see gender as having no ground in biology we will be unable to change the system of 'masculine domination' (Bourdieu 2000, 103). The dualisms that postmodern theorists contest, he argues, are 'deeply rooted in things' (Bourdieu 2000, 103). The field of social relations is mobile, but it can only be mobilised if one attends to its use of, and determination by, the powers of bodies. Bourdieu's approach sets itself against what he takes to be the defining feature of postmodernism, its reduction of gender to mere appearance or performance. But what Bourdieu shares with those postmodernists he criticises is the location of gender in created and temporal social relations, and not in some timeless or unchanging order. Today, when various parties contest whether one's sexual identity is natural or cultural, a border between matter and form, which is also a border between what is real and what is supplementary, is still assumed.

Feminists have responded to this supposedly central binary in Western thought in a number of ways. Western metaphysics, despite differences in history and culture, has often been defined as structured by a binary opposition, a series of overlapping and related dichotomies. Regardless of modern, pre-modern or postmodern approaches, something like a gender binary has been fundamental to Western thought. That is, even though there have been epochal changes in how we understand the world, ourselves or being, something like the opposition between male and female has structured our knowledge. We will look at the subtleties of this argument when we consider recent and contemporary debates regarding the relation between sex and gender. For now we can characterise two broad approaches to the claim that Western thought in general – from Plato to the present – has been structured around the male–female binary. On the one hand, there are those who define the gender binary alongside a series of other oppositions, with gender difference being one value among others, reinforcing, and reinforced by, a series of dichotomies. On this picture, male is to female, what reason is to body, what light is to darkness, what order is to chaos, what identity is to difference, what Occident is to Orient and so on. Helene Cixous is the most quoted example of this schema (Cixous 1981). On the other hand, there are those who consider sexual difference to be more than one difference in a series of oppositions; here, sexual difference would be a fundamental or possibly 'transcendental' difference – a difference through which all other differences are explained and made possible.

The first claim – that the male–female binary is one of a series – argues for a form of historical and cultural association. Traditionally, reason has been associated with qualities that have also been used to define men and male bodies. As we have already seen, Thomas Laqueur has traced the way this opposition informed medical knowledge. The male role in procreation was that of an immaterial, forming and creative power, while women provided formless matter. A gendered opposition – an opposition between masculine and active form, and feminine and passive matter was used to explain sexual relations of bodies. Sex, or biology, was seen through the lens of gender, or the relation between male and female principles – principles that could be expressed to a greater or lesser extent in any body (Laqueur 1980, 62). It was not the body itself, what today we would call biology, which determined gender. Use of masculine and feminine figures and oppositions extended well beyond medical knowledge, and well beyond arguments about marriage, sexual relations and social power. The opposition between male and female was a general structuring principle that could then be used to explain social, medical and scientific questions.

One of the most commented upon texts of the tradition is Plato's *Timaeus*, in which Plato, through the figure of Socrates, describes the generation or genesis of being. Before something can be said to be it must take on form; that from which it is formed is non-being, a non-being that has only a 'bastard' or secondary existence. This original text of Western thought has been seized on by twentieth-century critics as both the foundation and the undermining of traditional ontology and the dichotomy of gender (Butler 1993; Derrida 1995, 92; Irigaray 1985, 321–322; Kristeva 1981, 133). On the one hand, the *Timaeus* insists that only what is formed, ordered, present and nameable has true being. On the other hand, it admits that there must have been some unnameable, unthinkable formlessness from which being was generated. This not-yet-original, unthinkable and formless ground is feminine, for it has being only in relation to the masculine and originating power. There is the originating power, the modelled beings created by that power, and then the nurse or receptacle, which can only be spoken of 'dimly' (Plato 1963, 1176 [48e–49b]). Plato therefore invokes one of the most common cultural myths of a feminine ground, formlessness or otherness from which the world of identities is generated.

This metaphysical 'marriage' of male and female that explains the origin of being is neither confined to ancient texts, nor to the Western tradition. Even modernist and postmodern authors see creativity as possible only with the interaction of male and female elements: only through an encounter with the irrational and feminine forces of chaos can an artist or thinker begin to produce. According to Virginia Woolf, 'Poetry ought to have a mother as well as a father…Some collaboration has to take place in the mind between the woman and the man before the art of creation can be accomplished. Some marriage of opposites has to be consummated' (Woolf 1977, 99 [1929]). The figure of the male poet who receives the muse has not been confined to classical or traditional literature, with the interaction between male and female contraries often described in violent terms. W.B. Yeats's poem 'Leda and the Swan' describes the rape of the barely passive Leda as a metaphor for creation (Yeats 1982, 241), while the twentieth-century French philosopher, Gilles Deleuze, employs the sexual metaphor of creation, but does away with the passive female body altogether: 'I saw myself as taking an author from behind and giving him a child that would be his own offspring, yet monstrous' (Deleuze 1995, 6).

In the *Symposium*, Socrates describes the philosopher as a 'midwife,' as aiding in the labour of reason. Reason will give birth to eternal truths – far more worthy than the actual offspring of bodies (Plato 1963, 561 [209d]). It can only arrive at this pure birth by ascending from the apprehension of beautiful bodies to the love of beauty itself, and then to that which is desired eternally: the pure and disembodied form of truth. This birth does not then have a distinct material object; the philosopher who, through reason, contemplates truth becomes or achieves his creation, a creation that exists eternally. This notion of the light of reason that gives birth to itself – a power of truth in man that allows any man to see the truth of reason that is already within him – is an image of self-fathering or self-insemination which at once relies upon the image of material birth, but also negates and distinguishes itself from that birth. According to the French philosopher Jacques Derrida the concept of reason has always relied on this metaphor of self-fathering. Further, in order to think outside this metaphor, or in order to think reason in a pure and autonomous fashion free of all images and materiality, would still require that one depended upon the figures of self-generation that are tied to images of man (Derrida 1981).

Deconstruction

Derrida's deconstruction has raised a number of issues in relation to gender. One of the most significant has been the gendered metaphors that have marked the history of reason. According to Derrida it is not so much the male–female metaphors that are important so much as the structure of these metaphors – and the structure of metaphor as such (Derrida 1978). The very concept of metaphor distinguishes a real and literal ground from a figure or likeness, once again repeating a dualism between origin and representation. The dualism of metaphor is neither neutral nor innocent: for one term is seen as self-sufficient and real – the literal – while another term is secondary, dependent and inessential – the figure or image. Consequently, the metaphors upon which Western thought is structured, such as the light of reason as opposed to the opacity of the body, are asymmetrical. One term is not just valued more than another; it is seen as ground, cause and the true being of the other. It is not just that masculinity is identified with form and reason, while the feminine is identified with an inessential and not fully real matter that requires the light of reason. What is important for Derrida is that one term in the binary is self-sufficient and defined as the origin of the other. Reason, truth, light or form is regarded as original, foundational and self-sufficient. Matter is only real when it takes on form. One can think of the way in which Western thought presents certain terms as self-sufficient and others as accidental: goodness is capable of existing in itself, while evil is the corruption or negation of the good; being can exist in itself, with absence occurring only as the lack of being; error is merely the corruption of truth; darkness is only the absence of light and – by extension – man is the human norm, while woman is merely a lesser version or deviation from the centre.

Deconstruction, then, does not just look at the binaries that structure thinking; it also looks at the hierarchy of a binary, and the ways in which the first term structures and determines its other. It is not that reason is deemed to be better than unreason, or that men are deemed to be better than women. It is that reason and masculinity are seen as the ground or basis from which unreason and femininity are explained. There is a single norm of humanity – exemplified by the male – and there is a single standard of reason.

The feminine and the irrational are deviations from this assumed originating and self-generating power. Derrida's tactic is not to reverse the opposition. Rather, he wants to show how the supposedly secondary and inessential weaker term is essential to the structure of the supposed origin (Culler 1983, 174). Reason or the aim of pure, uncorrupted, disembodied and image-independent reason – reason as opposed to fiction and prejudice – must rely upon some image or fiction, such as self-fathering metaphors, or images of light. In order to be thought of *as disembodied*, reason must rely upon some expulsion or distance from the body, must depend upon an original decision or hierarchy that cannot itself be reasoned. All the images of gender, self-generation, fathering, light, disembodiment, purity and activity that characterise reason cannot be disengaged from an original violent hierarchy.

Deconstruction exposes the ways in which a binary of supposedly two distinct terms is actually a single privileged term and its dependent, accidental and derivative other. In all such binaries the ground or decision that determines this privileged term is itself undecided. In the binary of sex and gender, for example, sex is usually understood as the real, natural and immutable ground with gender being the accidental, secondary and dependent representation or mediation of that ground. Gender is the way in which we think about or relate to sex. Deconstruction does not elevate one term over the other but shows the ways in which such a binary inhabits a single logic: the binary of sex and gender presents a natural ground (sex) that then presents itself in some differentiated form (gender). However, all those features which are normally deemed to be secondary, derivative and attributable to gender – all the accidental or inessential features of gender – are essential to sex. Derrida's deconstruction famously insists that if an event is possible – if speech can be represented through writing, or if sex can be represented through gender – then this possibility is *structural*; it tells us something about what the supposedly original term is. If sex can be represented through gender, if it can become organised through a system or norms, differences and relations this is because sex is already other than itself. There is no natural, original or essential sexuality that has the *possibility* of becoming cultural, for sex is essentially differential. The supposed origin, Derrida insists, is not just *known through* difference; it 'is' difference. In the case of sex, which Derrida explores in his readings of Freud, that original life that supposedly underlines and precedes culture and writing already takes the form or character of writing. Sex is a process of anarchic movement, genesis, becoming or difference which we may like to think of as a natural essence before all gender, but which only appears to be original *after* its organisation into supposedly secondary terms. Derrida suggests that it is this repression of a radical, anarchic and non-conceptual difference, or *différance*, that has been effected through the figure of the man of reason, the subject or consciousness who would be at the origin of all language and culture. Derrida also suggests that one can begin to think the otherness of this man of reason through the figure of the feminine: not an essential feminine before all language, but the idea or image of that which resists the determining logic of fixed identities.

Now some feminists, such as Luce Irigaray whose work we will consider in a later chapter, suggest that there is a reason why metaphors of gender have structured the concept of reason. Irigaray explains the emergence of philosophy and reason as a direct result of the production of the masculine body as the only sex (Irigaray 1985, 134). The image of rational man creates, for itself, the feminine as the irrational body that must be repressed and brought to order. For Irigaray, then, the male–female binary is crucial to the establishment of the Western ideal of reason; without the fiction of the male subject who distances himself from the maternal natural body there could be no idea of pure and self-determining thought. Irigaray insists that the gender of Western thought can be explained and demarcated; by looking at the ways in which reason has produced an image of the feminine, we can imagine *another* mode of the subject that recognises and affirms its becoming from its bodily genesis or gender: 'If gender were to develop individually, collectively, and historically, it could mark *the place where spirit entered human nature*, the point in time when the infinite passed into the finite, given that each individual of a gender is finite and potentially infinite in his or her relation to gender' (Irigaray 1993a, 139). Irigaray's work can, to a certain extent, be included within a broad project of deconstructing gender. Rather than appeal to the feminine as it has already been defined in the male–female binary her classic reading of the history of philosophy looks at the way reason has always defined itself through an opposition. Reason is the form, movement, sense or concept that re-presents a body, nature, sensible or matter that, in itself, has no subjectivity or becoming of its own. The autonomous feminine to which Irigaray appeals recognises that the formation of such a binary depends upon a 'sensible transcendental' (Irigaray 1993b, 115). The very idea of a ground or genesis of being has always been thought through bodily images. If we imagine a subject who relates to its world not in terms of logic and judgement but as gendered, as living through a specific and sexed body in relation to another sexed body, then we replace the static binary of subject–object, with a relation between two subjects.

For Derrida, however, it cannot be possible to give a reasoned account or origin for the gendered metaphors that mark the history of Western reason. Any attempt to return to the origin, to explain the birth of our founding metaphors would, once again, rely upon an image of reason that can author and give birth to itself, that can step back from all its material instances and see again its pure origin. No opposition, such as the opposition between male and female, or reason and unreason, can explain the emergence of thought, for the act of thinking and reasoning is already located within a series of decided oppositions (Derrida 1978, 33).

For Derrida, then, the male–female binary emerges from a differentiation that is before or beyond all other structuring differences (Derrida 1983, 80). One cannot, for example, explain the masculinity of reason by looking at biology, for the very concept of 'biology' is itself only possible through the opposition between nature and culture, an opposition that already relies on the distinction between an origin and its effects. Any story of an origin can only be told from a point that sees itself as after the origin; we are always located within some structure of difference. The only way in which deconstruction can approach the gender binary is to look at its working and effects. No opposition, neither nature–culture, nor form–matter, nor male–female could legitimately be seen as the cause and ground of all the others. For any such opposition is already within a structure of differences and oppositions, and so cannot step outside and explain the origin of all opposition.

From this it follows, according to those feminists who have followed Derrida, that the feminine cannot be seen as an essence outside language (Cornell 1991, 104). Rather, the very notion of essence, and the very distinction between, say, structuring language on the one hand and pure undifferentiated reality on the other is already caught up in the system of differences that is also structured through gender (Kirby 1997, 151). Derrida's own tactic has been to try to think the process of difference, or *différance*, from which oppositions emerge but which itself escapes all conceptualisation and identification. Beyond the identities and differences of male and female, and before all notions of an origin, there must have been some differentiating process that can only be known in its effects, only 'known' as other than any knowable binary. On such an account gender is *one* of the ways in which Western thought has been structured. There is nothing essential about this structure. Indeed, the notion of essence – as that which is original, originating and unchanging – is itself caught up in this structure (Derrida 1983, 72). Gender is one of the crucial figures that has been deployed to establish the rational and the human.

Binaries of reason and gender: Genevieve Lloyd

Even when gender is not mentioned explicitly, philosophy, theology and other stories of genesis employ an opposition between an active, forming and immaterial power and a passive, formless and inert stuff. In so doing, these active–passive or form–matter oppositions reinforce the ways in which male–female genders have also been defined. We can think, alongside Plato's *Timaeus*, of the divine introduction and cre-ation of light in the book of Genesis. When God said, 'Let there be light' and created the world, he illuminated darkness; but this darkness before all being and creation cannot have had any *being* – for God must be the origin of being. In the series of oppositions that underlies Western thought one term is said to have true being – form, light and reason – while its other is merely the negation of what is: darkness is the absence of light; irrational is the lack of reason; matter is lacking in form; and woman is the other of man. Plato gives a typically gendered account of this generation of being from non-being. That from which form, space, truth and harmonious order emerges is the *chora*, which receives form but 'is' not, in itself, a being. The birth of the universe is self-engendering and autonomous, with the *chora* or receptive stuff being only an inessential element (Plato 1963, 1178 [51a]). Similarly, in the Judeo-Christian tradition, God does not create the world *from* some substance that has its own existence; there is no existence or being before divine creation. The darkness or chaos from which being emerges is non-being, nothing, parasitic, inessential and unreal.

In Christian theology this positing of an original absence or neg-ation from which form and creation emerge has been deployed to account for the presence of evil in this world, where evil is not created by God but is that which works against creation. In both the Judeo-Christian and ancient Greek traditions the originating principle is self-generating, with its other being the mere negation or absence of form – not a being in its own right. And this binary parallels the trad-itional explanation of gender, where male reason is the power to return to and account for itself, while the female body is that which remains resistant to form and order. On the one hand, the very image of reason seems to borrow from maternal images – reason gives birth to itself – while also repressing natural birth: reason is the capacity to free oneself from any bodily or physical process in order to form and intuit eternal truths and forms.

Many feminists have argued that Western thought begins with this privileging of a rational, self-sufficient, detached, disembodied and timeless *form* over chaotic, external, material and dispersed unreason; they have also argued that the metaphors to describe this opposition have more often than not been gendered (Spelman 1990). The very features used to define reason, order and being, have also been used to define what differentiates men from women. Men are detached from their bodies, freed from physical generation, liberated from the passions, capable of thinking in terms of universal truths. Women, by contrast, are embodied, irrational, passionate, other-directed and concerned with physical and particular generation.

One of the most important articulations of this connection between masculinity and reason came from the Australian philosopher Genevieve Lloyd. Whereas feminists had previously either demanded that women were equal to men *or* that women were essentially and valuably different from male reason, Lloyd looks at the way maleness and reason are produced in the same conceptual complex. In *Man of Reason*, Lloyd wants to 'de-essentialise' gender by looking at the ways in which the binary of reason and unreason has used, and been used by, the binary of male and female. One of the key points of Lloyd's work is that definitions of both reason and gender vary historically, with women sometimes being identified with nature, passivity and the body, and at others with virtue, domestic cultivation and care; but in all cases, and with a shifting attribution of values, reason has been defined through a gendered conceptual matrix, and gender has been defined through the establishment of a norm of reason (Lloyd 1984, 104). What is significant, according to Lloyd, are not those moments when philosophers are blatantly sexist, nor those other moments when philosophers concede that women are just as rational as men. Rather, gender politics lies at a far deeper and structuring level (Lloyd 1984, 105), and it is the figure and image of 'man' that determines the sex of Western thought. Reason has a number of historically varying definitions but it has always been defined through the values and differences that have characterised masculinity. Even when women are accorded the capacity of reason they are defined through norms and values that are associated with what it means to be male (Lloyd 1984, 49). Philosophers frequently, Lloyd argues, ostensibly support the equality and dignity of women but maintain an implicit gender dichotomy through their definition of reason. Plato, whose *Timaeus* establishes a crucial dichotomy between female formlessness and male reason, nevertheless felt that women ought to be liberated from the demands of child rearing and become rational and political individuals (Saxonhouse 1976, 195). The problem of reason and gender lies, Lloyd notes, with the definition of reason itself, rather than who is deemed capable of reason. Even when women are defined as rational, all those features that are used to define reason, such as autonomy, detachment, self-consciousness, impartiality and self-assertion are precisely those qualities that have been used to differentiate one gender from another. Further, as definitions of what counts as rational vary historically, so does the differentiation of men from women. If, for example, reason is no longer, as it was for Plato, a singular, disembodied and purely theoretical power and comes to be associated with, say, heightened moral sensitivity, then it is men who are defined through these positive attributes.

For Lloyd, there is nothing essentially masculine about reason. Indeed, there is nothing essential about masculinity or the male body; the form of reason and the form of masculinity vary historically and culturally. But reason is always a norm for human life in general, and that norm is invariably exemplified in what counts as masculine. Lloyd has also argued, more recently, that if feminist philosophy is defined by a capacity to recognise the images and figures that define the philosophical landscape, feminist analysis can also be turned to questions of racial exclusion (Lloyd 2000, 33). Feminist philosophy's attention to gender has exposed the ways in which philosophy's imaginary attachments to the body and other concrete figures have determined supposedly neutral and universal values. Lloyd's argument is therefore one of complex historical association. She does not want to affirm intrinsically feminine values in opposition to the supposed violence of male reason (Lloyd 1984, 106). She does not assume that reason has been valued *because* one gender in possession of reason has dominated another gender who are, say, more passionate and caring. Rather, she argues that gender and reason are mutually produced and defined historically. The opposition between male and female is produced with the opposition between what counts as rational and what is defined as secondary or supplementary. This would mean that even when writers celebrate the mystery, darkness, passion, beauty and enigma of femininity, they create a masculine reason of clarity, light, logic, disembodiment and transparency. Whatever values are attributed to the irrational, and however desirable the reason's 'other' might seem to be, the very concept of *reason* (which is the concept that is presupposed in all argument and justification) cannot be dismissed as one quality among others. Reason is just that necessarily assumed norm in all discussion and cannot be taken as just one value among others; at the same time, however, the inclusive ideal of reason should enable us to use reason itself to expand and enrich the practice of philosophy (Lloyd 1984, 107).

Lloyd's argument locates gender bias and gender determination precisely where it is *not* mentioned. Lloyd concludes that claims to gender neutrality – claims for a reason that is disembodied and knows no sex – are implicitly masculinist, for it is always the male body that is seen as having the power to abandon its physicality, while women are inevitably deemed to be governed by their sex (Lloyd 1984, 107). By claiming, for example, that there is one standard of reason, that all bodies (including women) are capable of participating in that ideal, *and* that the ideal is gender-neutral, philosophers create a single norm. Masculinity is, in fact, just this assumed norm which presents itself as sexless. It is precisely when a philosopher insists that women are and should be rational that he also, therefore, submits women to an implicit male standard. What it means to be a male body – self-contained, active, autonomous and well ordered – is also what defines reason. The gender dichotomy and the value of reason are produced in relation to each other.

Lloyd's work on the 'man of reason' has particular relevance for the domain of philosophy, where reason is obviously a fundamental value. But reason also has a forceful literary and imaginary heritage. Indeed, Lloyd's recent work has stressed the extent to which human political life is formed through fictions and ideas the self has of its own body. The ideas and images of reason have been crucial to the philosophical imaginary: the shaping of the self through the imagination of the body. Prior to the modern emphasis on science and material determinism, where sexual difference can be located in the body, differences of gender were explained according to different degrees of participation in the form of reason (Lloyd 1984, 33). But this structuring reason could itself only be imagined through figures of the body and relations among bodies. Gendered bodies were, in particular, crucial to the definition and 'mapping' of reason.

One of the achievements of the enlightenment, which was crucial for the development of feminism, was a shift in the very concept of reason. Whereas reason had once been *substantive*, almost considered as a quality or power that a soul could or could not have, reason in the enlightenment became purely formal and disembodied. Reason was no longer a portion of divine existence within man, no longer an inner light bestowed by God. Reason was not, as it was up until the seventeenth century, the possession of innate principles and laws. In the enlightenment the *only* principle of reason was that every principle ought to be justified and demonstrated. Reason became a structure of arguments – avoiding contradiction, justifying one's premises. This shift in emphasis had major implications for gender. First, as long as reason was an innate capacity, or something one possessed, one could locate reason in the soul or form of man, and reason could be used to differentiate genders – with men and women participating in reason to varying degrees. In the reading of *Paradise Lost* that follows we can see how John Milton saw reason as something one could discern and intuit in one's own soul. Because of this, men and women were submitted to the same standard. All beings ought to be rational, and gender differences were determined by the degree to which the standard of reason could be fulfilled. Second, as long as reason was defined as the ordering principle of the world, gender was also determined by what lay beyond mere matter. The opposition of male and female expressed, justified, and was grounded in, an eternal and divine structure of binaries. The enlightenment idea that gender might be grounded in the body, and that reason should know no gender and be a purely relational structure of arguments, was alien to a Miltonic world, where a body's realisation of its gender was also an expression of divine reason. There is no clearer expression of this way of thinking than *Paradise Lost*, a text that was written just as modern science, political revolution and developments in metaphysics were challenging the idea of an immutable and transcendent order which human beings ought to obey.

Paradise Lost

In *Paradise Lost*, it is precisely the demand that women ought to have the same standard, but not the same realisation, of reason as men that allows for a gender hierarchy in a text that otherwise refuses all forms of worldly or unjust hierarchy. Milton uses the relation of gender to differentiate between the legitimate rational hierarchies of form and order, and the spurious worldly hierarchies of mere force and imposition. Indeed, Milton criticises a misogynist view of two sexes, each of which bears a different essence or mode of reason (Wittreich 1987). Rather, there is one essential reason, which in its distribution in varying degrees, determines the distinct form of each gender. Furthermore, gender is not only explained *through* a rational hierarchy; gender difference is presented as *the* exemplary cosmic difference. If we can understand how it is that male relates to female we will then be able to discern harmony and relations in general. Milton uses the relation between Adam and Eve to express proper and due subordination, and thereby marks a difference between rational relations of warranted reverence and tyrannical impositions of power.

The relation of gender in *Paradise Lost* helps to explain how there can be hierarchy in a just universe. Like any revolutionary writer, Milton must *both* attack an existing illegitimate power – in his day, the monarchical power which was not rationally decided but was merely received, and which is reflected in his description of Satan's 'pomp,' display, rhetoric and seductive appearance – *and* justify a legitimate power – in Milton's case, the power of reason which decides for and determines itself. The binaries of legitimate and illegitimate, original and derived, authentic and corrupt, rational and irrational, and good and evil are mapped around a series of dual relations, with Adam and Eve providing the first couple. The opposition of gender structures *Paradise Lost* both at the level of image and of argument: Milton opposes self-determining reason to mere appearance and allure, opposes logic and universal truth to display and the seductions of immediate pleasure, and he also opposes a hierarchy in which reason recognises proper authority, to a hierarchy in which reason is enslaved by mere force. The opposition between true reason as order versus the mere power of seduction and display mirrors and reinforces the opposition between masculine rationality and feminine embodiment.

Milton's description of wedded love in paradise argues for a form of love that is ordered by reason, that produces domestic harmony, and that can be contrasted with the chaotic, derivative and surface appearances of the arbitrary power of the court. Love, the source of human creation, is ordered by reason, and is justly expressed in the marriage of Adam and Eve, whose position within the cosmos is clearly bounded by what can and cannot be known; they are ordered by a reason that transcends their own point of view:

> Hail wedded love, mysterious law, true source
> Of human offspring, sole propriety,
> In Paradise of all things common else.
> By thee adulterous lust was driven from men
> Among the bestial herds to range, by thee
> Founded in Reason, loyal, just, and pure,
> Relations dear, and all the charities
> Of father, son, and brother first were known.
> Far be it, that I should write thee sin or blame,
> Or think thee unbefitting holiest place,
> Perpetual Fountain of domestic sweets,
> Whose Bed is undefiled and chaste pronounced,
> Present, or past, as saints and patriarchs used.
> Here Love his golden shafts employs, here lights
> His constant lamp, and waves his purple wings,
> Reigns here and revels; not in the bought smile
> Of harlots, loveless, joyless, unendeared,
> Casual fruition, nor in court amours
> Mixed Dance, or wanton mask, or midnight ball,
> Or serenade, which the starved lover sings
> To his proud fair, best quitted with disdain.
> These lulled by nightingales embracing slept,
> And on their naked limbs the flowery roof
> Showered Roses, which the morn repaired. Sleep on,
> Blest pair; and O yet happiest if ye seek
> No happier state, and know to know no more.
>   (Milton 1971, 241–242 [*Paradise Lost* 4.750–775])

Mitlon's distinction between legitimate and illegitimate authority bears directly upon what many interpreters have described as Milton's 'feminism.' Milton rejected the idea that women were the source of corruption and evil, and insisted that they could be included in the exercise of reason; he also rejected the then common idea that the subordination of women was evidence of the fallenness of the world (Wittreich 1987). The subordination of women to men is not evidence of a fallen world where God allows oppression to continue; rather, women's subordination in its proper form is evidence of the rational capacity of the human soul, a capacity to order itself by submission to right reason. It is this proper subordination of the less rational to the rational that allows Milton to be a revolutionary writer demanding the overthrow of imposed power, while at the same time asserting the legitimate deference of women to men. One can, as Milton did, demand the overthrow of tyrants and kings precisely because no *man* can justly be subordinated to another man; such subordination would preclude the exercise of reason, where each man must look into himself to discern divine authority, not receive it from without. But women can reasonably submit to men because in doing so they realise the form of reason that is their own proper end:

> The *good man* or *master of the familie* is a person, in whome resteth the private and proper government of the whole houshold, and he comes not into it by election, as it falleth out in other states, but by the ordinance of God, setled even in the order of nature. The husband indeed naturally beares rule over the wife; parents over their children, masters over their servants: but that person who by the providence of God, hath the place of a husband, a father, a master in his house, the same also by the light of nature, hath the principalitie and soveraignitie therein and he is *Paterfamilias*, the father and chiefe head of the familie: to him therefore the true right and power over all matters domesticall, of right appertaineth.
>
> (Milton 1958–1982, 2.353)

Milton uses gender to distinguish between rational and irrational subordination, a distinction that is necessary to the ultimate and explicit aim of *Paradise Lost*: the justification of 'the ways of God to man' (Milton 1971, 44 [1.26]). Milton's image of the creation of the universe, where God gives form and light to dark matter (Milton 1971, 143 [3.11–3.12]) is repeated in Milton's own description of the creation of *Paradise Lost*. Just as spirit entered the abyss 'And madest it pregnant' so Milton asks the spirit to, 'what in me is dark / Illumine, what is low raise and support' (Milton 1971, 43–44 [1.21–1.23]). The writer penetrates darkness, gives form and life to matter and chaos. To make this claim about poetic creation is to reinforce the logic of gender: there must be a hierarchy between forming, creative and harmonious order and the inert, merely potential matter which takes on true being only by receiving that order. Just as darkness, negativity and evil cannot be said to have real being, for it would be heresy to suggest that something exists that is *other* than God – what is other than God can only be the absence of creation and production – so what is other than the penetrating, forming and actively masculine power of poetry can only be that which awaits form and reason. Woman is not positively other than man; she realises and becomes fully herself by recognising man's reason: 'man is not to hold her as a servant, but receives her into a part of that empire which god proclaims him to, though not equally, yet largely as his own image and glory' (Milton 1958–1982, 2.589). This is reinforced in *Paradise Lost* when the unfallen Adam refers to Eve as 'Best Image of my self and dearer half' (Milton 1971, 5.95).

Milton's epic does not just use the figure of gender in his description of Adam and Eve in paradise; without the logic of gender the epic as a whole loses its coherence. And cohere it must, for Milton wrote *Paradise Lost* in response to one of the most important political questions in the literary and philosophical tradition: why do people choose their enslavement? How do rational and divinely created beings choose irrationality, servitude and disharmony? The political context for *Paradise Lost* was the same political context that led to the emergence of enlightenment feminism and the radical rejection of all supposedly natural hierarchies. If human beings are free, divinely created and rational, why are they enslaved to monarchy, tradition, superstition and prejudice? Like his revolutionary contemporaries, Milton wanted to reject imposed, arbitrary and illegitimate forms of power. Much of *Paradise Lost* depicts Satan as an artful tyrant, capable of persuading the other fallen angels to pursue what is clearly a futile, humiliating and fruitless rebellion against God. And all the qualities that mark Satan as both seductive and dangerous are also those that are traditionally associated with the feminine: Satan is self-regarding, physically captivating, and capable of turning reason against itself by employing arguments that merely sound or appear correct but which lack logic and reflection. It is not surprising that Satan targets Eve in the garden of Eden, and persuades her to eat the forbidden fruit, by appealing to her beauty and her (illusory) sense of self-sufficiency. The evil of Satan, and his capacity to corrupt humanity through Eve, is not a positive quality that can compete with reason and creation; it is the distortion and simulation of reason. His arguments, Milton insists, always *seem* reasonable. Eve is both seduced by Satan's seeming reasonableness and halted in her ascent to true reason by being captivated with her own form. Milton uses the legend of Narcissus to emphasise Eve's beauty and to warn against the seduction of the image of human self-sufficiency. It is Adam's *voice* – the intervention of reason – that lures Eve away from her own image. As Eve recalls in her later narration to Adam of her captivation by her reflection: 'there I had fixed / Mine eyes till now, and pined with vain desire, / Had not a voice thus warned me' (Milton 1971, 222 [4.465–4.467]). Later, Satan's flattering rhetoric will persuade her to disobey, and he does this by referring to Eve as self-sufficient, as liberated from any order or power beyond herself: 'Thee all living things gaze on, all things thine' (Milton 1971, 471 [9.539]). When Eve submits to Satan she therefore turns against her proper reason, submitting to what merely appears to be her own interest; had she remained loyal to Adam she would have also been loyal to herself – to the ideal of reason, which is not imposed so much as recognised. Eve's due reverence for Adam is both part of, and a symbol for, a chain of hierarchically arranged essences: 'God is thy law, thou mine: to know no more / Is woman's happiest knowledge and her praise' (Milton 1971, 232 [4.637–4.638]). Both Adam and Eve express God's glory, but Eve's form is 'less expressing,' and bears a tendency towards 'outward show.' In *Paradise Lost* Adam relates to Raphael the attraction he felt for Eve after their 'wedding':

> Nor vehement desire, these delicacies
> I mean of taste, sight, smell, herbs, fruits, and flowers,
> Walks, and the melody of birds; but here
> Far otherwise, transported I behold,
> Transported touch; here passion first I felt,
> Commotion strange, in all enjoyments else
> Superior and unmoved, here only weak
> Against the charm of beauty's powerful glance.
> Or Nature failed in me, and left some part
> Not proof enough some object to sustain,
> Or from my side subducting, took perhaps
> More than enough; at least on her bestowed
> Too much of ornament, in outward show
> Elaborate, of inward less exact.
> For well I understand in the prime end
> Of Nature her the inferior, in the mind
> And inward Faculties, which most excel
> In outward also her resembling less
> His image who made both, and less expressing
> The character of that dominion given
> O'er other creatures…
>   (Milton 1971, 425 [8.526–8.546])

Milton insists that Adam has the free will to resist such commotion but maintains the ideological association between women and the power to make men 'vehement' or irrational. Raphael warns Adam against Eve's power with the rebuke, 'what transports thee so; / An outside?' (Milton 1971, 426 [8.567–8.568]). When Adam relates his dream of Eve's creation he says it is her 'looks' which 'infused sweetness' into his heart (Milton 1971, 421 [8.474]). Part of Milton's assertion of Adam's capacity to have withstood the fall lies in situating Adam's failure, not in his reason, but in his attraction to Eve's physicality: 'Against his better knowledge, not deceived / But fondly overcome with female charm' (Milton 1971, 495 [9.998–9.999]). Eve's bodily appearance causes a suspension of reason in Adam; her '*heavenly* form' – the aspect that is not so much feminine as divine initially stuns Satan and overawes his malice (Milton 1971, 465 [9.457]). However, when Eve's beauty is seen as self-sufficiently perfect – when Adam sees the world 'in her summed up, in her contained' – her beauty causes distraction (Milton 1971, 421 [8.473]).

The feminine, for Milton, is therefore *capable* of reason but tends towards a greater degree of embodiment, is 'less exact' in its fulfillment of form. Once Adam has received the story of his creation from Raphael, Adam relates the story to Eve. Eve requests that Adam, rather than the angel, relate God's warning because he will 'intermix / Grateful digressions, and solve high dispute / With conjugal caresses, from his lip / Not words alone pleased her' (Milton 1971, 398 [8.54–8.57]). The feminine is not simply devalued by Milton; any unthinking misogyny would fail to do justice to man's capacity to recognise divine order in all creation. Like the body, the feminine is a valuable aspect of experience if subordinated to masculine reason. If due hierarchy is maintained the feminine can be rational; if this hierarchy is disrupted the feminine can contaminate and ensnare reason. Christ tells Adam that his failure to acknowledge this natural law of gender is the cause of his fall and that Eve's visual adornment ought not have been allowed to affect the 'real dignity' of male reason. Adam's failure is a failure of self-knowledge and a fall to the outwardness of 'attraction':

> Wherein God set thee above her made of thee,
> And for thee, whose perfection far excelled
> Hers in all real dignity: adorned
> She was indeed, and lovely to attract
> Thy love not thy subjection, and her gifts
> Were such as under government well seemed,
> Unseemly to bear rule, which was thy part
> And person, hadst thou known thyself aright.
>   (Milton 1971, 514 [10.149–10.56])

If God is the very principle of reason, obedience to God is not *servitude* so much as a recognition of the harmony of creation, which is also the harmony of one's own being. The soul that submits to God (and reason) gives order and well being to itself. By contrast, the soul that strives to be a law unto itself turns against creation and suffers from inner turmoil and chaos. One becomes servile or subject to tyranny only in refusing one's reason, in allowing other, contingent and merely physical forces to govern one's being. Obeying God is not obeying an external authority; it is recognising the rational power within oneself, a power *not* to be a mere body of passions. Obeying God's law is not submission; it is becoming what one properly is, realising one's form.

The passage which most clearly demonstrates this principle of due form in *Paradise Lost* is the speech of Raphael (here significantly called 'the winged hierarch') to Adam:

> O Adam, one Almighty is, from whom
> All things proceed, and up to him return,
> If not depraved from good, created all
> Such to perfection, one first matter all,
> Indued with various forms, various degrees
> Of substance, and in things that live, of life;
> But more refined, more spirituous and pure,
> As nearer to him placed or nearer tending
> Each in their several active spheres assigned,
> Till body up to spirit work, in bounds
> Proportioned to each kind. So from the root
> Springs lighter the green stalk, from thence the leaves
> More airy, last the bright consummate flower
> Spirits odorous breathes: flowers and their fruit
> Man's nourishment, by gradual scale sublimed
> To vital spirits aspire, to animal,
> To intellectual, give both life and sense,
> Fancy and understanding, whence the soul
> Reason receives and reason is her being,
> Discursive or intuitive; discourse
> Is oftest yours, the latter most is ours,
> Differing but in degree, of kind the same.
>   (Milton 1971, 286–287 [5.469–5.490])

Milton insists that evil arises not from some inherent corruption of natural being but in the very dynamism and creative potential of nature – '*if not depraved from good.*' What is other than goodness or reason is potential reason; there is no positive principle outside reason. God expresses himself, and *is*, the ability of human wills to aspire upwards towards God, becoming more spiritual, or downwards towards the less rational positions in the ontological hierarchy. Milton therefore places the origin of evil not in matter as such ('one first matter all') but in the possibility, which stems from free will, that human beings can either aspire to their appropriate form, or refuse God's grace and remain bound to the fallen disruption of the will and passions. The assertion that all things proceed from and return to God (an idea of Plato's *Timaeus* which influenced Christian neo-Platonism) enforces the idea of a totality in which all being is subsumed beneath its transcendent source.

The expression of hierarchy in this tradition sees the upward progression as a process of spiritualisation. Entities are 'by gradual scale sublimed.' The traditional concept of the chain of being also sees the character of each member of the hierarchy assigned to a particular sphere of activity: 'Each in their several active spheres assigned' and 'in bounds / Proportioned to each kind.' The presence of reason in the soul expresses the position of human being in the hierarchy, and it is the possession of reason which characterises the appropriate mode of activity for human life: 'whence the soul / Reason receives, and reason is her being.' The idea of the proper station of being is repeated throughout *Paradise Lost*, both for angels – 'Each had his place appointed, each his course' (Milton 1971, 188 [3.720]) – and for human beings. Raphael warns Adam against both aspiring beyond his capability for knowledge and against 'attributing overmuch to things / Less excellent' (Milton 1971, 426 [8.565–8.566]). The appropriate kind of knowledge is knowledge of one's own proper mode of being: 'but to know / That which before us lies in daily life, / Is the prime wisdom' (Milton 1971, 407 [8.192–8.194]). Not only does Raphael assert the existence of the chain of being; he also prompts the recognition by Adam that an awareness and contemplation of this hierarchy is the appropriate and edifying object of human knowledge:

> ...and the scale of nature set
> From centre to circumference, whereon
> In contemplation of created things
> By steps we may ascend to God...
>   (Milton 1971, 289 [5.509–5.512])

The acknowledgement of hierarchy and degree is here connected with moral knowledge in two respects. First, as we have just seen, knowledge of the 'scale of nature' provides the contemplative wisdom that yields a moral life capable of spiritualising human being. This idea is reiterated in Book Seven where the ascension towards God is qualitative and by steps: 'till by degrees of merit raised' (Milton 1971, 366 [7.157]). Secondly, like Plato and Augustine, Milton asserts a hierarchy within the individual. The idea that the mind itself had both spiritual and temporal aspects is evidenced in the distinction between reason and the will. The unfallen Adam insists upon the distinction between certain aspects of inner experience which are duly subordinated to reason: 'in the soul / Are many lesser faculties that serve / Reason as chief' (Milton 1971, 261 [5.100–5.102]). Even in Eden, Adam is warned by Raphael to maintain the subordination of will and the passions to reason: 'take heed lest passion sway / Thy judgement to do aught, which else free will / Would not admit' (Milton 1971, 431 [8.635–8.637]). Rather than be transported by the 'outside' of Eve's appearance, which would lead to 'subjection' as opposed to 'honour' (Milton 1971, 426 [8.568–8.570]) Raphael states that the appropriate love:

> ...refines
> The thoughts, and heart enlarges, hath his seat
> In reason, and is judicious, is the scale
> By which to heavenly love thou mayst ascend,
> Not sunk in carnal pleasure...
> (Milton 1971, 428 [8.589–8.593])

After the fall the subordination of the lesser faculties to reason gives way to a disruption of hierarchy. Adam and Eve, like the fallen Satan, now have minds that are divided. What was once a 'calm region' for Adam and Eve is now an inner hell; this disturbance of inner harmony is a consequence of the usurpation of reason by the appetite, which sways the free will to its demands:

> ...nor only tears
> Rained at their eyes, but high winds worse within
> Began to rise, high passions, anger, hate,
> Mistrust, suspicion, discord, and shook sore
> Their inward state of mind, clam region once
> And full of peace, now tossed and turbulent:
> For understanding ruled not, and the will
> Heard not her lore, both in subjection now
> To sensual appetite, who from beneath
> Usurping over sovereign reason claimed
> Superior sway...
> (Milton 1971, 503 [9.1121–9.1131])

Through the figure of gender Milton can, then, resolve a seeming contradiction. Adam and Eve express a rational hierarchy, which is distinct from mere force and imposed tyranny. Indeed, it is primarily through marriage, where individuals recognise a divine creation in the partner they love, that individuals can also realise their spiritual freedom. Milton can embrace worldly political revolution and *equality*, including the overthrow and execution of kings, only because of a rational hierarchy. It is because reason is an ordering power that we do not require blind submission to priests or kings. We can recognise this natural, due and right submission in the condition of marriage in Eden. Eve's recognition of Adam's authority is recognition, not of physical force or seized power, but of his godly reason. As long as human beings submit to worldly authorities or tyrants they cannot exercise their reason. They become *self*-governing only by recognising what is divine and eternal in their being. A wife's recognition of her husband's right reason is therefore a step towards her own liberation and reason. Milton can stress due and natural order, alongside a revolutionary commitment to the overthrow of kings, precisely because certain forms of subordination – such as marriage – are the exercise of reason, while others – submission to kings, priests, tyrannical husbands or irrational wives – impede one's reason. The relation between Adam and Eve, and the opposition of gender, become crucial to a theory of power *and* the justification of why the world is as it is. And this is not just the case for Milton.

Many political theorists rejected political hierarchy – the subordination of men to other men – but allowed for gendered hierarchy, for the latter was deemed to be a hierarchy of reason. Submission, as Milton describes it, can take two forms: arbitrary or rational. The first is pathological, inessential and corrupt; here, in following the desires of one's body, one merely responds almost mechanically to immediate interests and pleasures. The fallen angels are persuaded by Satan because he appeals to their vanity, their own powers, *or what they already are*. When Satan tempts Eve he appeals to her beauty as something fully sufficient and valuable in itself. The tendency to evil is a tendency to what *already is* – the body – rather than the creative power or reason that flows through that body and connects it to a higher order. When the fallen angels and Eve follow Satan they merely act on the basis of what they already are, with no sense of the cosmos or order which gives them their being, and which allows them to ascend beyond themselves to what they ought to be. Eve falls, Milton insists, not because God made women too weak to obey male reason, but because all bodily life is free either to realise its divine form by ascending towards God and reason, or to refuse reason and act on what is merely pleasurable or appealing. Tyranny, illegitimate sovereignty and (for Milton) marriages worthy of divorce are all caused by a submission to powers below that of right reason: the body, vanity or force.

The second form of submission, justified by Milton, is rational. Here, Eve obeys Adam, not because Adam exercises brute force, but because she can see in Adam a rational or well-ordered form of human life. Adam, in turn, tempers his desires and orders his passions, not because of a calculating interest, which would simply maximise pleasure, but because acting rationally is merely becoming what he properly is: an expression of the divine reason that illuminates all creation. Eve's relation to Adam, like Adam's relation to the angels, and like the angels' relation to God, is a relation toward the reason or form that orients one's own body. Milton grants Adam and Eve, and all creation, a form of reason – a tendency to strive towards God – but he also acknowledges differing degrees and expressions of this rational form. Satan, in turn, is depicted as the very principle of a will or force without any end or proper form, a force or will unto itself: evil is the negation of form; it is a will that can will nothing other than itself. The picture of Adam and Eve, by contrast, is of two bodies who recognise reason and a greater harmony in each other, with Eve's body being the sign of divine physical creation, and Adam's less embodied reason being a sign of the human potential to become more divine, more rational.

Milton's epic was, however, written just as many philosophers, poets and scientists were contesting the notion of a pre-given order. Milton insisted that a system of subordination achieved through the exercise of pure force or will, a subordination that was merely the outcome of forces that in themselves possessed no order or predetermined relation, was illegitimate. He also rejected the divine right of kings precisely because no one rational being could claim the power of reason over others. Milton rejected the putative divine hierarchy of kings *because* of the divine hierarchy of reason. And it was just this hierarchy of reason, which not only justified and explained, but also produced, the hierarchy of gender. Only with the overthrow of kings, bishops and other worldly powers that demanded irrational submission could true reason be exercised. But the exercise of true reason would also, for women, require due deference to those who expressed reason in its better form: men. Milton opposed a divine and rational harmony to the merely historical seizing of power. Adam ruled over Eve *not* because she was weaker or dominated by the condition of child rearing – not because of any bodily essence – but because of her gender: the form that rendered her duly and happily subordinate to one who was merely a greater expression of her own true being.

Many of Milton's contemporaries, and the enlightenment and Romantic writers who followed Milton, saw his rejection of illegitimate, seized or tyrannical power as applicable not just to kings and magistrates but to life in general – including the power of men over women. In so doing they had to reject the reality and rationality of forms and insist that *all* relations were the outcome of physical powers – the interaction of forces without any preceding order – and that there was, therefore, no such thing as due subordination. Reason, for the writers of the enlightenment, was no longer the recognition of an inner law that reflected a transcendent order; reason was the capacity to give a law to oneself. In the absence of any law, in a world of nothing but competing and *equivalent* forces, reason would be nothing more than the refusal of external power. Reason was negative – it was the rejection of received orders – rather than positive – it was no longer the recognition of an order beyond oneself.

Many eighteenth- and nineteenth-century writers – as we will see in the next chapter – took Milton's image of gender as due subordination as *the* political relation that needed to be refigured in the passage to modernity. William Blake's *Milton*, Percy Shelley's *Prometheus Unbound* and Lord Byron's *Don Juan* celebrated the image of a will that broke with all form, and tied that celebration to images of sexual union and excess. In Mary Shelley's *Frankenstein*, there is an even more compelling relationship between sexual binaries and the destruction of received orders, a relationship that will be examined in the final chapter. William Blake, in *The Marriage of Heaven and Hell* saw the constant interaction of 'contraries' as the only way to sustain the dynamism of life, and ward off the stagnation of fixed states: 'Without Contraries is no progression' (Blake 1988, 34). For Blake, the key figure of contrariety was the image of male and female bodies. It is when man sees the feminine as his shadowy other or 'spectre' – when religion presents the feminine as a 'harlot' figure – that he falls into guilt and despair. If, however, the feminine, nature, matter and embodiment are recognised as positive – as expressions of divinity rather than the negation or corruption of spirit – then 'man' will overcome his fallen perception of the world as divided and 'evil.' Redemption can be achieved only through conflict and difference. In *Visions of the Daughters of Albion*, Blake expressed the vibrant marriage of contraries quite literally, celebrating 'happy copulation' and condemning images of the feminine that were nothing more than reflections of man (Blake 1988, 50). Sexual liberation was the first step to a new world, or new Jerusalem, where male and female could exist in relations of productive *difference*, rather than the female merely mirroring or expressing the male: 'Sexes must vanish and cease / To be, when Albion rises from his dread repose' (Blake 1988, 252 [92.13–92.14]).

3 Modernity and the Materiality of Gender

Sex and matter: Modern empiricism and liberalism

Plato's *Timaeus* is one of the most important texts for both ancient and contemporary thought, precisely because it established the problem of what, if anything, can be said to precede or exceed the formed world. For Plato, only the forms existed properly speaking, with their material and worldly embodiment being a mere copy. But even those who wrote after Plato and who rejected his otherworldly separation of forms still insisted that the ultimately real beings of this world – individual substances – could be what they were only by having essentially defining properties. Something *is* or has identity only by being something specific. To say that something exists is to say that it exists *as* this or that kind of thing. That which precedes all identity, naming, possible representation or identification cannot really be said to be.

This emphasis upon determination and form applies to both premodern and modern understandings of gender; we grant reality or being to that which has a repeatable and sustainable identity. If we ask whether there 'is' such a thing as 'woman' we are asking whether there is some feature all such bodies share, and we may reject this notion and demand that we do away with such general concepts of gender. Similarly, we might also reject any appeal to an immutable or essential 'femininity' that precedes and lies outside all naming and reference. Some feminists have indeed argued that there is no such thing as 'Woman,' while others have insisted that any appeal to an essential feminine that exceeds language, reference and communication cannot have any validity. Plato may have argued that only forms or those immaterial ideas that have a stable and unchanging essence have real being, but in the turn towards modernity and experience there has been even more emphasis on granting reality only to what could be determined. Not only was enlightenment defined as the refusal of any mystical or fanatical appeal to what could not be proved or experienced; there was also a stress on defining experience and knowledge as that which can be conceptualised and represented (Kant 1993). The philosophical and rational rejection of the formless, ineffable and singular was intensified in modernity and the enlightenment. For it was precisely the achievement of the enlightenment to reject any notion of a transcendent or mysterious law or ground to the world: if something has being and force then it must be subject to legitimation, verification and justification. According to Jürgen Habermas, modern thought is post-metaphysical because it refuses to posit that which lies beyond language and communication; all truth claims are articulated in language and, by virtue of that very fact, are subjected to the scrutiny of all possible language users (Habermas 1992, 47). For Habermas, our recognition of language is also a recognition of intersubjectivity: that which lies outside the common world of experience and language can only be known and posited *from language*. This means that we need to negotiate the limits of language from within language and communication. For the feminists who have followed Habermas this means that we need to reject any notion of immutable genders or sexes that underpin language, at the same time as we need to see gender as a political category that inflects how one is positioned and recognised as a subject (Benhabib 1992).

Habermas's critical theory is an example of a much broader trend in modern thought that rejects the pre-modern dependence on a law or order beyond human representation. The widely accepted notion of the 'social construction' of gender presupposes that our experience of the world is necessarily mediated by forms or structures that 'we' as language users construct, and are constructed by. When we insist that we only know the world as it is rendered meaningful through language, we privilege the differentiated and the identified over that which cannot be referred to in any meaningful way. We maintain, then, an implicit privilege of the knowable and representable over the unknowable. Indeed, one of the common arguments of twentieth-century thought was not only that it made no sense to refer to what lay beyond language; it was also stressed that the pre-linguistic is only known *as* pre-linguistic by being other than language (Wittgenstein 1958, 109). We should dismiss all talk of the unnameable, the pre-representational, the ineffable, and recognise that we only know and experience something as already formed, determined and contextually located (Rorty 1982, 14–15).

It might seem that such an approach would privilege the activity of the human mind and its power of social construction over the matter or physicality of the body, but this is not really the case. The emphasis on language, communication and social construction acknowledges the existence of body and matter but merely insists that this materiality is known, lived and experienced only through the distinct ideas we have of it. Indeed, it is our very character as physical bodies that subjects us to need, needs that are best met through human communication, society and order (Habermas 1972). Our bodies are, therefore, never brute natural objects that lie outside language and sense – never possessing some pure sexual specificity – for bodies are always *lived* bodies and therefore already mediated by our cultural and linguistic condition.

On the one hand, this refusal to give weight to what lies outside language overturns the Platonic and mythic image of an underlying, undifferentiated and formless matter from which the universe is actively formed. On the other hand, we could also say that this refusal of anything beyond the bounds of sense, context, culture and meaning intensifies a tendency of Western thought to give true being only to one side of the implicitly gendered binary. The formless, pre-representational matter of the world is dismissed as a mythic, metaphysical, mystical and 'feminine' origin; what is real is what can be represented, justified, legitimated and communicated. Indeed, it is this emphasis on the rational, accountable, justifiable and communicable which, for many social theorists, constitutes the hallmark of modernity (Habermas 1985).

For many liberal feminists – those concerned with equality – the modern and enlightened emphasis on reason and justification enables the inclusion of women and precludes notions of a radically 'other' femininity. A commitment to the universality of reason should lead to the dissolution of gender *hierarchy*. Even if there are two genders, and even if one affirms the role of women in the family or private sphere, women's capacity to exercise reason should lead to the affirmation of equal rights (Okin 1989). Further, if the world we live is experienced and constructed through language – if our world is contextual and social, then it cannot be legitimate to exclude women from the practice of reason on the basis of some supposedly pre-linguistic feminine essence. Insofar as we speak and inhabit the same life-world we are all subject to the same norms of communication, argument, reason and justification. Certainly, no speaker can be excluded on the basis of any claim regarding their physical or biological being (Richards 1982). Sex must be strictly irrelevant once we recognise that men and women are known only through their genders – the social meaning given to the body and not the body itself.

Liberal feminism therefore insists both on the separateness and the irrelevance of the body: sex cannot affect our subjectivity, because as speaking and social subjects we have already distanced ourselves from our merely bodily being. Liberal feminism proceeded, from the eighteenth century to the present, to criticise any gender norms that would allow the body to determine one's identity. Many liberal feminists accept that we can have different gender norms – women can be domestic and maternal carers, while men can be public negotiators and wage earners – but such social roles have no essential or finally determining ground in the body. Such roles are decided socially and rationally, with each gender having an equal right in social construction and decision. Gender is a social role; it is certainly not an essential bodily determination. Once modern and enlightenment thinkers recognised that reason must be an all-inclusive power – that reason must be legitimate and available to all if it is to be self-evident – then no one could be excluded from the activity of reason on the basis of any physical difference. It is the very character of reason to transcend the body: our capacity to reason liberates us from physical determination and necessity and subjects us to a world of communication, justification, argument and *rights*. To demand equal rights is not to demand that we all be the same, but it is to demand that we all be granted the power to be self-determining.

Liberal feminism's appeal to rights, as it was first articulated in the eighteenth century, is sustained in contemporary liberal feminism's refusal to grant one's body any determining status. Contemporary liberal feminists have admitted that women's sexual capacities may impede their participation in the public activity of reason, but this admittance should prompt us to create the social conditions – such as available childcare, contraception and freedom from violence – that would place women on the level playing field that earlier liberal theories have claimed as a reality. Ideally, one's body ought to be irrelevant to one's social and political being, but this freedom from one's sex needs to be achieved (Richards 1982, 17). Whereas early liberal feminists asserted the equality of women, later liberal feminists saw equality and rights as political goals that could only be achieved through the management of sexuality. But in order for feminists from Mary

Wollstonecraft to Janet Radcliffe Richards to insist on the (ideal) meaninglessness and irrelevance of sex, sex had to be situated as radically distinct from one's social, decided and meaningful gender. There is then an implied, and often explicit, distinction between biological and unchanging sex, and socio-historical and determinable gender.

The sex–gender distinction is also maintained by those post-liberal or radical feminists who recognise the relevance of sex. We still need to distinguish biology from social representation, but we do this in order to show both the ways in which the supposedly generic human 'rational' self is actually a male self, and the ways in which women's sexual specificity has been socially represented as subordinate and less worthy of political consideration. Far from being gender-neutral, the ideal of reason and objectivity has been constructed to justify the interests of one social group – men – at the expense of another. For reforming feminists like Catherine MacKinnon, who still write within the liberal tradition of granting women as a group more rights and recognition, we need to see the ways in which the notion of rational man is gendered. Men's bodies are represented as universally human; the self of rights and reason is *masculine* and produced by a certain type of body and sexuality that has enjoyed violence, rape and pornography. Women's sexuality, with its quite different relations to questions of rape, reproduction and fertility control, has not been considered to be of political relevance. According to MacKinnon:

> If feminism is a critique of the objective standpoint as male, then we also disavow standard scientific norms as the adequacy criteria for our theory, because the objective standpoint we criticize is the posture of science as a specifically male approach to knowledge. With it we reject male criteria for verification. We're not seeking truth in its female counterpart either, since that, too, is constructed by male power. We do not vaunt the subjective. We begin by seeking the truth of and in that which has constructed all this – that is, in gender.
>
> (MacKinnon 1987, 54)

MacKinnon rejects any direct appeal to sexuality. We live our sexuality in a gender system where, for example, women's sexuality is denied the freedom of abortion or expression in non-pornographic forms. There is, as yet, no femininity outside this system, but there are features of women's sexuality – such as reproduction – which demand a change in the gender system. Indeed, what MacKinnon regards as the 'unmodified' nature of her approach is her appeal to a possible sexuality outside the current gender system, and the inequity of gender as it is constructed. Gender, according to MacKinnon, is constructed, but is constructed on the basis of real sexual difference; questions of rape, pornography and abortion leave no doubt to the pre-linguistic and real nature of sexual difference. MacKinnon's argument, like many of those who insist on the *constructed* nature of gender, both insists on the social creation – and therefore mutability – of gender, at the same time as she insists on the difference and reality of sexuality. Gender must be addressed by the problems encountered by women's bodies. MacKinnon's work is both an extension of first-wave or liberal feminism and a recognition of second-wave feminist concerns. Like first-wave feminists, MacKinnon regards the legal system and the public sphere as the primary area of reform. But we can only achieve such reforms – only give women the right to control their bodies and to see themselves as worthy individuals – with recognition of the gender system, the way in which individuals regard themselves as sexed. It is this concern with gender – not just women's bodies, but the social representation of those bodies – that marked second-wave feminism.

One of the classic texts of the second wave, Kate Millett's *Sexual Politics*, had declared that the personal is political, and in so doing had shown that ideas and representations were as significant to questions of oppression as were the liberal demands for education, pay and property (Millett 1971). Radical feminism therefore refused to see women as simply excluded from the traditional rights of man. The rights of man were *men's* rights, and many of these rights – the rights of property, autonomy and reason – had been established through the oppression of women. Second-wave feminism rejected the idea of an inclusive humanity and argued for the specificity of women. Behind the traditional gender system of male and female virtues were sexual differences, differences that needed to be revalued and reconfigured. Only the masculine illusion of a single humanity for whom the body is irrelevant could maintain that selves could be liberated from their sex. Women were *different* and would require different rights. Most of these significant sexual differences lay in women's reproductive capacities, but it was also argued that men's power had been achieved not just through freedom from childbirth and childbearing but also by a greater degree of physical power and violence over women (Firestone 1979).

Second-wave feminism argued that masculinity as such had been constructed through power and violence, and that femininity had been oppressed through a history of uninterrupted patriarchal domination. The only answer to this history of domination was to free women from men: from the practices of pornography, the nuclear family and rape that had oppressed women as a group. For second-wave feminists differences in gender – such as the lesser value placed on feminine qualities – had its basis in sex – the power men held over women, and the disadvantages bodies sexed as female would suffer in the current political system (Dworkin 1981). MacKinnon's sustained attack on pornography, and her demand for a change in laws regarding prostitution, abortion and rape, maintain an unmodified commitment to women as a group and women's sexual specificity, and demand that this specificity be recognised in order to challenge the current representation of women: 'women are human beings in truth but not in social reality' (MacKinnon 1987, 216).

Whereas first-wave feminists accepted that men's and women's bodies were different, they insisted that these differences were irrelevant for political agency. Radical feminists, by contrast, rejected the notion of a sexless reason or humanity and insisted on the primacy of different bodies and desires. Third-wave feminists rejected both the reality of some general humanity, and the reality of sexual difference; if the world is constituted through systems of difference, language or representation, then *no* category of sex or gender can be ultimately grounded (Adams 1979, 52). Today, the debates among various positions in gender theory concern just what can be counted as real: *are* there really two sexes, or is this just an effect of language and social construction? Are the differences of language and culture the only reality we have? If first-wave feminists appealed to humanity's rational essence, and second-wave feminists flirted with the idea of a sexual essence which demanded women's difference, third-wave feminism was characterised by an almost unanimous agreement that essentialism or biologism was both mythic and ideological.

Third-wave feminism: Reality and essence

In order to negotiate how the politics of gender has been negotiated in modernity we need to recognise the shift in the status of what was taken to be ultimately *real*. On the one hand, the anti-metaphysical stress in modern thought, or the refusal of anything that cannot be known and verified, led to an emphasis on evidence and materiality.

There were no transcendent forms or essences that preceded and ordered the world; essences would need to be understood as what a thing is intrinsically, before all concepts or ideas. Essences could now be seen as intrinsic physical properties. If something has an essence, this is not its meaning or relation to a whole; it is its status when considered objectively, free from its relation to a subject or any other thing. According to John Locke, whose definition of essence at least set the terms of debate for what could count as real or essential, we can understand the notion of essence in two ways. *Real* essences exist before experience and relations and *cause* those relations, and so real essences are the foundation of the basic properties of the world, certainly not divinely ordained forms or ordering principles (Locke [1700] 1975, 442). Nominal essences have their existence only in human knowledge; a nominal essence is how something is known, the features something must have in order for us to call it, say, a man (Locke [1700] 1975, 453). Locke's understanding of essences was typical in its grounding of essences within the physical world, either in what things are intrinsically or in our predictable relations to those things. Essences were regarded as the ultimately real basis of the world, but they were neither Platonic ideas (forms that transcend the world), nor Aristotelian forms (what something strives to become). Essences were explained and distinguished by what caused perception, by what produced relations and by what could legitimately be known.

The modern stress on science and observation also led to an awareness of the subject as observer or knower. Once we acknowledge that the aim of science is to perceive the world *without* imposing our own forms, then we become aware of just what those forms are. If we wanted to know the 'real' essence of women, we would have to posit some specificity independent of social norms, observation and expectations. If we want to know the nominal essence of 'woman,' we need only refer to those properties that we insist a body must have in order to count as feminine.

When Monique Wittig in the twentieth century argued that 'lesbians are not women,' she did so because she took 'woman' as a nominal essence: to be a woman is to be defined in relation to man, to be heterosexual, and to be determined by social and political demands (Wittig 1992). Those features that define what it is to be a woman cannot be shared by the lesbian. Wittig appeals to perceived predicates – what is essential for us to call someone a woman – and not some underlying 'real' essence that causes social definitions. The vexed topic of essentialism, today, oscillates between these two understandings of essence. When Gayatri Spivak insists on a 'strategic essentialism,' she suggests that women need to appeal to, or act *as if* they expressed, a real essence or underlying identity in order to make political claims (Spivak 1990, 11). If there were no such thing as woman, if the feminine were nothing more than a fiction, then women could not make demands, claims or interventions. However, women can speak *as if* they form a distinct group precisely because gender ideology has produced them as such. Such an essence is a 'strategy,' or only *appears* as real, because 'woman' is actually a historically and politically produced name, a nominal essence constructed from a patriarchal history. On the one hand, then, essences are fictions, imagined identities or imposed categories; this is certainly the case for feminists such as Spivak or Drusilla Cornell who want to *use* the concept of woman but deny that anything real or pre-linguistic answers to the name. Whereas for Spivak one can employ the name as a tactic to challenge the dominant and naming ideology, for Cornell one might also imagine a new mode of identity that is *other than* the already constructed fiction of 'Woman.' And one can do this precisely because 'woman' is produced in language. There will always be a difference between the term 'woman' and what that term signifies, for no signifier is grounded fully in a self-present essence. Cornell sets herself against an 'Aristotelian approach to the feminine' (199) and advocates a 'mimesis' whereby one uses the name of woman to produce an outside to the current gender system, but does not commit oneself to any real essence of woman:

> But is there 'her sex' beyond or, more precisely, irreducible to the definition of the current gender hierarchy? As we have seen, the answer is yes, at least in the sense that 'her sex' is only presented in language and, therefore, cannot be reduced to the unshakeable reality, supposedly constructed by the male gaze, in which we are as they have made us. . . .
>
> Gender identity is a prison for both sexes, but given 'the reality' of masculine privilege, the two genders do not suffer the same entrapment. . . . The feminine is not an established set of properties of the female. The feminine, as continually re-metaphorized, does not demand that we re-instate a unified, identifiable subject, Woman. The feminine through *mimesis*, is an affirmation, a valuation, but even so, is not a traditional, ethical concept that would identify the good of Woman with her fundamental properties.
>
> (Cornell 1991, 199)

After the advent of post-structuralism and third-wave feminism, which questioned radical feminism's affirmation of the intrinsic difference of women, many feminists not only followed Cornell and Spivak in questioning the assumption of women's specificity. They also affirmed the possibility of thinking beyond identity, gender and distinct kinds. On this picture, feminism would no longer be the affirmation of women, women's issues or women's identity, but would, in its criticism of conventional maleness, identity and power, take the criticism of essentialism to include all forms of supposed naturalness, distinct kinds or stable norms.

Rosi Braidotti, whose *Patterns of Dissonance* outlined the distinction between first-wave feminisms that demand equality, and second-wave feminisms that asserted women's specific identity, warned that post-structuralist affirmations of difference and non-identity occurred just when women were gaining a specific voice and power. Braidotti's answer to this problem was not simply to assert the difference and uniqueness of each gender. She did, following her own post-structuralist insistence on the genesis of gender from mobile systems of difference such as language, refuse to assert the simple existence either of a generic humanism or of distinct genders. But she also argued that the true thought of difference would not simply dissolve genders and identities into some arena of free play. Rather, the classic subject of modernity was already produced *as sexed*, through the expulsion of certain qualities (such as embodiment) as feminine, and the elevation of other qualities (such as autonomy) as masculine. Braidotti draws upon the work of Luce Irigaray to argue that sexual difference is neither some brute biological given, nor an effect of social construction. On the contrary, all our images and ideas of modernity, including the separation of mind and body, form and matter, reason and passions, have been produced by subjects who also position themselves as sexually different and differently embodied. For Braidotti, overcoming modernity and the notion of the disembodied and universal subject must begin with sexual difference, for it is the refusal of this difference which is the hallmark of the modern 'neuter' self. If a masculine fantasy of neutrality is at the heart of modernity, then only the thought of feminine difference can open the way to a future of affirmative difference:

> ...one cannot ask the question of the crisis of modernity without raising the issue of sexual difference, or of gender. Modernity and sexual difference contain each other as two sides of the same coin.

> The female feminist subjects of the historical era of post-metaphysical uncertainty are the subjects of enunciation of the question of sexual difference.
>
> (Braidotti 1991, 276)

Braidotti aims to chart a middle way between two poles in the politics of gender. If one does away with gender entirely then one merely celebrates difference as such; all sense of how differences, such as gender, have been determined politically, historically and socially is lost. However, if one merely asserts that there are female subjects, and that these subjects might provide some radically innocent outside to a system of patriarchal oppression then one risks a nostalgic and misguided celebration of a fantasy of woman that exists before all relations, language and power. For Braidotti, the 'female feminist subject' is produced *through articulation*, by asking just *who* the subject of modernity is. By asking about the sex of 'universal man,' by interrogating the pure 'self' of modernity the feminist creates a position of questioning and dissonance. Femininity is not some stable essence, thing or ground that *then* questions the masculine subject. Rather, the subject of philosophy who has always been disembodied, universal, autonomous and rational is exposed as sexually different through the feminist project. Braidotti's rejection of essentialism does not, therefore, put difference, play and non-identity into some newly valorised position of an unquestioned good. As Rita Felski has argued, the celebration of difference may just become one more orthodoxy if it does not negotiate the ways in which differences are articulated and the ways in which identities are produced from contestations of difference (Felski 2000). After all, the celebration of difference can, as Braidotti also shows, be one way of robbing feminist politics of its force, just as the affirmation of multicultural difference can be a way of avoiding recognising the claims of dissident cultures. What the question of sexual difference achieves, according to writers like Donna Haraway, is neither the traditional assertion that bodily sex is meaningless and that we can do away with the fiction of gender, nor the naively 'post-modern' assertion that there are no material determinants outside the differences of language. Rather, the sex/gender question enables us to think of how different bodies come to be socialised and stabilised as gendered, how material bodies are taken as signs or grounds of timeless essences or genders. Haraway insists that 'gender' analysis does not simply assume the sameness of all women, regardless of race or class:

But 'alterity' and 'difference' are precisely what 'gender' is 'grammatically' about, a fact that constitutes feminism as a politics defined by its fields of contestation and repeated refusals of master theories. 'Gender' was developed as a category to explore what counts as a 'woman', to problematize the previously taken-for-granted.

(Haraway 1991, 147)

Braidotti's and Haraway's attempts to save the specificity of feminist politics from the charge of essentialism or the fate of dissolution rely upon an expanded horizon of the concept of gender. Gender is not, they insist, an idea *within* Western thought. For the very category of the thinking subject has always been male. The history of Western thought is already gendered; the thinking subject is produced through the fantasy or image of the male body, a body that masters itself and has an instrumental relation to its own physicality. One can, therefore, refuse the inclusion of women within this ideal, and affirm the difference of women without appealing to some essential feminine awaiting discovery, for the mythic feminine has always been crucial to the self representation of man. Haraway, in particular, is adamant that her feminism is neither a humanism nor an essentialism, for the 'nature' or 'sex' that supposedly precedes culture is, she insists, itself a contested and constructed term (Haraway 1991, 135).

Those feminists who were *accused* of essentialism were attacked because they posited some biological – and therefore unchanging and inhuman – reality of sexual difference. Michele Barrett, for example, wanted to go further than the radical feminist affirmation of women's difference by asking both how women were produced as a distinct group and why this specific group had suffered the form of patriarchal oppression that seemed resistant to historical change. For Barrett and others, 'essentialism' or the notion of a difference in gender that transcended culture and politics would not only hamper liberation, by assuming one category of woman across differences of race and class; it would also sustain the association of women with domestic, child-bearing and child-rearing duties (Barrett 1980, 13). It was the fear of essentialism – the very idea that social genders might have some cause that was not itself fully malleable and social – that led to the attacks on essentialism that distanced the gender theory of the 1980s from the earlier radical feminist assertions of women's difference. Toril Moi's attack on the 'bad' feminism of Luce Irigaray was based on the assumption that an appeal to women's difference, and the possibility of thinking or writing differently, located an essence outside language

(Moi 1985). Moi favoured the feminism of Kristeva precisely because she argued that the difference between man and woman was 'metaphysical.' Because essentialist feminists insist on the existence of a femininity that is not reducible to masculine definitions and fantasies they are guilty of imagining some reality or being beyond the realm of discourse. To be essentialist in this sense, Moi argues, is to make a claim about the body before all language and culture; it is to abandon all hope of political and linguistic change. For Moi, then, essences would be qualities that inhered in biology or matter. Her anti-essentialism shares with radical feminism a specifically material understanding of essence, where essential determination would be grounded in one's biology. The essential is no longer deemed to be an otherworldly or transcendent form that determines language and bodies. Whereas the physical world was once seen to be determined by an ideal and essential order, essences have – since Locke's day – been defined as either what really exists physically or as the stable features that physical world must have for human observation. Essences are not ideal forms that are expressed in the world; they are the physical world before all relations (real essences) or the world as it is known and predicated (nominal essences).

Subjectivity, ideas and experience

The anti-metaphysical stress in modern thought, or the refusal of anything that could not be known and verified, led to an emphasis on evidence and materiality. At the same time, however, this stress on science and observation also led to an awareness of the subject as observer or knower (Foucault 1970, 241). This shift from a world of forms within which 'man' was located to a realm of matter that was observable and quantifiable had two broad consequences for the politics of gender. First, if physical matter was now the basis of reality, with forms being effects of observation, it would now be possible to think of *sex*: the bodily, physical or genetic substrate of one's being, which may or may not determine one's social gender. Second, once matter is defined as pre-linguistic and meaningless, then it makes sense to think of the *subject* as the point from which that matter is known and ordered. From 'man' as one animal among others in a hierarchy of forms, we move to the 'subject,' as the being for whom matter is representable and quantifiable (Foucault 1970, 247; Irigaray 1985, 180).

One of the key features of modernity is not only a positive emphasis on matter; it is also the assertion of the reality of matter. Forms and ideas, which were once seen to reside in a transcendent order, were from the seventeenth century onwards seen to be effects of matter or experience. Forms were produced from the relations of forces. The form of the world, *from the point of view of science*, was the effect of interacting material forces; while the form of the world, *from the point of view of knowledge*, was the effect of those material forces on the senses. Empiricism had a long philosophical history, but in its modern form it asserts the primacy of experience: there are no ideas, concepts, truths or meanings outside the organisation of the flux of perceptions by the receptive mind. According to philosophers such as John Locke (1632–1704) or David Hume (1711–1776), the mind formed concepts in response to the flux of experience; the mind itself had no character or innate qualities before its encounter with experience, and sensations are only formed into conceptual order through experience: 'what we call a *mind*, is nothing but a heap or collection of different perceptions, united together by certain relations' (Hume 2000 [1739–1740], 137). We know the world as organised matter; the substances or essences that precede this organisation or synthesis of the world are strictly unknowable (Hume 2000, 139). Indeed, we only know ourselves through the flow of experience; we have no knowledge of any substantial soul that precedes experience. The self was, for Hume particularly, no longer a determined essence in the hierarchical order of things; selves and identities were produced through experience: 'The identity, which we ascribe to the mind of man, is only a fictitious one, and of a like kind with that which we ascribe to vegetables and animal bodies' (Hume 2000, 169). The mind, according to Locke, was a *tabula* rasa, or blank slate, that had no innate qualities, and was nothing more than a capacity to receive sensations. The self or personal identity was just an awareness of these collected experiences (Locke 1975, 341).

The subject, then, differed from earlier theories of 'man' as an animal within the cosmos with a certain nature. The subject was nothing more than a capacity to perceive and represent the world (Foucault 1970, 247). From this, it *should* follow that all subjects would relate to each other equally, and that social orders and hierarchies could not have any transcendent order. Any system or order would need to be explained from its basis in the physical world, and no order or hierarchy could be justified either by asserting the existence of some divine harmony, or by claiming that certain forces had simply gained power or precedence over others. If the world was made up of powers and forces that produced relations, then each individual had the right to challenge and question any already constituted system of relations. In the eighteenth century the widespread assertion of human rights was based on just this affirmation of equality before the world. Not only did advocates of the rights of man assume that each self had the power to question, decide and determine worldly relations for himself, rather than receiving some moral doctrine from without; liberals and empiricists insisted that no quality other than the force of social relations ought to decide one's position in the whole. Early feminists insisted that no assertion about one's bodily sex could justify precluding women from the exercise of reason. Mary Wollstonecraft demanded a return to first principles. Reason, she argued, had been used to justify all forms of prejudice, including slavery, but the renewed exercise of reason would allow a conquering of bodily passions and prejudice and produce a world of happiness and equality: 'Where is then the sexual difference, when the education has been the same? All the difference that I can discern, arises from the superior advantage of liberty' (Wollstonecraft 1989, 92).

Gender, for early liberal feminists, was a *social division* and not a quality of bodies. Maintaining gender distinctions could be justified only if women's position within the home were rendered as dignified and rational as men's position in the public and political sphere. But despite the fact that consistency demanded that women, as subjects, could not be deemed irrational or inferior to men, most philosophers continued to assert a gender hierarchy that preceded and gave sense to social relations. At the same time that modern philosophers rejected any immutable social order by insisting that laws arose from experience, they quite happily explained the ways in which a sexual identity and social relations could be produced from the material relations of bodies. Typically, women's position was explained as a result of their bodily predicament: their physical weakness, or their role in childbirth and child rearing.

Even though matter was now seen as quantifiable and devoid of all divine order, and therefore the basis of scientific laws, there was still an association between women and matter, and men and determining reason. Matter was now that which needed to be observed, represented, mastered and ordered by the subject, while the subject was nothing more than a capacity or power to represent nature. On the one hand, the shift towards matter was a rejection of idealism and transcendent order (Montag 1994, 71). Gender could no longer be seen as dictated by some divine cosmic principle; it had to be derived from the matter of the world – one's sex. On the other hand, while the turn to matter might suggest a shift in the gender binary, which had once associated matter with the feminine element and form with masculine activity, the binary merely re-inscribed itself in a different form. Whereas divine forms had once been opposed to an inessential matter, the newly affirmed reality of matter allowed for the scientific and physical justification for the gender binary. Women were subordinated by men because of their sex. Mind and reason were quite distinct from matter, which was the physical substrate of the world, but women's physicality meant that it was quite acceptable to accord them a domestic and subservient role in society. Subordination was no longer ordained by a cosmic order, but was the result of the relations of stronger and weaker bodies. And despite women's weaker physical force it was also still the case that women were associated with physicality rather than reason. Even the feminist Mary Wollstonecraft argued that if women were to become rational and liberate themselves from enslavement to their bodies, they would have to strengthen their bodies (136). The weak woman who is subject to fits of nerves, fainting spells and dizziness, is in no position to think rationally. Only an exercised body can command and transcend itself: 'she was not created merely to be the solace of man, and the sexual should not destroy the human character' (Wollstonecraft 1989, 122). Indeed, women have to resist the 'tyranny' of controlling men and reason through their physical appearance and physicality: 'Yet, to their senses, are women made slaves, because it is by their sensibility that they obtain present power' (Wollstonecraft 1989, 130). Wollstonecraft was typical of liberal feminists in demanding women's cultivation of reason, insisting that only when women were educated and rationally motivated could they both free themselves from sexual subordination, and benefit humanity as a whole, for it is only the exercise of reason, not physical pleasure, that constitutes the worth of human life. Reason is the power to distance oneself from material forces and pathology (81), the capacity to decide and determine oneself. The world itself may be grounded in physical forces, but human subjects have the power to reflect upon those forces, and no *body* can be subordinate if it has the power of reason: 'Happiness is not material, it cannot be seen or felt! Yet the eager pursuit of the good which every one shapes to his own fancy, proclaims man the lord of this lower world, and to be an intelligential creature, who is not to receive, but acquire happiness' (Wollstonecraft 1989, 143).

Despite the positive modern re-evaluation of matter as now bearing a force and reality, liberal theorists positioned the human mind as a power to decide and know its place within the world. Precisely because the world was reduced to a system of competing forces without a transcendent law, 'man' could be positioned as the creature who must give a law to himself, for man was now blessed with the power to distance himself from, manage and represent physical forces. He no longer had an ordained position within nature. Human reason was, as Wollstonecraft herself made clear, just this capacity to decide one's relation to nature (Wollstonecraft 1989, 81).

Many twentieth-century feminists have argued that the long-standing gender binary elevating form over matter was sustained and intensified in the modern turn towards a matter that gained its form only though a process of relations. Some forming power is required to give matter determination; this forming power shifts from a transcend-ent source – God or the forms – to the subject. Luce Irigaray's *Speculum of the Other Woman* provides the most provocative account of how the philosophical subject, despite historic shifts, has always been imagined as a masculine body that is other than the flux and unreality of matter. Whereas man was once part of matter who had a privileged relation to reason, in modernity he becomes a pure princi-ple of reason and representation, divorced from all genesis:

> Once upon a time, something related to genesis and becoming used also to appear and even to precede the specific predicates attributed to the substance, the sub-jec-tum. But now, by a stroke of almost incredible boldness, it is the singular subject who is charged with giving birth to the universe all over again, after he has brought him-self back into the world in a way that avoids the precariousness of existence as it is usually understood.
>
> (Irigaray 1985, 182)

The world is mere flux and quantity without the subject who per-ceives and gives sensations their logic and order, a logic which all male subjects recognise as universal. For this reason many contemporary feminists have seen the theorisation of matter in Platonic metaphysics as governing the entire Western tradition, both modern and pre-modern (Butler 1993, 52). There is always some opposition between the known, formed, shared and recognised world that is representable, and the fluid, changing, merely potential world of a matter that awaits determination. What underlies the form–matter hierarchy is not just an association with gender, but the dismissal of one side of the gender binary as having no real being. Man or the male forming principle is what can be known, repeated, represented and rendered transparent to itself. Matter can only be known from the forms and logic imposed by man and, as such, cannot be referred to, named or known in itself. Man is not only *privileged*; he exhausts the notion of the subject. The subject as such – the rational power to know, represent and order the world – is determined as *other than a feminised matter* that has no being or possibility outside its capacity to be formed. The insistence on the universality of reason and the rejection of what lies beyond reason both produces and denies gender. There is only one gender, only one kind of human: the man of reason. Man has no other: to be a subject is to be set over against materiality, with the 'feminine' being defined as that which is not yet, or not fully, rational.

Man and modern subjectivity

Pre-modern thought was dominated by the stress on a reason and order to which human bodies ought to submit. Reason, though it was a feature that gave human beings their specific form, was not reducible to human life. To be reasonable was to be governed by a law beyond one's self-interest. In modernity, however, this picture shifts dramatically. Writers from the seventeenth century onward no longer accepted that the world itself had a reason, nor did they maintain the image of human reason as the reflection of a divine ratio. The world itself had no preordained system of moral law. Scientific knowledge was no longer considered to be the interpretation of a divine book of nature. Scientists catalogued and ordered various genera and species. But whereas pre-modern discourse had seen the order of the world and the order of the heavens as expressive of divine creation, modern science recognised the importance of human observation in the representation of the world. The world's laws were mapped by reason, not bestowed by God. And the basic categories through which the world was mapped – quality, quantity and so on – were created by the activity of the mind. The enlightenment philosopher David Hume insisted that ideas in the mind were nothing more than the reflection of observed and sensed ideas. And even those like Immanuel Kant who, against Hume, wanted to insist that there was some immaterial mind or subject nevertheless refused to see the reason of that mind as something that possessed an innate or divine order. Reason could only be known and enacted in its encounter with the sensible experiences of this material world. Enlightenment thought, in general, refused to accept any imposed law or order of reason. If something was deemed to be rational then it needed to be demonstrated from and through experience. There may well be ideas or truths which hold for all experience and give form to experience, but such ideas can only be known *from* experience (Kant [1781] 1998, 136).

Human reason was no longer a lesser version, or expression, of the divine world soul; it was no longer God's Inner Light implanted in man. Reason was a *capacity* to observe and judge. Reason was emptied of any specific quality; it became a power to represent the world, rather than a thing within the world with its own determined qualities. Reason was not, as it had been for Milton, the recognition of true authority; it was the rejection of any authority other than itself (Lefort 1988, 92).

What changes dramatically in this assertion of reason as a power, rather than an innate quality, is the relation between reason and gender. On the pre-modern cosmological model, the world itself is a rational and ordered totality of kinds, which human reason is capable of recognising and expressing. From the seventeenth century onwards, philosophers and scientists saw the world as possessing an order, not of moral qualities, ends and hierarchically ordered kinds, but of uniform relations, and of quantifiable forces that generated, rather than tended towards, different kinds. The relations and forces of matter, such as forces of attraction and repulsion, produced specific entities. Instead of assuming that genders or kinds could explain relations, genders needed to be accounted for from the fundamental relations of force and difference. Just as the mind's ideas emerged from an interaction with sensible experience, so gender and differences of genera and species needed to be accounted for from the basic laws of force and interaction.

Even though nature was recognised as having a lawful and scientifically reliable causal structure, the very notion of law changed. Law was no longer an order or command; the world was not seen as being structured by some external lawgiver. Laws were regularities; from the observation of constant relations, effects and causes one could produce a law that would allow prediction of the future. Political laws and hierarchies could, then, no longer be based on some supposed divine law or will on the model of external command, but needed to be justified by referring to the basic mechanisms of matter. Political structures could be justified by referring to the ways in which they furthered or maximised human interest, but it would no longer be possible to subordinate human interest to the supposed rationale of a political structure; one no longer simply accepted one's position in a social hierarchy because it was ordained to be natural.

It was the very lawfulness of nature – its scientific reliability – that precluded philosophers from assuming natural hierarchies. Whereas Aristotle had argued that each being moved according to its own tendency and towards its own place – heavenly bodies ascending, earthly bodies descending – modern science established *universal* laws of matter and motion which had no reference to timeless kinds. If women in modernity were subordinate to men, this was not because of some divine hierarchy, but because their weaker physical force and the capacities of their bodies would best be located in the protected domestic sphere. Genders were produced from the forces of bodies. Instead of matter taking on form – with men's and women's bodies realising their position in a cosmos where masculinity and femininity were principles that transcended bodies – forms were the effect of material relations, and relations were the effects of the powers of matter. The human eye, for example, had the power to see the substance of gold as coloured yellow, but gold in itself did not have that colour, nor were there colour ideas independent of the relations of sensation. Similarly, there was no such thing as 'femininity' but there were women's material bodies which, in this world of political relations, were weaker and subordinate to the physical and rational powers of men. Relations were produced from the material forces of nature. Behind the world of perceived and qualitative differences there was a uniform world of material substance, obeying the same mechanistic laws.

Various historians of ideas have given competing and overlapping accounts of this epochal shift from traditional to modern societies (Lefort 1988; Blumenberg 1987; Tonnies 2001; Koyré 1994; MacIntyre 1981; Hardt and Negri 2000). Perhaps the clearest contrast comes from Karl Popper who contrasts 'closed' to 'open' societies: the closed world is bounded by an already determined law, while open societies create their values from relations (Popper 1945). Like other historians of ideas, Popper argues for a relation of resemblance between political theory, scientific understanding and ideas of the cosmos. Modern societies no longer understand law as emanating from some ideal or order beyond the world; nor is the world in its physicality structured hierarchically (Collingwood 1945). There is one uniform matter from which various points of difference or quality are produced, with the production of these differences being the effect of a single system of relations (such as relations of attraction and repulsion). Louis Dumont has described modern ideology as 'equalitarian': whereas earlier cultures were ordered by a hierarchy that emanated from a transcendent source, such as God, modern cultures have no external principle of law and must derive law from the interaction of elements (Dumont 1977).

Dumont, like Popper, cites a number of philosophers and theorists who exemplify this shift. In political theory one of the key figures is Thomas Hobbes who refused to accept that the world or cosmos simply had an order which human life ought to obey. Hobbes insisted that we needed to explain how a chaotic and disordered nature without hierarchy or order comes to be structured or 'civilised.' Hobbes is still important today precisely because he sought to give an account of sovereignty, or how one part of life seizes power over another (Hardt and Negri 2000, 83–84). He was also one of the few modern political theorists to assume that men and women did not occupy a natural hierarchy and that gender hierarchy – however justifiable – required explanation. For Hobbes, there was nothing timeless about genders or kinds. Relations are not ordered because of the inner nature of each thing; forms and structures are generated politically *from relations* among individuals. Prior to social relations individuals are mere atoms of power, the power to strive to preserve their own existence with no reference or subordination to a higher order. Hobbes refused to see women as essentially and eternally subordinate to men, 'For there is not always that difference of strength, or prudence between the man and the woman as that the right can be determined without War' (Hobbes [1651] 1991, 139). Rather, Hobbes explained the ways in which various material conditions, such as the dependence of children on their mothers' bodies, and the need for mothers to defend their children from the ruthless and brutal world of violent disorder, led to a political opposition between men and women. For Hobbes, one could not explain power relations by referring to a divine or transcendent hierarchy. One needed to see power and force – competitive relations of attraction and compulsion – as the purely mechanical plane from which an ordered world of distinct kinds emerged.

Whereas Plato, Aristotle and writers as late as John Milton regarded form as true being, with the body as dependent matter destined to realise its form, Hobbes and other writers of his time insisted that order and hierarchy were precisely what required explanation. Matter was real and primary – forces of attraction and repulsion. What was secondary was the world of relations and forms generated from that matter. Genders or kinds were not the forms from which, or through which, the material world was generated. Rather, genders and kinds were the outcome of generation, created from a nature that was essentially meaningless. This modern argument that focuses on how kinds or differences are generated from material forces marks the beginning of the possible distinction between sex and gender: on the one hand a material body that is meaningless and pre-social, and on the other hand a gender or social role that is determined by historical and political forces. The possibility of this type of distinction is made clear in the opening of *Leviathan*, where Hobbes refers to 'man' as the 'matter' of his enquiry (10). Man is the 'artificer' who brings matter into the form of the commonwealth or ordered body politic. What Hobbes makes clear is that the formed commonwealth needs to be created and that this creation is not a development of matter's innate potential, but has to be imposed on recalcitrant material.

Modern science and mathematics

There are many ways in which we can approach the dramatic break that takes place with the modern shift to the physicality of substance: through the history of science, the history of ideas, or the history of philosophy. Instead of focusing on forms and order as the true being of the world, modern science shifts its attention to physical forces as the principle of explanation. One influential account of this shift in attention is given by Martin Heidegger – whose work has also been important for twentieth-century feminists (such as Luce Irigaray) and post-structuralist critics of Western phallogocentrism (such as Jacques Derrida). Heidegger's account of the transition to modernity is particularly important because he also sees a continuity in the shift from the pre-modern to the modern, or from ideal forms to extended matter as what is ultimately real or substantial. For Heidegger, Western metaphysics is united by a commitment to substance as that which remains the same and grounds all perception, observation and representation. As Luce Irigaray has argued, the commitment to a single logic is also a commitment to sexual indifference: there is one mode of difference, one system of relations, and all matter is subsumed by this single measure. Mind or judgement gives form and order to a matter that forms a ground or medium through which logic can always represent itself (Irigaray 1985). For both Heidegger and Irigaray, this commitment to presence is always a *subjectivism* (Heidegger 1967, 104; Irigaray 1985, 133). There is always a continuing ground or substratum, which provides a logic or system from which all experience will be determined. The turn to modernity and the 'subject' shifts this ground from a *world* of ordered and formed substances to a *mind* – now a 'subject' – that represents the world according to an already determined logic. Bodies no longer have their intrinsic differing forms; the determination of bodies is produced only in relation to the subject who views or represents them. For Irigaray, this persistent subjectivism is also masculine. The very logic of the subject – as one who represents an inert matter and gives it form and order – establishes the relation to matter in advance and precludes the possibility of other relations, such as physical proximity. The possibility of another body or relation, the possibility of the subject encountering what cannot be calculated in advance from his own imaginary cannot be considered. What is excluded is any encounter with another subject – such as the feminine – whose being cannot be reduced to the sameness of a single logic, whose embodiment might imagine a different relation to the world. There is only one point, one system and measure of all relations:

> The 'subject' plays at multiplying himself, even deforming himself, in this process. He is father, mother, and child(ren). And the relationships between them. He is masculine and feminine and the relationships between them. What mockery of generation, parody of copulation and genealogy, drawing its *strength* from the same model, from the model of the same: the subject. In whose sight everything *outside* remains forever a condition making possible the image and reproduction of the self.
>
> (Irigaray 1985, 136)

According to Heidegger, whereas Aristotle had thought of the world in terms of beings with their own essence, modern metaphysics is mathematical; there is one single extended substance that is known through one system of spatial measurement (Heidegger 1967, 80). Heidegger focuses his reading of modernity on Descartes, but Descartes's 'mathematical' approach to being – where all kinds are explained as versions of one underlying substance – is one more version, according to Heidegger, of a tendency in all Western thought to reduce being to one single principle (Heidegger 1967, 100). In Descartes's case, that principle is that of substance: that which in itself remains the same, requires no other being in order to be, and under-lies accidental or inessential changes. Descartes's single extended sub-stance is experienced as having various qualities, but these qualities are all effects of our relation to an underlying substance with only one essential property: the property of extension or the occupation of space. The essential properties of extended substance are quite differ-ent from the qualitatively diverse world we perceive. Substance in itself has extension; that is its essence, the quality that makes substance what it is. All other qualities, such as colour, are inessential. This has two major implications for the understanding of genders.

First, as Heidegger and those who follow him make explicit, human beings now become 'subjects.' Before the modern scientific positing of one single extended substance that can be known systematically and mathematically, 'man' was one being among others in the world, with all these beings bearing their own essence. To know what one *was*, one could study the order of nature, recognising a rational form reflected in the highest and lowest levels of being. 'Man' could be described as hav-ing a specific position in this order, as being determined by his position in a larger whole, the rationality or logic of which was beyond the mind. With Descartes and modern science, man becomes a subject. He is now a separate substance, with one essential quality – the capacity to think; he is *res cogitans* set over against *res extensa*. There are now two essen-tial qualities, extension and thought, the two essential qualities of the two substances. Man is a subject because he is a separate substance, but he is also a subject in that it is this substance – thinking substance – that gives the world its logic. Man is not one thing in the world among others, with a form like other forms; he is the subject, the basic condi-tion or substratum for the world. Subjectivity, in this sense, is not just a rational aspect or elevated part of the world; subjectivity is the immate-rial, distinct and radically disembodied point from which the world of matter might be known and measured (Heidegger 1967, 106–107).

Descartes distinction between *res cogitans* and *res extensa* creates an essential dualism, which theorists of gender have both criticised and exploited. If it is the case that human beings are subjects and radically divorced from their bodies, then no bodily difference, such as sex, can determine one's subjective or individual being. For this reason, many feminists have emphasised the ungrounded nature of subjectivity, its difference from any material or bodily determination. Not surprisingly, the movement of enlightenment that defined reason as a *critical* capacity, a power to judge that was liberated from any determined law, was also a movement of universal rights and the rejection of intrinsic genders. Reason was not the reflection or expression of a divine order; it was a principle of self-determination, radically distinct from any existing, perceivable, or finite thing. The first overwhelming consequence of Cartesian subjectivity, we might say, was its creation of the idea of the subject as that which is entirely other than the material world of determined causes and fixed kinds. One's material being or sex was radically distinct from one's subjectivity or capacity to think. This enabled the movements of liberalism and liberal feminism, which insisted that one's particular bodily being could have no bearing on one's political rights – for rights were generated from each subject's capacity to decide and determine themselves.

Second, not only do human beings in modernity become subjects – pure knowers of the world rather than bodies within the world; mind and body are radically opposed. Feminists have seen Descartes's dualism as the intensification of a tendency in Western thought in general (Benhabib 1992, 207; Bordo 1987; Fox Keller 1992, 39; Grosz 1994, 6–10; Lloyd 1984, 50). Whereas philosophers had always devalued the body and associated it with femininity, Descartes's separation of mind and body as distinct substances, along with his recognition of the extended world as a substance, now allows for a completely mindless or soulless matter – a substance without any meaning, quality or form other than its occupation of space. Opposed to this soulless extended matter is the other of the two substances: *res cogitans* or thinking stuff. While, *in theory*, women ought to be subjects just as much as men, the emphasis on the radically disembodied nature of mind reinforced the binary prejudices of Western thought that associated women with space, the body and matter. Once mind was radically disembodied, it became possible to see body as no longer tending towards the condition of mind and reason, but as radically opposed to mind. This separate mind had no other quality or essential property than the power to think. It was distinct from the body, unaffected by the body, and related to matter only through the thought or representation of matter. As the gap between mind and body becomes definitive, so, we might say, becomes the elevation of pure, disembodied mind, and the concomitant devaluation of that matter which is metaphorically tied to the feminine.

Many writers have noted that with the modern turn to a nature that is no longer a divine book to be read and interpreted so much as a uniform substance, a huge gap opens between facts and values. Nature itself has no meaning, and all values are generated from the perceiving, evaluating and ordering subject. Science is no longer the recognition of a divinely ordered and harmonious universe; it is the observation of one substance that can be measured, known in advance, and that is now emptied of any essence other than that of extension in space. Scientific knowledge is 'disenchanted,' and whatever intrinsic or causal powers bodies have, such properties are distinct from perceived qualities (Adorno and Horkheimer 1979, 5). One could no longer say, for example, that the human body was the *sign* of a divinely ordered cosmos, that women's bodies were to men's, what men's bodies were to the divine; human bodies were no longer 'read' as expressing an order or meaning. Something like the body as matter existing before all gender, relations and form was now possible. The body can now have an intrinsic sex or biological being that has nothing or little to do with its form or any essential relation to other bodies.

Not all writers agreed with Descartes that substance had only one essential attribute – extension – but the debates of the seventeenth and eighteenth centuries concerned just what essences could be attributed to substance. Substance, what was ultimately real, was now the physical stuff of the world, and essences were its intrinsic properties – not immaterial forms in which the world participated or aimed to realise. It would no longer be possible to see qualities like justice, beauty, goodness or reason as essences or true forms, while the bodies of the world were mere vehicles or participants. Now it was bodies or physical stuff that was real, with ideas being the reflection or representation of matter. This meant that order was no longer transcendent or granted to the world through some divine principle of reason.

Political theorists would need to explain the emergence of order, and the generation of genders or kinds, from a uniform world of extended substance on the one hand, and human subjects who are nothing other than a power to think and represent on the other. For this reason Thomas Hobbes is usually seen as the father of modern political theory. Hobbes explains the production of society from a chaotic 'state of nature' – where human beings are nothing more than pre-social atoms with the desire or will to maintain their own existence, and where nature is so much appropriable property. John Locke, who had defined the mind as nothing more than a blank slate or *tabula rasa* set over against a world whose real essences were nothing like the perceived qualities we know and represent, also saw the world as so much property. Locke defined the human political individual as the owner of one property: labour or the power to work upon nature (Locke 1988, 291). This definition of the political individual as having no quality or form other than the power to labour, where labour was also one marketable and exchangeable property among others also became crucial for the development of the concepts of sex and gender. One becomes a social and political subject through the exchange of labour, through the subjection of the power of one's body to a system of mutual efficiency and co-operation for the sake of production. Political being is no longer determined by some pre-given nature – man as a rational animal who engages with others in order to realise his divine potential – but is achieved through relations of power. Power, here, is not the specific potential of each body – say, the power of some bodies to give birth and other bodies to exercise physical strength; power is not, as it had once been, each being's essential and specific *potential*. Power is now uniform and quantitative; one's position in the social whole is determined by quantity of power, with one single power of struggle, labour and appropriation defining the whole.

When Karl Marx and Friedrich Engels, in the nineteenth century, criticised modern political theory for its capitalist assumption that the market and relations of exchange ought to dictate the social whole, they nevertheless agreed that it was the power of labour and appropriation that explained and created society and, in Engels's case, gender. Private property, or the acquisition of goods as one's own, did not always exist. There were societies that owned goods collectively, and in such societies women were not necessarily subordinate to men: 'One of the most absurd notions taken over from the eighteenth-century enlightenment is that in the beginning of society woman was the slave of man' (Engels 1942, 49). However, once men began to produce more, and to produce efficiently, it became possible for them to retain and *own* the surplus of their labour; they were no longer just fulfilling needs, but were capable of producing beyond need, and in this increased production, and ownership, there lay a certain power. The desire to pass this owned property or stored power onto the next generation as capital meant that something like a family would need to be formed, where fathers could pass property on to their own sons. For Engels, like so many of the seventeenth- and eighteenth-century theorists of whom he was critical, the family is formed through the institution of property. But Engels wrote a history of the family, insisting that the modern form of father–mother–child was contingent on economic relations. Engels's disagreement with his predecessors lay in the supposed universality of the arrangement of gender. There had been matriarchal societies (Engels 1942, 15). Like Locke, Hobbes and others he agreed that it was the power to labour and appropriate property that explained the emergence of society and then the subordination of women (Engels 1942, 25). Only in a society where production and acquisition could be held by an individual, rather than distributed collectively, could men's power of production and acquisition result in the 'world historical defeat of the female sex' (Engels 1942, 59). Engels, and the Marxist feminists who followed and criticised him, regarded as lamentable and historically contingent, what the seventeenth-century political theorists had regarded as natural and justifiable. The confinement of women in the domestic sphere and their reduction of status to men's property occurred through the ascendancy of men's labouring power, their increasing domination of nature and liberation from immediate need. Gender was no longer explained as the expression of some just order or hierarchy; gender was a relation of power produced through the striving and conquering of nature.

From Locke to Karl Marx and contemporary Marxist feminisms, gender has been described as a consequence of the division of labour: as a political rather than an essential difference. Women are differentiated and subordinated because their bodies do not produce sellable property. They are confined to the reproduction of other labouring bodies, while men can sell their labour and enter a system of exchange relations and appropriation. On the other hand, while the theory of the self as a 'possessive individual' clearly favoured the man of labour and acquisition (Macpherson 1962), early feminists also seized on the insights of modern writers like Locke to argue for equality. If bodies had no essential position in a political order, and if political hierarchies were achieved through exchange, labour and property then there was nothing to justify the gendered division of labour. Gender relations were now political – to do with powers and relations – rather than essential (to do with pre-given forms).

Patriarchy

This modern and materialist rejection of forms at a metaphysical level was tied, not only to science and the insistence on order as emerging from human observation and relations, but also to the political and economic ascendancy of capitalism and the defeat of classic patriarchy. Locke, for example, argued against Robert Filmer's *Patriarcha* of 1680 and insisted that there could be no received historical power of the first father (Adam) over all subsequent sons (Locke 1988, 151). Hobbes had argued that we need to think of social man as fatherless, 'as if but even now sprung out of the earth, and suddenly, like mushrooms, come to full authority' (Hobbes 1991, 205). If there were to be an open market of exchange and a maximisation of production, then there would also need to be a shift from a theory of 'man,' with specific qualities, to a theory of the subject. The self could have no essentially moral and constraining properties, but must recognise the flow and exchange of the market as the ultimate producer and regulator of order. The subject produces himself through acquiring property, through the transformation of nature; he does not *have* properties, for he is nothing other than a power, and that power is determined in relation to others: 'The Passions that most of all cause the differences of Wit, are principally, the more or lesse Desire of Power, of Riches, of Knowledge, and of Honour. All which may be reduced to the first, that is Desire of Power' (Hobbes 1991, 53). Man was no longer an animal with moral qualities and a determined position within the world; he was no longer subservient to an external authority. Man was a subject in relation to other subjects, collectively and freely producing a civil society.

On the classic and pre-modern patriarchal model of power, just as Adam was given rule over Eve, and thereby established the first position of God's order on earth, so kings rule over subjects. There is a natural hierarchy of fathers over sons – evidence of a due order in nature. The natural order of the family both displays and leads to a divinely rational hierarchy of kings over their subjects. Such a political theory is possible only if the order of nature *includes* human beings. Rather than human beings being the subjects who generate and represent political order, humans were, on a pre-modern patriarchal model, *subject to* a law of nature. Classic patriarchy also relies on nature being more than extended physical substance; it must somehow express the forms and orders of the world. The book of nature is also a book of morals.

The order of nature reflects divine order: kings govern subjects as God governs man, and man governs woman, as God governs his sons. If, however, nature is nothing more than extended substance it can bear no moral message. And if human beings are *not* nature, not of the same substance as the observable world but detached minds – if they are subjects or powers to represent nature – then there can be no natural human order. Order must be generated and explained from the subject faced with a world of meaningless matter. This, as no shortage of commentators have pointed out, was crucial in the formation of modern man. The ancient self was one who contemplated the forms of the world, engaged with others to discern the true forms, and who formed himself as an image of good reason and harmonious order. Modern man is quite different. He is nothing more than a capacity to represent, transform, own and manipulate the world. Modern man is not *homo hierarchicus* but *homo economicus*; he is not situated in a world of kinds so much as set over and against a world whose order is generated from exchange, labour, acquisition and relations (Dumont 1977).

This reduction of the world to a system of exchange, where relations and forces create forms and kinds, rather than kinds being the determinant of forces, should lead to the dissolution of gender hierarchy. If there are no intrinsic hierarchies, and if the world of matter is given form and order only through the acts of subjects – all of whom are equal precisely because they are liberated from their physicality through rights and reason – then women as well as men should have been included in the public order of self-determination. This was not the case. Both seventeenth-century feminist writers and political theorists explained how it was that even in a world without natural political hierarchies, women were still seen as 'naturally' subordinate to men. Writers like Wollstonecraft claimed that while all subjects possessed the right or power to reason, social conditions, such as the lack of education for women, had not realised that right: 'Where is then the sexual difference, when the education has been the same?' (Wollstonecraft 1989, 93). Earlier theorists had insisted that even though powers preceded kinds and relations, the relation of gender 'naturally' followed from the relative powers of men's and women's bodies. Fathers no longer had authority because they mirrored God's relation to man, and Adam's relation to all his sons, but because the family itself was a self-generating order. Familial relations could themselves be justified on the basis of men's and women's bodies. Modern patriarchy situated the ruling father within the domestic unit of the family, defined through the relations and needs of childbearing and labour, and not in some distant past where all power derived from the divinely ordained Adam. Classic patriarchy – the rule of all by the father-figure of the king, where power once instituted governed posterity – gave way to a different form of patriarchy, where the social order was still centred on, and defined through, man. The structure of power was no longer imposed by the past and received as a traditional or eternal order, but generated through the equilibrium of social relations.

There is a distinction to be drawn, then, between classical and modern patriarchy: what unites the two, however, is an explanation of the political order from the power relation of men over women. Whereas the relation of persons in the classical polity – such as slaves and masters – was previously dictated by the *kinds of beings* men were, relations in modern society were among equals with no distinction in kinds. But this levelling out did not apply to gender, for the one form of natural hierarchy that was maintained in this new equalitarian universe was the family, with the subordination of women to men allowing for male individuals to enter the marketplace of labour without the encumbrances of the private sphere. Sovereignty, in both classical and modern forms of patriarchy, was described and explained from the family, which was assumed to be the basic or minimal political unit. In classical patriarchy, the king was 'like' a father, a protecting and naturally elevated authority; in modern patriarchy men were all literal fathers, dominating a domestic sphere. There was no longer a father who transcended the political order:

> At the turning-point between the old world of status and the modern world of contract another story of masculine political birth is told. The story of the original contract is perhaps the greatest tale of men's creation of new political life. But this time women are already defeated and declared procreatively and politically irrelevant. Now the father comes under attack. The original contract shows how his monopoly of politically creative power is seized and shared equally among men. In civil society all men, not just fathers, can generate political life and political right. Political creativity belongs not to paternity but masculinity.
>
> (Pateman 1988, 36)

Modern 'man' has neither parents nor children. He is, ideally, a fully independent, autonomous and self-determining unity, a being of pure decisions and self-creation. By contrast, 'woman' is figured as the guardian of the private sphere, maintaining all the sentimental attachments, virtues and partial sympathies that men must abandon in order to become individuals engaged in exchange (Elshtain 1993). As many literary theorists and historians have noted, it is the modern emphasis on the family as a distinct sphere that accounts for the radically new force of the novel (Armstrong 1987). Early novels of the eighteenth century had already focussed on private plots of marriage, while the nineteenth century eventually saw the development of a specifically domestic fiction.

By the time Jane Austen wrote *Pride and Prejudice*, relations among individuals and families took place against a backdrop of marriage and property relations; this was no longer Milton's epic world of good and evil cosmic struggles. Whereas the family had once been a metaphor for the polity, with the king as a God-like father figure, and with political subjects as sons who hand over their freedoms to a benevolent sovereign, in modernity the family is clearly differentiated from the polity. The state is no longer like a family, and the ruler is no longer like a father. Rather, the polity is presented as an equal gathering of brothers, distinguished from familial life. But this is because the family is now the site of emotional life, generation, the creation of subjects and the passions. On the one hand, then, early novels could present the escapades of free and detached individuals, disengaged from all mythic, social or political structures. On the other, such individuals, who made their way in the world of fortune, also defined themselves through marriage, thereby creating their own domestic haven of virtue and order.

The very structure of the early novel detached the individual from all ties and displayed his power both to make himself and the world anew (Goldmann 1975). Robinson Crusoe reinvents the minimal relations of production and society after he has been shipwrecked; Tom Jones, and other foundlings, make their way in the world without the benefits of fortune or tradition. At the same time as the early novel stresses the power of the individual to make his way in the world, it also stresses the importance of the marriage contract. If *Robinson Crusoe* and *Tom Jones* are tales of fortune and labour, novels such as *Pamela*, *Clarissa* and *Moll Flanders* describe women whose social position will be decided by economically prudent marriages. As the novel as a genre develops there is also an increasing development of the private sphere in 'domestic fiction,' an entire tradition of literature that focuses on the family as a site of moral and personal development. The novel is not just, as many Marxist critics have noted, a genre associated with the 'modern individual' who is defined through social forces of exchange, labour and acquisition; it is also a genre made possible through gender. Not only do the novels of Jane Austen describe the economic necessity of marriage for the maintenance of property relations, inheritance and social stability; relations of love and the emotions are now described as operating in tension with market relations. Individuals must negotiate the stability of an economically prudent marriage with the need for emotional recognition, affection and respect. A novel, such as *Tom Jones*, can be propelled by the conflict between true love on the one hand, and financially advantageous marriage on the other. Typically, narrative pleasure derives from resolving this conflict. In *Tom Jones* the lovers choose to marry regardless of fortune, thus demonstrating the importance of the private virtues of love, fidelity and altruism. But then fortune is bestowed nevertheless; the lovers receive an inheritance despite their privileging of morality over financial calculation. In *Pride and Prejudice* Elizabeth refuses to marry Darcy as long as he appears as a figure of blind snobbery, unjust elevation and inherited power. However, when she perceives his estate, and recognises him as an individual who puts his wealth to work for the sake of the social whole – the servants praise his benevolence and charity – she can now go on to marry him through a relation of love and due respect. Elizabeth's regard for Darcy begins when she recognises him as one capable of transforming nature through good form: 'She had never seen a place for which nature had done more, or where natural beauty had been so little counteracted by an awkward taste' (Austen [1813] 1972, 267). Darcy's wealth and property is not merely acquired but made over as his own: 'The rooms were lofty and handsome, and their furniture suitable to the fortune of their proprietor; but Elizabeth saw, with admiration of his taste, that it was neither gaudy nor uselessly fine' (Austen 1972, 268). Darcy no longer represents mere wealth and received right, and this transformation lies in Elizabeth's capacity to recognise his social power. Their love is based on just this recognition of just, rather than inherited, value. The novel as a genre plays out the relation between the private sphere of marital love, partial attachments and bodily passions, and the public sphere of profit, self-interest and social order. The novel does not just represent two pre-existing genders; without the distinction of gender there could be no private/public distinction – the very distinction between (feminine) sentiment and (masculine) wealth that gives novels their narrative momentum.

We could say, following Judith Butler, that novels are *performative* in their inscription of a boundary between private and public, female and male:

> If a subject becomes a subject by entering the normativity of language, then in some important ways, these rules precede and orchestrate the very formation of the subject. Although the subject enters the normativity of language, the subject exists only as a grammatical fiction prior to that very entrance.
>
> (Butler 1997, 135)

Butler insists that language produces the distinctions it seems to name. Rather than seeing the novel as a genre that turns to women, or that begins to represent women, we could see the novel as producing 'woman' as a private individual set over against the male world of wealth and power. The novel does not *describe* two genders and two distinct spheres; without the discourses of politics on the one hand, and private emotions on the other, there could be no difference of gender. It is in the very act of referring to and negotiating the relations between public and private that such distinctions come to appear as natural.

According to Carole Pateman, it was precisely because modern political theory began its questions and problems *from* the description of the family and the assumed femininity of the private sphere that such distinctions were taken to be natural and pre-political (Pateman 1988). We could also say, following Pateman, that the novel is patriarchal in a modern sense; for without the world of freely interacting brothers there could not be a fiction focussed on self-creation and reinvention; and there could not be this realm of detached brothers if women were not charged with the labour of the private sphere. Indeed, patriarchy becomes even more important from a modern materialist point of view, which can no longer rely on a divine hierarchy of kinds, but must explain relations from the forces of bodies.

Patriarchy and the sexual contract: Carole Pateman

Classical patriarchy, where power and subordination can be explained because the king is the father or natural ruler of the polity, was, according to Carole Patemen, comprehensively defeated in the seventeenth century. Writers like Locke, Hobbes and Rousseau insisted that the polity did not take the form of a family. It may have been composed of families, but one needed to distinguish the political order of equal men, from the familial order of men and women. Pateman describes this new distinction between the familial sphere of natural order and the public sphere of created relations as modern patriarchy. In modern patriarchy, all men are equal and entitled to appropriate and sell property, including the property of their own labour. What distinguishes modern from classic patriarchy is that the rule of father – where the king is a representative of divine order – is replaced by the rule of brothers. Here, Pateman argues, despite the proclaimed emphasis on a world of forces and powers, a natural gender hierarchy is smuggled back in. Women's subordination can no longer be explained as the expression of some cosmic hierarchy; gender has to be explained from a non-hierarchical state of nature. The very meaning and politics of nature has to shift, and this takes us back to the nature of essences. In modernity, nature's essences are physical; women are subordinate, not because of any divine or rational ordering, but because of their physicality. Something like *sexual* difference becomes politically important, and this importance will increase as medical knowledge amasses more and more 'evidence' regarding reproduction and sexuality, intensifying a supposedly biological difference in kinds that precedes all sociality (Pateman 1988, 119).

What was significant about the beginnings of modern patriarchy, according to Pateman, was that a world in which order and hierarchy was rejected at a political level, nevertheless maintained subordination within the family unit. This tension presents, as Pateman details, a major problem for political theory and the explanations of gender that were articulated from the seventeenth century onwards. On the one hand, humans were self-determining subjects capable of forming and representing their own world, creators of the polity rather than subordinates within some divine order. On the other hand, women were still 'naturally' subordinate. How was it that the meaninglessness of nature could, on the one hand, eliminate all pre-given hierarchies – leading to a capitalist world of free exchange and self-determination – but could also, on the other hand, intensify the association between women and mere embodiment? There are two answers to this question. First, the modern patriarchal theorists, such as Hobbes and Lockes, insisted that while all men were equal in labour, women were not included in the labouring fraternity, for they were confined to the (still) hierarchical order of the family. The second extended answer, offered by Pateman, is that these modern patriarchs were able to sustain the supposedly natural state of the family hierarchy because they refused to consider an earlier *sexual* contract. Before brothers can band together and form a labouring market, they must be produced *as* brothers within a family form, which had already established a distinction between women, whose labour is unpaid and uncalculated, and the wage-labour of men (Pateman 1988, 109).

In modern contract theory, according to Pateman, it is the absence of any natural or paternal order that creates modern man as a brother rather than a father – as an individual with the right to share and exchange women, rather than a single patriarch who governs all women. In classical or pre-modern patriarchy the order and rule of society was, supposedly, derived from Adam, who was the first father, and who inaugurated a line of kings who would then bear a paternal role towards their naturally subordinate subjects. As Pateman notes, however, for Adam to be a *father* and to be established as the model and origin of all subsequent rule, he must have already established a hierarchy over Eve. A man can, after all, only be a father if some woman has given birth. For classical patriarchal theory, all subsequent fathers are both, like Adam, rulers over their wives and sons and, like Adam, subject to the fatherly rule of God, and God's anointed – the king. Classic patriarchy therefore presents the natural rule of the world on the model of the family, where the father holds natural right over his sons. The 'man' of classic political theory is, therefore, a gendered individual, marked by a specific sexual relation (Pateman 1988, 27), and this sexual relation is retained in modern patriarchy. The rule of the father has been overthrown, but 'man' is still an individual who has conquered and feminised the private domestic sphere.

According to many anthropologists, historians and political theorists it is not just Western culture that has established political order on the model of the family. The idea of the ruler as analogous to a father – the father of the tribe or head patriarch – is the first image of natural rule. Political theory then develops, supposedly, by transferring allegiance from this literal father of blood-ties, to some ruler or sovereign who, like a father, holds power for the benefit of his subjects. David Hume, for example, insisted that without our initial familial sympathies and attachments to others we could never develop social virtues and extend our deference to more abstract figures of rule (Hume [1777] 1975, 192). Sigmund Freud also described the father as the first figure of authority, an authority that could then be extended to society as a whole, and internalised as the individual's own conscience

(Freud [1930] 1985, 318–319). Patriarchy is, in its modern form, not the rule of a single father-figure, such as the king, over the tribe or community, but it does retain 'man' as a basic political unit. And this man, who has supposedly liberated himself from all paternal authority, can only achieve this independent state by being in the literal position of fatherhood: located in a nuclear family where women take over domestic labour and men are free to relate to each other as unencumbered brothers. 'Man,' as Pateman insists, can be a disembodied, rational and labouring individual of reason, only because he is other than, and holds power over, the domestically labouring body of woman. The modern ideal of a world of brothers assumes that women have already been displaced from the political sphere, and confined to domestic labour through a prior relation where men establish themselves as fathers. What makes modern patriarchy different from non-Western and earlier forms is that the father is no longer the model for public and political power, but he is still assumed to be the ruler of the family, and the family is then assumed to be the private political unit that precedes and makes possible the social contract.

David Hume was not a social contract theorist strictly speaking; he did not insist that political society emerged from all members renouncing certain immediate freedoms for the sake of submitting to the stability and safety of law. But Hume did think that the only way to explain morality, society and humanism was from the family. We are born with natural sympathies and affections – children for their parents and parents for their children – and as civilisation progresses we are capable of expanding our sympathies and concerns for those not immediately present: from families to tribes, from tribes to societies (Hume 1975, 192). If societies emerge from the natural sympathies of families, it is also the case that families themselves have an order of natural sympathies, where wives are naturally deferent to their husbands. It is also assumed that this primitive social unit is the family of mother–father and dependent children. Once again, even if political order is now seen as something to be explained, it is explained from the supposedly natural binary of mother and father (Hume 2000, 221–222). While natural order and hierarchy are definitively rejected at the divine or extra-human level, it is nevertheless assumed that while the family is not a prototype for order, it literally functions as the basic political unit, and is ordered from within by a sexual relation. Gender is no longer the expression of a larger order, the sexual relation is the basic relation from which all society is explained:

But suppose the conjunction of the sexes to be established in nature, a family immediately arises; and particular rules being found requisite for its subsistence, these are immediately embraced; though without comprehending the rest of mankind within their prescriptions. Suppose that several families unite together into one society, which is totally disjoined from all others, the rules, which preserve peace and order, enlarge themselves to the utmost extent of that society; but becoming then entirely useless, lose their force when carried one step farther. But again suppose, that several distinct societies maintain a kind of intercourse for mutual convenience and advantage, the boundaries of justice grow larger, in proportion to the largeness of men's views, and the force of their mutual connexions. History, experience, reason sufficiently instruct us in this natural progress of human sentiments, and in the gradual enlargement of our regards to justice, in proportion as we become acquainted with the extensive utility of that virtue.

(Hume 1975, 192)

The social virtue of justice is an extension of the natural sympathies of the family. Not only does Hume begin with the family as a basic unit, he also suggests that there are natural propensities or directions in which sentiment flows. From the high regard of great objects, such as the father, we pass readily to a high regard of his family, but we are less inclined to move in the opposite direction: 'our passions, like other objects, descend with greater facility than they ascend' (Hume 2000, 222). Hume's family is, therefore, already hierarchically ordered, and indicates the directions in which our social and political passions will flow. We esteem those of a different country if we have high regard for their rulers, but do not quite so easily value a ruler on the basis of one agreeable citizen. We judge a family on the virtues of the father, who is the natural symbol or representative. Hume's construction of society from the family assumes the inherent sociality of individuals, a sociality that is directed by gender – with fathers holding priority over sons and families.

In contrast with Hume's gradual enlargement of sympathies from the family to the state, social contract theory assumes that some sacrifice or submission is required for individuals to pass from a chaotic state of nature to an ordered polity. But even here, where a break with nature is required, the character of political 'man' – the supposedly pre-social unit from which society is built is really the modern father, who possesses right over women. Social contract theory is one of the

most persistent and clear examples of a political theory that begins
from the explicit refusal of natural kinds and hierarchies, but also
relies on a hidden assumption about sexual hierarchy. Social contract
theory had its clearest early articulation in Hobbes, who wanted to
explain sovereignty from a brutish state of competing nature, and
continues today in modern liberal theory. In all cases the basic political unit – the individual who engages with other individuals – is a
rational individual, where reason is just the power to abandon
immediate and partial interests for some calculated recognition of
maximum benefit. The basic individual from which society is to be
explained is, invariably, the independent male, unencumbered with
children but existing within a family – for he is also liberated from
domestic labour. The twentieth-century liberal theorist, John Rawls,
for example, assumes that the society we would all agree to would be
one where we factored in concern for our dependants, but Rawls
assumes that one simply has dependants – not that one gives birth
(Rawls 1971; English 1977; Green 1986; Pateman 1988, 42). In modern
patriarchy, there is an equal order of individuals whose subordination can no longer be explained through some cosmic or eternal
order. Rather, individuals submit to power *because* the world has
no order. Nature, in itself, is chaotic and violent; individuals agree to
abandon anarchic freedom and submit to a world of law for the sake
of greater stability, along with the efficiency and advantage of social
co-operation. From the rule of fathers, who have a supposed natural
and divine right, we shift to a rule of brothers, united by nothing
other than a recognition that they are *all subjects* – all self-
determining and self-creating – bearing no essential qualities that
could elevate one over another.

According to Pateman, however, this supposedly liberated band of
brothers, freed from all imposed or assumed patriarchal order relies
on a sustained sexual contract. Modern contract theorists freed the
world from all political order, insisting that nature in itself had no
moral qualities. But this very 'denaturalisation' of man, this creation
of the subject as autonomous and self-constituting, raised the problem of sex and gender. If it was the case that man was now, ideally, an
individual liberated from any imposed order or determination from
without, and if social order was an effect of autonomy – produced
because there is no preordained law – then one would need to produce an individual who was freed from the determinants of sex and
embodiment. The liberal individual is marked by nothing other than

his power to exchange, decide, and relate to others. His particular, private or pathological qualities should, ideally, have no force in determining the political order. According to Rawls, for example, a liberal society is one that *could* be chosen by each individual, regardless of their particularity (Rawls 1971). I could not, *rationally*, choose a society where, say, persons of a certain skin-colour other than my own had no power; to do so would be to choose a society on the basis of what *I am* – not a society any possible individual would choose. Reason is just this capacity to be no one in particular. I could rationally choose a society where children, in general, benefited from their parents' affections – for such a society could be chosen by all – but it would not be *reasonable* to choose a society where only *my* children benefited. This would be a private desire, neither universalisable nor justifiable. A liberal society is a rational society, where reason is simply the capacity to adopt a decision-making procedure where one is not any individual in particular. The modern political individual must at least be able to imagine himself from a universal point of view. This is what differentiates the modern *subject* from *man*. It is precisely because we are subjects – liberated from any notion of a determined essence – that we must create our own social order without relying on any normative notion of what the self *is*. The ideal individual must, therefore be of no particular sex. This raises two problems. First, what if one can only be freed of sexuality through a gendered division of labour? According to Pateman, one could become this disembodied man of political theory, adopting free and rational choices in a world of market forces, only because *some* bodies had taken over the domestic labour of childbearing with all its embodied and particular attachments (Patemean 1988, 109–110). Second, if one is of no particular gender, or if maleness and femaleness should *not* determine one's political decisions, what happens to sex? What happens to the undeniable biological differences and conditions of reproduction?

The answers to these problems inaugurated the first wave of feminism. According to the liberal feminists of the eighteenth century, a rational society ought to include conditions that would allow women to take up the free and universal viewpoint of reason. This could only be achieved if domestic labour was no longer the *sole* activity of women. Second, one would need to distinguish more rigorously between sex and gender. One's sexual being – such as the capacity to bear children – should no longer determine whether one could be considered as a rational subject. Women, no less than men, must be allowed to consider themselves as freed from their bodies and biology. The self of liberal theory – the self of rights who must face a world of meaningless forces and decide for himself – is a self who is also liberated from any pre-given notion of human nature.

4 Sex without Gender

First-wave feminism and the sex/gender distinction

Many writers on gender today have seen René Descartes as a crucial figure in the history of ideas, precisely because his differentiation between mind and matter exacerbated a tendency of Western thought to define thought and reason in opposition to matter. If women had always been associated with embodiment and men had always been in greater possession of reason, then the distinction between mind and matter as two distinct substances could only exaggerate the irrationality of nature and, by association, of women. The first-wave feminist response to the modern elevation of disembodied reason was to reject the association of women with embodiment. This rejection took two related and overlapping forms. First, a distinction was made between sex and gender. One's body or sexuality was a merely physical quality and had nothing to do with one's subjectivity. If reason was a distinct and disembodied substance, entirely other than the body, then women and men – at least as far as minds were concerned – were of the same substance; they were both rational human subjects. There could be no justification for arguing that the bodies of women led to any specific, immutable and subordinate gender. Once essential genders were rejected, women could insist on the irrelevance of sex and demand inclusion in a single and genderless humanity.

It was not until the twentieth century that social theorists explicitly distinguished sex from gender, with sex being one's biological and bodily being and gender one's social and cultural being. One reason why this distinction became so important in the twentieth century lay in the theory of the social construction of reality. The social construction argument was explicitly articulated in the twentieth century, but it had its origins in Descartes's turn to the subject – where the world we know is always mediated by representation, known only as it is given through the senses. In the twentieth century it was primarily the work of sociologists who insisted not only that the world was given through experience, but also that the experience that 'constructed' reality varied according to the cultural, linguistic, historical and social conditions within which it was embedded. Here, it was argued that there could be no way of knowing the world in itself, for the world we see and experience is mediated by our particular world-view. Furthermore, we can never know what men or women would be like 'really'; all we can know is their gender: the ways in which maleness and femaleness are constructed by society. Our sex or biological being would therefore be largely irrelevant. Power and political order lies at the level of gender, or all the ways in which sex has been represented and valued.

The twentieth-century distinction between sex and gender also helped to explain how many women could still assent to traditional prejudices, despite their real interests. Early feminists, from the eighteenth century onwards, had insisted that women were just as rational as men. There was one universal reason, regardless of the body one happened to inhabit. But if this were the case – if women really were equals in reason – why had women's subordination been such a long-held prejudice, and why was it that women themselves often seemed to maintain this prejudice? A complex notion of gender ideology had to answer this conundrum. It would not do to attribute the false representation of women as irrational to male self-interest and prejudice; one would also need to see how women themselves assented to the notion of female weakness and irrationality. Ideology is, indeed, the recognition that a governing idea is not only false or erroneous; ideological ideas are crucial and structural to the ways in which we live and experience our world. Ideology structures reality and gives it form; ideology is the way in which individuals make sense of, or symbolise, their images of reality (Althusser 1971). Gender has, therefore, less to do with one's sexuality or the experience and knowledge of the body, and more to do with the way those sexual bodies are interpreted and valued. Gender is the representation of sex, the construction of sexed bodies into specific roles, norms and expectations (Barrett 1980).

With the separation of sex from gender, feminists and sociologists could explain how women saw themselves and their sexuality in terms that were manifestly contrary to their rational self-interest. The distinction between sex and gender also explained the difficulties of first-wave feminism. If women are essentially rational and equal, why do they so often not appear to be so? For first-wave feminists this was because their reason had not been cultivated, and this because of historical masculinist prejudices. Those later feminists who distinguished between sex and gender went further. Women were not only educated to be less than rational; they were also taught to think of themselves and their world in terms of gender binaries, representing their sexed bodies and biological differences as feminine. One could have a *female* body and sex, which would have no direct relation to one's reasoning capacities; but if one saw oneself as '*feminine*,' then one had adopted certain expectations of gender which would lead oneself and others to expect irrationality, passivity, weakness, or whatever other social and cultural constructions were imposed on women's bodies.

Enlightenment feminism

First-wave or liberal feminism, from the eighteenth century to the present, remains committed to the idea of equal and rational subjects who all have the right to be considered human. Gender representation, on this argument, should either be done away with or refigured to include women within the norms of reason. One's biological sex should not determine one's social being (Moller Okin 1994). Early feminists, prior to the explicit distinction between sex and gender put their faith in universal reason, believing that the errors and prejudices of the past could be swept away if women were given the political and concrete conditions that would enable them to think (Wollstonecraft 1989). Education and *inclusion* in the rights of man would lead to a society where sex no longer mattered in terms of the attribution of reason. These early feminists did not yet attack, or have any sense of, a social or cultural gender. Their faith in universal reason led them to assert the possibility of a single, united and sexless humanity, regardless of the body one inhabited. It would be possible, therefore, for women to go on being women – child rearing, tending the home, maintaining 'feminine' virtues and practices – without excluding themselves from the activity of public reason which should, by right, be open to all subjects regardless of their social or physical position (Wollstonecraft 1989, 109–110).

Seventeenth- and eighteenth-century writers did not yet feel the need to account for the ways in which supposedly equal human subjects could nevertheless be ruled or determined by the social and cultural stereotypes of gender. The early feminists were confident that once sex was recognised as entirely distinct from one's mind or reason, a thoroughly non-hierarchical and human society would follow. Sex was understood to be *merely* natural; humanity, as purely rational, should not allow itself to be determined by sex difference.

These early feminists, did, however, adopt a second strand of argument, which comes close to a theorisation of gender in its modern sense. If it is the case that reason is a disembodied, universal and equally distributed power, how is it that women have been oppressed? If bodies are entirely distinct from reason, and if bodies are irrelevant to a polity that is based on agreements among equals, how is it that certain bodies have been denied participation in rational self-determination? Many of the early feminists agreed with the *explanation* of gender that was adopted by modern patriarchal theory, but they also insisted that that explanation of gender was quite different from *justification*. Women had been enslaved because of their weaker bodies, but such an explanation could not legitimate their continued exclusion from a rational and liberated world, governed by right rather than force (Wollstonecraft 1989, 110). In a world where reason is an entirely different substance from the body, how have some bodies been deprived of the right to reason? The problem of sexual equality as it was articulated by early feminists articulated one of the central problems of political theory: how is it that subjects with an equal rational power, or equal rights, submit so readily to their subordination? If we are all equal, how do we explain the ready and unthinking submission of self-enslavement, the easy acceptance of gender as natural?

The theorisation of sexual inequality was one of the earliest inquiries – well before late nineteenth-century Marxism and twentieth-century Freudian psychoanalysis – into how certain groups willingly accept a way of seeing that is not only false but contrary to their self-interest. How is it that rational individuals can – quite irrationally, or contrary to the demands of life and self-interest – hand over their power and reason to another group? For the early patriarchal theorists, sexual difference *was* rational and prudent: the subordination of women allowed for a more harmonious social whole and a more efficient society. For the feminists of the eighteenth century, however, this explanation would not do. First, it was contrary to the interests of humanity as a whole for half of it to be held in slavery; the emancipation of women was necessary for the emancipation of 'man.' No man who tyrannically governs his wife and home is really maximising his reason, and no man with an enslaved and uneducated wife is fulfilling his true humanity.

Second, even if the subordination of women had once been efficacious, this was no justification for its continuation. Men may once, in an age of violent barbarism, have surrendered their freedom to a king or despot for the sake of greater security, but a past arrangement cannot justify a present in which men recognise each other as capable of creating a harmonious social equilibrium. Similarly, one might explain *how* women were defeated and enslaved, but this explanation should only serve to do away with, not justify, continued enslavement.

The most common explanation was a natural one. Women's child-bearing capacities and their lesser physical strength explained how power had been seized. But such a hierarchy is neither legitimate – for it is mere force not order – nor is it pertinent to modern society. In a rational world where bodies are no longer subject to strict force, and where we can recognise each other as fully human, then whatever powers have been seized in the past – whatever fictions of divine order have been imposed – these can have no bearing on the present. Eighteenth-century feminism, with its distinction between one's natural being and one's social being, was part of a larger movement of social liberation and enlightenment in which natural kinds, myths of origin and received values were overthrown in the name of reason. If we are rational – not just acted on by nature but capable of deciding and transforming nature – then no given or received order can determine our being. Whatever effects the sexual relation between men and women may have once had on political orders, this should have no bearing on the present. Reason is, essentially, autonomous and self-determining, and there is a strict distinction between the world of facts – say, that women give birth – and the world of values – just how we allow that fact to be socially structured. Many first-wave feminists, for example, accepted that women's bodies might *explain* an unfair division of labour and the restriction of women to the private sphere of the family, but they also insisted that the modern recognition of equality and reason should alter those natural conditions. A rational humanity can only be achieved with the levelling out of gender roles. Childcare should not confine women to the home; nor should the traditionally male spheres of politics and public decision-making be confined to men.

In its early forms first-wave feminism focussed on education, and it was this aspect that tied early feminism to the broader movement of liberalism. Human beings are ideally, or *in principle*, equal; no physical or traditional determination should impede the free, rational and self-determining powers of reason. Only universal education could both remove past prejudices and develop each subject's rational potential. Assuming *one* ideal of reason for men and women, and the capacity for all subjects to exercise reason, feminists like Mary Wollstonecraft argued that as soon as the light of reason was cultivated, gender hierarchies would be swept away. Wollstonecraft's theorisation of gender and her ideal of gender equality was not only a feminist argument. True, she was interested in the rights of women, and the inclusion of women within an already established and valued sphere of human rights. But she saw rights, justice and equality in general as possible only when reason was developed in all members of society. A man who relates to a woman who has not cultivated her reason is relating only to a body; he is not a true master and is as subject to the tyranny of beauty and feminine wiles, as the slave-owner is subjected to the brutality of the system that allows him to relate to persons as things (Wollstonecraft 1989, 109). For Wollstonecraft, then, the liberation of women will free men from their unreflecting position as tyrants. If marriages are based on the mutual recognition of individuals, and if the passions are educated and cultivated, then humanity will be self-governing and autonomous, no longer subject to the intoxication of power (Wollstonecraft 1989, 93).

The very concept of rights was possible only with the distinction between reason and material nature; each human has rights precisely because there is no preordained natural order and imposed law. In the absence of an already determined social structure, and in the absence of any essential character, each individual must determine for themselves their place in the world: 'Reason is, consequentially, the simple power of improvement; or, more properly speaking, of discerning truth. Every individual is in this respect a world in itself' (Wollstonecraft 1989, 122). Rights are not things an individual has, like bodily qualities; they are always rights *to* do, act and be. The inclusion of women in human rights would therefore be bringing the logic of rights, and the disembodied essence of reason, to its rational conclusion: nothing other than reason, which is shared by all, can determine what one *is*. Rights do not define what you are; one has rights because reason is self-defining, disembodied, and other than any natural or specified kind. The very concept of rights is at odds with an assertion of transcendent, determining and essential kinds. As long as one accepted the rights of man, one would have to accept the rights of woman: neither rights nor reason could be determined by sex.

Marriage and gender harmony

The reconfiguration of gender relations would, on this understanding, be beneficial to humanity as a whole, and essential to any just polity. This was not just because as long as men tyrannised over women they would not be living within a truly rational polity; it was also because something like a proper marriage or just relation between maleness and femaleness would be required to realise a full humanity (Wollstonecraft 1989, 106). To this day there are feminists who celebrate the greatness of writers like Wollstonecraft precisely because her ideal of the inclusion of women in the model of rational humanity would allow for a reason that was in line with, rather than repressive of, the emotions and passions (Findlen 2002, 189; Green 1995). We should not see reason as masculine, oppressive and disembodied. Through writers like Wollstonecraft we can see reason as the recognition of the power of justifying arguments along with the claims of the family and affections.

Karen Green has challenged the picture of a tradition of Western reason produced through a singular image of man; reason may have been defined through gender bias, but reason cannot be reduced to the partial (or not fully rational) images we have of it. Reason is also the capacity to expand, correct and criticise bias. The very feminists who challenge what has been defined as reason can only do so through reason, and thereby manage to give reason more purchase by including ideals that are traditionally seen to be exclusively feminine – ideals of care, nurture, empathy and affection. Like many liberal feminists, Green's defence of reason does not separate reason from the supposedly unruly and inessential body; she sees reason as the balance or harmony, the reflective equilibrium, between the particularity usually associated with the feminine and the universality of traditional masculinity:

> A just society needs to reproduce itself. Doing so requires institutions, like the family, within which love and sexual desire contribute to the reproduction of morally motivated citizens. These institutions need to be just from women's point of view (as well as men's). They need to reproduce women and men who are economically independent and who regard each other as equals.
>
> (Green 1995, 168)

Many anthropologists have pointed out that in virtually all cultures the generation of the universe and its continued harmony were

thought to depend upon a balance of male and female principles
(Bourdieu 2001; Ortner 1996). We have already seen the way in which
Western philosophy, in its Platonic origins, began with a relation
between active male form and receptive female matter. With the
enlightenment, authors were keen to rid human reason of any myths
of gender, any idea of two opposing and essentially different principles. There was only one principle, reason, which needed to be
exercised equally by men and women. The mythical image of creative
and productive marriage, or the idea of a God who inseminates the
universe with divine life, must be done away with. But if reason needed
to sweep away these myths of cosmic opposition and harmony, it was
literal marriage that took over as the principle of social harmony. There
can only be a true development of reason with the education of both
men and women, with women tending to the domestic virtues, and
men organising the polity – both through the exercise of reason
(Wollstonecraft 1989). Marriages in which men and women still had
distinct roles – women in the private sphere of the home, men in the
public sphere of the market – would allow reason to be expressed in
different and complementary forms.

The concrete consequences of granting men and women the right to
reason lay in political achievements, such as the right for women to
vote, the right to education, the right to property and the right to speak
and write. Such rights were, however, a long time coming; and one
could question, as many second-wave feminists were to do, why it was
that there was such a huge time lag between the recognition of
inequality and the actual political changes that would lead to equality.
Further, one might also ask why, even with the achievement of public
and legal reforms, women were still oppressed. Second-wave feminists
felt it was necessary to move beyond public and legislative questions
of rights to the private sphere, to address the fantasies, desires and
images – the ideology – through which women are gendered.

The rights declared by enlightenment feminists did not demand
what many today would consider to be a reconfiguration of gender. For
Mary Wollstonecraft and later nineteenth-century feminists, women
could exercise reason and still be the traditional mothers and home
keepers in a complementary, rather than hierarchical, relation. As long
as women are regarded as mere property, political life in general will be
impoverished; for men will be mere tyrants, exercising force rather
than reason in the household. But there could be a rational, enlightened and liberated marriage, where women cultivated their reason

alongside, and in harmony with, their roles as mothers. For Wollstonecraft, only a rational and educated woman can be a good wife and mother. A woman who relies entirely on physical beauty, charm and the illusory appeal of weakness and ignorance can neither fulfil her duties nor be a desirable partner in marriage. Enlightenment liberal feminism of the eighteenth century sought, therefore, to produce the image of the well-ordered family, where the conditions of natural sex – childbearing, embodiment and the passions – did not disrupt the mutual recognition of partners.

In twentieth-century liberal feminism this insistence on a proper and fruitful marriage was both an extension of an age-old reliance on the male–female polarity as a symbol of order emerging from difference, and a refusal of *essential* difference. Because both men and women were essentially the same – as rational subjects – they could both, in a marriage of different roles, fulfil and exercise their reason in different but complementary ways. On the one hand, gender difference was deemed to be something that ought to be overcome. All bodies were members of the one humanity, and society should, as much as possible, do away with conditions that would impede women from realising their rational potential. Granting women the right to vote, and other forms of legislation that would remove prejudice and inequality would allow women to become fully equal and human. At the same time, it was also acknowledged that while sex ought not to dictate one's social being – that sex was irrelevant and *not essential* – the traditional dichotomies of gender could be of relevance. Perhaps those qualities illegitimately but traditionally attributed to women were not just to be done away with; perhaps humanity in general would benefit from the inclusion of women within the public sphere. If it is the case, for example, that women have – traditionally – been confined to the roles of child rearing and domestic labour, then this may mean that they have developed certain virtues which ought, now, to be given value: all those altruistic virtues of care, compassion, unselfishness and conciliation. Whereas men have traditionally been defined as moral agents capable of detachment, judgement, autonomy and independence, women have been considered as lesser, but still valuable, representatives of domestic or caring virtues. One may wish to do away with essential differences, but still recognise that all humanity could benefit from traditionally gender-divided virtues – women could be rational, and men could be caring. But the assertion of masculine and feminine virtues that were not grounded in any sex would, it seems, either lead to the dissolution of gendered associations or result in an ideal of androgyny, where any body of whatever sex could participate in masculine and feminine qualities. Since the enlightenment there have, therefore, been two approaches to the recognition of the non-essential nature of gender. First, traditionally gendered qualities – such as masculine reason or feminine compassion – could now be available to both sexes. Second, we could redefine the relation between the sexes; women are not *less* rational – not lesser versions of men – but differently gendered, operating with a specific, but no less valuable, form of reason.

For first-wave and liberal feminists, this could have two consequences. The first would be to say that just because the division of labour constructed women as domestic carers and men as public legislators, there is no essential reason why such roles could not be reversed or done away with. There is nothing essentially male nor essentially female. By educating women and reforming the structure of the family – involving men with childcare, women with the work force – gendered oppositions could be done away with. If gender were nothing more than the social construction or representation of sex, then gender could always be otherwise.

The second consequence of acknowledging the constructed nature of gender would be to look at the value of that construction. Whereas early liberal feminists, such as Wollstonecraft, insisted that women could be equal *to men*, later feminists and political theorists saw more radical implications even in Wollstonecraft's own work. While there may be no essential sexual difference that dictates our social being, it may be the case that the historical and cultural construction of femininity can be appealed to positively. Women should not just be considered as equal to men and included within the norm of humanity. Qualities traditionally associated with women may enhance the norm of humanity in general (Green 1995).

Second-wave feminism and difference

Second-wave feminism radicalised insights that were implicit in early feminism's demand for equality. Liberal feminists had insisted that with education, suffrage and political reform gender dichotomies could be rendered politically irrelevant or reformed. Gender would be either dissolved or revalued. However, in explaining how gender inequalities had emerged from an essentially equal human nature, first-wave feminists had to give some account of the genesis of gender. In so doing, their explanations often arrived at two models of political subjectivity. If it was the case, as Hobbes had argued, that women were subjected because they were inclined to care for their children, and would therefore be hampered in any struggle or competition, then this suggested that women became political subjects or subordinates through caring for others. Their entry into the polity was not, as it was for men, achieved through ruthless competition, but was originally partial, interested and other-directed. Whereas first-wave feminists insisted that women could be as detached, rational and autonomous as men, later feminists began to question just how valuable the image of rational detached man was. What had been seen as women's inferiority and subjection – their 'failure' to liberate themselves from natural attachments – could also be interpreted positively to insist on women's difference.

Radical or second-wave difference took a number of forms and deployed a number of theories to account for gender difference, but in all cases difference was no longer to be deemed a mere impediment to reason. To be different from man was no longer regarded as a failure to achieve equality; to be different *as a woman* would require no longer measuring all humanity on the model of 'man.' What had been constructed or generated as feminine had a value of its own. Perhaps, then, one should not be striving to arrive at a world where sex did not matter. Perhaps the social and political effects of one's sex – the formation of two different genders – also allowed for a more valuable image of humanity than that usually associated with the universal 'man' of reason.

Despite their stress on the positive value of women's gender differences, many forms of radical or second-wave feminism were still anti-essentialist, for they relied on stories of how genders were constructed rather than appealing to timeless female qualities. There was no direct relation between bodies and genders; indeed, second-wave feminists often rejected the ways in which female bodies had been interpreted or gendered, and sought to represent those bodies differently by rethinking gender from the woman's point of view. Second-wave feminists asserted the difference and value of femininity, no longer accepting that women should strive to be equal to men. But such assertions of difference were also accompanied with explanations and justifications of this newly valued femininity; often, it was precisely because women had been excluded from the traditional positions of power, rationality and domination that they offered a new voice and model of subjectivity.

There were two dominant theories explaining the emergence of gender from nature: Marxist and psychoanalytic. On the Marxist account, which was also a critical account, gender differences were explained according to the economic division of labour. Political power is primarily economic because it is the ability to control production that creates relations and identities; the master becomes a master only by being liberated from the needs of life by the slave, and the slave becomes a slave only by producing more than he actually needs for the sake of the master. Relations among individuals are structured by work and production, with the individual acquiring their essence through their actions on the world. Slavery and disempowerment are *effects* of social relations and existence, not dictated by essence. Indeed, the very idea of *essential* mastery or slavery is ideology: the presentation of historical and economic effects as timeless and immutable causes. It is social existence and relations of power that precede and determine essence, or what one is.

From the point of view of gender, Marxism argues that women also become subordinate through labour and production. The family is essential to the structure of labour and private property; indeed the family and private property emerge with each other. The man becomes a worker and is subjected to the system of exchange and property by selling his labour, while the woman becomes subject to man by reproducing – creating more labour power – and performing unpaid labour in the private sphere. Traditional Marxism could therefore assume that it was economic relations of work and exchange that structured gender relations; class inequality, or subjection to capital, precedes sexual inequality. Women become tied to an unpaid private sphere when men sell their labour to others and exchange property. The division of labour is also a sexual division; capitalism produces sex difference alongside class difference. If the system of economic exchange and exploitation were done away with, Marxists argued, gender equality would follow accordingly. Economic differences and relations explain all subsequent relations.

This supposed primacy of the economic assumes the naturalness of the family. Even though Engels sought to explain the emergence of the modern family of mother–father–child, he nevertheless assumed that women were responsible for biological reproduction and were already a group distinct from men (Engels 1942). Marxists begin their explanation of the emergence of private property from the family, where women and men are already differentiated, and where women are responsible for childcare, homemaking and biological reproduction. Even the originally posited stage of 'matriarchy,' from a traditionally Marxist point of view, presupposed the 'natural' opposition between mothers and fathers, and the 'natural' association of child rearing with women. Women are 'defeated,' as an entire sex, Engels argued, when property is no longer owned collectively, but must be owned by distinct individuals, and passed on from fathers to sons. In this establishment of lines of ownership, women not only lose the right to property, they become property. Their position in the family can be explained fully by economic circumstances; they are oppressed because they neither own nor control property.

Many later Marxist feminists disagreed with this traditional assumption that one could begin economic explanations from an already constituted difference between men and women, and they did so because they saw sexual difference as having its own political dynamic. How did men come to be differentiated from women, and how were women formed as a distinct class? Perhaps the very conditions of childbirth and child rearing, the very institutions of motherhood and the family, had their own power structure and needed to be addressed on their own terms (Firestone 1979). As long as women were mothers in relation to fathers some form of oppression would be maintained. As long as women were *women* – defined as a coherent group in relation to men, marriage and heterosexual relations – there could be no liberation. Radical materialist feminism therefore took Marxism's insights on the relation between the family and the power to argue that the very concept of *woman* – as mother, wife and domestic labourer – was intrinsically oppressive. There could be no liberation from within the already differentiated gender system; to be a woman was to be defined as man's other (Wittig 1992). Overthrowing capitalism might liberate the male worker from his subjection to the market; but only a revolution and overthrow of the family would liberate women.

Marxist feminists disagreed over the extent to which the relation between the labouring man of production and exchange, and the domestically enslaved woman of biology and reproduction, could be tied to capitalism. Michele Barrett, for example, rejects both the idea that women's oppression can be strictly explained by biology, but she also insists that we need to explain why it is *women* who occupy the weaker position in the domestic hierarchy. Her answer is gender, or the way in which sexual difference is socially constructed into specific political roles and relations (Barrett 1980, 93). Barrett is critical of second-wave or radical feminisms that simply accept that women's bodies are the cause of oppression and that the answer to oppression can only come about through the separateness and affirmation of women's difference, or the ideal of women as somehow outside all power and tyranny. Radical feminists associated masculinity with domination, violence and oppression, and turned to women as a redemptive point outside patriarchy (Brownmiller 1975). Against this appeal to an innocent feminine outside patriarchy, Barrett insists that gender is an ideology, not caused by sex so much as representing sex in ways that are open to adjustment and rearrangement. Marxism's and feminism's value lies precisely in its explanation and demystification of oppression, leading to the possibility of change. The Marxist feminism that criticised the second-wave feminists' appeal to the intrinsic value of women, and that characterised itself as materialist, was highly critical of any utopian appeal to a female essence (such as Mary Daly's *Gyn-ecology* [1979]). Rather, only if one saw the ways in which sex had been gendered, or rendered socially and politically meaningful, could capitalist and patriarchal power structures be dismantled. It was no longer a question of appealing to the difference and virtue of woman, nor of demanding woman's equality, but of realising that both 'man' and 'woman' were products of ideology, the presentation of social roles as timeless and immutable kinds: 'If we examine the characteristics of men as radical feminists describe them – competitive, rationalistic, dominating – they are much like our description of the dominant values of capitalist society' (Hartmann 1981, 28).

Marxist feminism was one of the movements most insistent on the need to assess not only the position of women, but also the construction of 'man.' Liberal feminism had assumed that women could and should be included in the ideal of reason and subjectivity or the rights of man; radical feminism had stressed women's difference and value – their capacity to care and nurture in opposition to male dominance – but Marxist or materialist feminisms were the most strident in insisting that we see both men and women as gendered. Genders were, furthermore, not caused by biology, for biology is always lived, mediated and organised through systems of power and meaning. 'Man,' no less than 'woman' is a political issue.

The contested relation between economics and gender in Marxist theory is typical of one of the main problems in theorising gender: to what extent is sexual opposition created by, or creative of, other social oppositions? For Marxist feminists, the subordination of women, or women's unpaid labour, is what underpins the entire patriarchal structure. Simply waiting on an economic revolution will not ensure the overcoming of gender inequality. Rather one needs to address the very relation between man and woman, the very relation that constructs the family as the unquestioned, seemingly natural social unit from which all other relations are explained (Hartmann 1981, 26). Against this, Marxist feminists argue that one needs to account for the sexual relation: how does one section of humanity becomes a class of unpaid labourers devoted to biological reproduction and domestic labour? Marxism was radical precisely because it refused to accept the market and the production of the polity through exchange as natural; only in capitalism are individuals subjected to market forces. In a Marxist utopia, market forces are properly seen, not as forces that govern life, but as effects of human relations, decisions and powers. Marxist feminists extended the Marxist critique of the market to the family. Just as market relations – the relations of workers to those who own production – is anything but natural and is the effect of a seizing of power, so the position of women in the family is the effect of men's seizure of women's unpaid labour. Gender relations produced by the family structure are as oppressive and historically contingent as the class relations produced by the market. Unlike liberal feminists, who aimed to include women within the ideal of a self-defining humanity, Marxist and radical feminists insisted that freedom could only be achieved with a restructuring of sexual relations: 'We must insist that the society we want to create is a society in which recognition of interdependence is liberation rather than shame, nurturance is a universal, not an oppressive practice, and in which women do not continue to support the false as well as the concrete freedoms of men' (Hartmann 1981, 33).

Traditional Marxists insist that class difference precedes gender difference; the unpaid labour of women in the family is required for workers to sell their labour in the marketplace, and the ultimate explanation comes down to economics and relation of man to needs, nature and life. One of the key problems in such an explanation is that of the relation between *techne* and *praxis*. Man develops certain skills and systems (*techne*/technology) in order to *act*, fulfil himself and develop his being (*praxis*). From a Marxist point of view alienation or submission occurs when a skill or *techne* that is developed in order to enhance life – such as the technologies of labour-division which increase efficiency – appear as timeless laws of structures to which man submits. Factories become masters of the human life that built them; capitalism and the economy become enslaving systems, rather than means for life and exchange. Ideology is, indeed, the misrecognition of a created and human act as an inescapable law, mistaking a historical decision and act for a timeless essence and law. As soon as an activity, such as theory, skills or ideas, becomes detached from the needs and purposes of life it enslaves, rather than enhances, praxis. For Marxism, then, the primary value is *praxis*: a life that acts in order to enhance and create itself. The problem which Marxism confronts is the overtaking of *praxis* by *techne*; the skills we have formed *in order to* act now *determine* action. The revolution will occur when all those systems developed to enhance life, such as the increasingly liberating possibilities of technology, are returned to those who work and transform nature.

The family has its origin in this drive for increased efficiency and mastery, in praxis. Marxism explains the emergence of the family as required by the need to work and master nature, but it also allows for the possibility of liberation from that need. Technology will develop to the point where we can all benefit from productive efficiency. What is required is a worker's revolution; instead of increased efficiency leading to the enjoyment of greater and greater profits by the capitalist, production can be enjoyed by all. For traditional Marxists, this utopia can only be achieved by the worker, who must come to recognise himself as productive and active. What *seems* to be natural – the labour market – must be exposed as constructed. Overcoming ideology means recognising the ways in which what is presented as natural and immutable – the market – is actually the product of human relations; utopia can only be achieved when 'man' realises that he creates his own existence. He is not *subjected to* the market, so much as the agent from whom the market is generated; for this reason he can also re-create social relations by transforming economic relations. If all bodies enjoy the fruits of production, rather than allowing excess production to be channelled into further profits, then exploitative relations will be eliminated. All bodies will become fully human, and gender *inequalities* – but not gender itself – will wither away.

Radical feminisms contested this supposed primacy of economic relations, and contested the primacy of production. Not only must women already be subjected to the structure of the family in order that man may become a 'worker' – engaged with other men in a competitive marketplace – the Marxist image of the self is implicitly masculinist, and relies on a particularly heterosexual concept of man as self-determining, nature-conquering, active and technologically progressive – as opposed to the passive, acquiescent and nature-immured body of woman. Marxism assumes that 'man' must conquer and transform nature, that man develops technology or systems of efficiency in order to be liberated from nature, and that man is, as an economic individual, defined by his capacity to create and recognise himself.

Even though Marxism challenges the supposedly 'natural' hierarchy of the family, and explains the subjection of women, it nevertheless assumes that human life is motivated by the need to transcend and transform nature. Marxism intensifies a nature–technology opposition, an opposition that has been crucial in the production of gender. There is a good 'techne,' which unfolds and develops what nature ought to be, a technology that allows man to develop his nature by conquering nature, and a monstrous or derivative 'techne' that supplants and perverts nature, that prevents man from liberating himself from nature. Marxism's 'man' is a subject who adds technology to an otherwise inert nature, who uses technology to liberate himself from chaotic and primitive need. Anything radically other than man, anything alien, inert, unproductive or resistant to the active creation of progressive man, must be recognised and internalised.

While Marxism was critical of capitalism's capacity to present the 'laws' of the market as timeless and natural, and insisted that liberation could be achieved only when man seized control of production, it nevertheless retained one aspect of capitalist ideology: the dichotomy that privileges production, activity, work and self-realisation over the merely natural, unproductive, passive and un-self-conscious. Woman's role as agent of reproduction is left out of the equation.

For many forms of radical feminism, 'woman' should not be accepted as a natural category in need of liberation, for the very concept and class of woman has been produced through structures of power (Guillaumin 1982). This should not necessarily mean that all those features associated with woman should be abandoned. If women were traditionally confined to the natural, private and passionate attachments of the family, then they could also provide a way of thinking beyond a ruthless, uncaring and systemic capitalism.

Some radical feminists argued for separatism, insisting that women could form alternative communities not corrupted by the competitiveness of male reason. But other radical feminists insisted that the cultivation of what had traditionally been seen as feminine could be incorporated into a new model of humanity, where both men and women could take on virtues that were once divided between masculine and feminine. Today, for example, many eco-feminists, criticise the capitalist assumption that humanity's role lies in the exploitation and appropriation of nature. Rather than including women within the male labouring force, eco-feminists turn to women as offering a more valuable model of labour – forms of work that recognise and care for nature, rather than seeing nature as so much inert and appropriable property (Warren 1994; Warren 1997). If men become men by detaching themselves from immediate needs, transforming nature and selling their labour, women become women by cultivating and tending nature – both their own children and their homes. Whereas capitalist individualism celebrates man as detached from any natural or determining values – capable of thinking with universal logic and reason – radical feminisms see women's maintained relation to unpaid labour, care and the family as offering a more compassionate model of the subject.

Marxist feminism, like so many other forms of radical and second-wave feminism, rejected the liberal idea that women ought to be included in the already established political sphere. They insisted on the transformation of the political sphere, including economic relations of paid labour, and sexual relations of reproduction, in order to achieve a true equality. Unlike liberal theories of gender it was not assumed that sex could be rejected as irrelevant in order to arrive at a single, universal and genderless humanity; it was often acknowledged that if 'man' had been constructed politically, what had traditionally been defined as 'woman' could offer a social alternative. Perhaps women's traditional 'failure' to become detached, reasoning and competitive citizens could be reread as a virtue. And because such a traditionally constructed femininity was a *construction*, there was no reason why these alternative virtues could not apply to humanity as a whole. Instead of arguing for the inclusion of women within the rights of man, as liberal feminists had done, many radical feminists argued for the rejection of 'man' as such in a feminist utopia that would question the reality and legitimacy of sexual difference: 'All feminists reject the sex/gender hierarchy, but very few are ready to admit that the logical consequence of this rejection is a refusal of sex roles, and the disappearance of gender' (Delphy 1993, 7).

Psychoanalytic feminism

Apart from Marxism and materialist feminisms, which sought to explain the difference of men from women through processes of power and oppression, the other dominant narrative for explaining the emergence of gender from nature was psychoanalysis. Indeed, many Marxist feminists saw psychoanalysis as a necessary supplement to the theory of economic oppression, allowing a critique of the sexual relation that Marxism had taken for granted (Mitchell 1974). Marxism insists on the social and political nature of human existence: nature is never known in itself, but is always mediated through human relations. This mediation would include the human body, which is known only in its relations with nature, history and social power. Marxism and materialist feminisms had insisted that 'women' have their essence in the institutions of the family and the relation between private and public production (Barrett 1980, 251). Women, as a class, are produced through processes of labour and power; any appeal to women's essence or femininity would be ideological: the misrecognition of a historical production for a timeless truth (Guillaumin 1988). Marxism therefore assumes a distinction between sex and gender: 'No one would want to deny that there are physiological differences between the sexes, but what is at issue is how these natural differences are constructed as divisions by human social agency' (Barrett 1980, 250). Woman's biological sex is one thing, but her construction as a mother within the private bourgeois household is politically and historically constituted. Gender is thoroughly transformable. There is no reason why all bodies might not become fully human, liberating themselves from their gender. One's biological being or sex may have originally played a role in determining social relations, with women being confined to the family and being incapable of selling their labour; but, ultimately, humans determine their own existence. Once technology develops to the point where human life can be liberated from natural determinations, there need no longer be any gendered hierarchy: 'We require regeneration, not rebirth, and the possibilities for our reconstitution include the utopian dream of the hope for a monstrous world without gender' (Haraway 1991, 181).

Not only does Marxism, with its explanation of gender from economic structures, privilege the model of labouring and nature-conquering man, it also – according to many feminist critiques in the Marxist tradition – fails to explain the intransigence and seeming universality of gender. Can the subordination of women to men be explained solely through the institution of private property? Is the structure of the family, and the relation of the sexes constructed economically, or is there a deeper reason and structure that might explain sexual difference? The problem is not only that pre-modern and non-Western societies – without private property – operate from a male–female hierarchy and binary, it is also the case that economic and political changes seem to have made very little difference to gender inequality. Why is it that, despite the reasonable recognition that there is no natural basis for gender inequality – despite suffrage, contraception, anti-discrimination legislation and other developments – men and women seem to see themselves as so different? And why do these differences seem to be trans-historical and trans-cultural, occurring well beyond Western and capitalist societies? Is there something more to gender than socially constructed representations and economic conditions? Do we need to attend to a specifically sexual politics that precedes specific economic and historical epochs?

Marxism's insistence on overcoming ideology by recognising the human creation of political structures, both elevates the image of a man who creates his own being, and refuses the possibility that political relations might be determined by events that cannot be rendered conscious. Marxism privileges consciousness, activity and the creation of one's own being, whereas the psychoanalytic emphasis on the unconscious focuses on those elements in human life that we neither choose nor recognise. Marxism's explanation of ideology and capitalism ultimately refers back to human intention; we develop technology for the sake of liberation from need, and all subsequent enslavement to technology lies in a forgetting or concealing of this aspect of our 'species being.' Psychoanalysis, by contrast, does not assume that the self begins with intentions and life-enhancing interests, for the drives that propel the human organism towards life are also always deflected by aims that are contrary to life. The central notion of the Oedipus complex in Freudian psychoanalysis begins from the recognition that individuals are self-punishing; oppressed by a function of the psyche rather than a wholly external political system. The unconscious is not only what we do not know; it is also that which resists knowledge.

Unlike Marxism, which assumes the ability of conscious human life to overcome myth and illusion, psychoanalysis insists on the ways in which human desire masks its own workings. Psychoanalysis sets itself the task of explaining not just the economic and political need for the family, but the reason why the structure of the family has such a deep hold on our most basic categories. For psychoanalysis the family is itself a myth; the child relates to its mother and father through fantasies that then structure the relation to reality in general.

The Oedipal production of gender

The first form of psychoanalysis that we will consider here is one that maintains a strict opposition between sex and gender. Sigmund Freud's own work on sexual difference and gender has been variously interpreted, with commentators in his own time – and today – criticising his assumption that women's gender can be explained by their 'lack' of a penis. But Freud has also, just as often, been cited as the most radical theorist of gender precisely because he explains, rather than assumes, the difference between male and female, and because he therefore offers the only way in which gender relations might be transformed and revalued (Mitchell 1974). Indeed, as many queer theorists have insisted, Freud's description of heterosexual masculine development describes the production of the male gender as both fragile and traumatic, with the heterosexual norm being neither inevitable nor stable. Indeed, many of the radical rereadings of Freud begin from the insistence that Freud *describes*, rather than endorses, the difference between the sexes, and that his description enables us to understand why gender opposites are so persistent, even if they have no biological or natural necessity. One of the clearest defences of Freud as a theorist of gender, rather than a biological determinist, comes from the American tradition of psychoanalysis, in particular Nancy Chodorow's *The Reproduction of Mothering* (1978) – a book that was highly influential in philosophy, literary theory and anthropology.

Chodorow follows Freud in explaining the emergence of masculinity and femininity from the Oedipal structure of the family. Not only do women, as the primary caregivers, have to relate compassionately to their children; male and female children develop different personality structures because of the structure of the family. The child begins as dependent on its mother and can only develop an ego, or sense of self, in being other than the mother. For Freud, this transition from the un-self-conscious position of infant fulfilment – the child at the breast – to the independent ego, is relatively easy to explain in the case of the male child. The child must abandon his mother as an *object* of desire and identify with his father. Here, he no longer desires his mother but takes on the father's identity and relates to other women as objects. The boy must become like the father – a *subject* who is different from the mother. Notoriously, Freud explains the motivation for this abandonment of the mother through the threat of castration. Seeing that the female lacks a penis, the child can only assume that she has been castrated (Freud 1977, 311); he therefore chooses to identify with the father who, in his obvious position of social superiority, must possess the power to castrate, and power over the castrated. The boy therefore becomes a detached and social self – a bounded ego – by being other than the mother, and by having a separate, punishing and social authority figure with whom to identify (Freud 1977, 319).

For girls, however, as no shortage of feminists have noted, the story is not so simple. Indeed, the inadequacy of the Oedipal structure to explain the girl's development was noted in Freud's own time: 'The fear of castration being thus excluded in the little girl, a powerful motive also drops out for the setting-up of a super-ego and for the breaking-off of the infantile genital organization' (Freud 1977, 321). Freud himself admitted that female sexuality was a puzzle he had failed to solve (Freud 1977, 372). One way of approaching this theoretical difficulty is to accept that the Oedipal structure *is* less conducive to the separate and autonomous development of female subjects. Perhaps, then, we need to question the values of detachment, autonomy and distinct ego boundaries. Freud's explanation of femininity required that the girl's development proceeded with the same assumptions as the boy's. The girl sees the mother as lacking a penis, and *wants* to have what the mother lacks. If we accept this structure, this may go some way to explaining why women in patriarchal culture regard themselves as weaker or lesser versions of men; their psychological development has proceeded along a phallic model, where women are seen as defined by lack: 'When she comes to understand the general nature of this characteristic, it follows that femaleness – and with it, of course, her mother – suffers a great depreciation in her eyes' (Freud 1977, 380). If the girl does, as Freud suggests, perceive the mother as lacking a penis – whether we take the penis literally, or symbolically, as lacking social power and authority – the girl cannot simply abandon her mother and identify with her father. For the girl, unlike the boy is *already castrated*, and so she cannot hope to take on the position of the father. She can no longer desire the mother, for the mother who lacks the phallus is no longer a full object, but her sense of self cannot simply be opposed to her mother. Unlike the boy she is not *other than* the feminine. According to Freud, all she can do is aim to become a mother *for* her father, to one day have a baby of her own; this baby would be a substitute penis. She cannot – or should not – aspire to a position of male authority. This explains, according to Freud, women's weaker moral development: 'Their super-ego is never so inexorable, so impersonal, so independent of its emotional origins as we require it to be in men' (Freud 1977, 342). Boys abandon mere pleasure and need through the threat of castration; they identify with the punishing figure of the father, and themselves take on the role of moral, judging and punishing agents. In becoming like their fathers, they become subjects – detached from nature and the biological conditions of life. Women, by contrast, never identify with or internalise the authority of the father; they can only aim to please or become desired objects for men. They will always be passive objects of desire, prone to narcissism, rather than active agents who renounce desire for the sake of cultural law.

According to Chodorow, Freud's tale is only half the story, for it assumes one model of ego and social development. It is true that if we take individuality to consist in impartial judgement, domination of nature, detached reasoning and autonomy, then women will fail. Chodorow wants to explain gender relations, following Freud, but she does not want to assume the value Freud places on the masculine gender – neither the value of the penis nor the structure of masculinity that supposedly follows from possessing a penis. Chodorow wants to look at the picture positively, in terms of what the girl child does identify with – not her failure to identify with her father. Because the girl does not abandon the mother or sever her first ties of love to identify with her father, she has less strict ego boundaries: 'She is preoccupied with issues of symbiosis and primary love without sense of the other person's separateness' (Chodorow 1978, 115). The self with whom she identifies – the mother – is also the self on whom she is dependent and for whom she feels love. Whereas the boy must become other than his first loved object to become a boy, the girl maintains her first object as both desired object and ego ideal. Second, this mother with whom she identifies is not a punishing father but a caring other, an other who does not threaten and oppose the self, but who – like one's first self – is also loving. If men become social subjects by being liberated from their first object of love, women never fully detach themselves from the first relation of care. Women, then, are structured as caring, compassionate, other-directed, less autonomous and more sympathetic. It is not that they lack morality or sociality; rather, they demonstrate a different mode of sociality. Women are not the nature-conquering, disembodied, calculative, detached and self-directed agents of classical moral theory. Of course, given our social and political values, it is not surprising that women do indeed accord lesser worth to their own and their mother's femininity, but Chodorow insists that Freud describes gender – or socialisation – and not sex, and that we need to revalue the structures he describes (Chodorow 1978, 150). Women's specific virtues of care, compassion, other-directedness, sympathy and negotiation offer a positively desirable model of selfhood. Because this selfhood is not natural – grounded in biology – but gendered, or produced through the structure of the family, it can also be considered as a model of moral development that is desirable in general (Chodorow 1994, 82–83). It can also help us to break down the strict differences of gender binaries and see how particular men and women, including those who are attracted to the same gender, or those who have ambivalent relations to their mothers, negotiate their own Oedipal resolutions (Chodorow 1994, 90–91).

Many criticisms of masculine ideology in literature and culture have drawn upon Chodorow's insights. Many feminist critics have suggested that English Romanticism has been constructed through specifically masculine norms of subjectivity (Levin 1987; Mellor 1993; Ross 1986). The poet confronts nature, asserts his autonomy, mourns a once integrated natural origin (with mother nature), but overcomes that loss through self-creation and poetry. The male Romantic poet is typically narcissistic, capable of seeing nature only as an object to be negated, only as a medium through which he can be self-creating. Women authors, by contrast, were other-directed, less concerned to objectify and transcend nature and more capable of recognising nature's own force and value: 'many women experience their own bodies as the only available medium for their art, with the result that the distance between the woman and her art is often radically diminished' (Gubar 1986, 296). Female Romantic poets would not, then, exemplify the 'subjectivity heightened to an absolute pitch' which Harold Bloom defines as typical of the male poet wrestling with his poetic forefathers (Bloom 1973); nor would female Romantic poets be striving to eliminate self-consciousness to arrive at a point of anti-self-consciousness that, according to Geoffrey Hartman, seeks reunion with nature and an overcoming of separation (Hartman 1970). Far from living out these Oedipal dramas of struggle with a maternal nature that is at once desirable but prohibited, women authors were other-directed – turning positively to other women writers in an attempt to forge a position of authorship: 'she can begin such a struggle only by actively seeking a *female* precursor who, far from representing a threatening force to be denied or killed, proves by example that a revolt against patriarchal literary authority is possible' (Gilbert and Gubar 1979, 49).

The attempt to retrieve and revalue women's writing in the wake of the different structures of gender described by Nancy Chodorow and psychologists such as Carol Gilligan (1982) goes beyond the inclusion of women's writing within traditional values, and suggests that we need to rethink just how we value a text or a subject (Jaggar 1989). First, it may be the case that what we assume to be 'great' literature already commits itself to specific gender norms (Tompkins 1989). The male Romantic poets do not, then, express universal and existential questions so much as typically masculine anxieties. The 'anxiety of influence' described by Harold Bloom as definitive of great English poetry from Milton to the present – an anxiety the author feels regarding any sense of indebtedness or threat to his autonomy – could not be felt by women poets who were far more capable of acknowledging dependence and relations to others, and had to struggle with a tradition that could not acknowledge their capacity to write (Gilbert and Gubar, 1979). Second, not only are our decisions as to what counts as great literature embedded in values about what it is to be a (gendered) subject; it is also the case that reading literature can help us to challenge and rewrite gender norms. While certain feminist critics, particularly in the 1970s, did appeal to a specifically feminine mode of writing (Showalter 1986, 248), most critics, like Anne Mellor, insisted that gender was constructed, and that we need to see how texts both produce masculine and feminine norms, and how women writers challenge such divisions and values.

Anne Mellor's work suggests that decisions regarding literary value are open to revision and this is because her work operates from a second-wave version of feminism that distinguished sex from gender. Neither Mellor nor Chodorow suggest that feminine other-directedness and care are *essential*. The values and modes of subjectivity exemplified by the caring and other-directed woman offer a new mode of selfhood for both sexes. Indeed, the masculine subject who is opposed to nature, otherness, ambiguity and embodiment may lie at the heart of a series of oppressive structures, such as racism, colonialism, homophobia and fascism. There have been, and still are, forms of second-wave or radical feminism that insist upon, and value, the specifically different qualities of women, and insist also that one can simply turn back to the history of literature and construct a great canon of essentially different and feminine women's writing (Spender 1986; Showalter 1986; Todd 1988). Literary theorists who have drawn upon Chodorow and similar modes of psychoanalysis, however, have refused to see femininity as a simple given that one can read behind texts that are written by women. Instead, they look at the ways gender norms and ideals have constructed, and been constructed by, the literary canon. The inspired, tradition-breaking, assertive and individual poet is a masculinist ideal that rejects all those qualities of dependence, compromise and acknowledgement that are not only associated with, but are constitutive of, femininity.

Chodorow's psychoanalysis insists that male and female genders are created in social familial structures and have less to do with biology than the way in which that biology is socialised. True, it is women's capacity to give birth that establishes them as the primary caregiver, and therefore it is the mother who will need to be abandoned in the male child's identification with the father. But the familial structure is nevertheless a social structure, and just as the boy's autonomous masculinity is achieved by identifying with the cultural figure of the father, so the girl's caring femininity is achieved by identifying with the mother. Chodorow's psychoanalysis explains how relations among bodies produce social roles, and how those social roles produce different modes of subjectivity. The male subject is necessarily *other than* his natural and biological origin, *other than* his caring and loving mother; he becomes male only by *not* loving an other, and by identifying with one who owns and prohibits love with the mother. The father with whom he identifies is a figure of authority, legislation, judgement, autonomy and law. The mother from whom he must be separated and whom he must devalue is associated with love, care, embodiment and concern.

Chodorow neither questions nor asserts the structure of the family. We have already seen that, from the pre-modern point of view, it is the essential nature of genders that produces the family. It is because each material body is expressive of a kind or cosmological position that the family is the very image of order: the father is analogous to the creative and active God; the mother is analogous to the passive and receptive matter, and the son is analogous to the world's produced forms. Similarly, the polity is structured like the family, precisely because the family is itself expressive of an essential order: the king is both God's divine anointed, and the father to his subjects. Gender, from a pre-modern viewpoint, is more than a familial and sexual relation; gender is the very order of the world, which, from the basic polarity between male and female, is structured through a series of hierarchies and analogies.

In modernity, all this changes. Far from being expressive of a divine order, the family is used to describe how a nature of pure forces and matter becomes social and hierarchical. The gender binary of the family – the active father who labours in the public domain, and the passive mother who nurtures in the domestic privacy of the home – is literal, material and created socially. Indeed, it is because there are no essential genders, no natural and immutable positions for male and female, that the family takes on so much importance in *explaining*, rather than expressing and symbolising hierarchy. The hierarchy of the family is neither purely natural, nor purely cultural. It is the essence of human subjectivity to be other than natural: not a thing within the world but a power to represent and transform the world. But this necessary transcendence of nature also explains women's continued association with nature. The man of reason, labour and self-transformation must be distinguished from the biological conditions of reproduction, and the private conditions of familial attachment and bodily passion. The family is, on the one hand, different from the public world of equal and rational individuals, who are all equal by virtue of their reason and capacity for self-determination. On the other hand, the family is also the condition for such purely rational individuals; only with women taking on the burden of nature do men become other than nature. Gender is, on this modern picture, *not* biology. According to a prominent contemporary feminist, 'gender is the social organization of sexual difference' (Scott 1988, 2).

Simone de Beauvoir represents a particularly forceful expression of this desire to liberate gender from sex. Men, she insists, have achieved their proper freedom, becoming fully human in their transcendence of nature. Women, by contrast, are still mired in the condition of nature, and this because of the bourgeois structure of the family (Beauvoir

1972). Change that structure and you change gender. The ideal for enlightenment and liberal feminists, and the existential feminism of de Beauvoir, was to allow women to achieve the freedom from sex and embodiment that had been granted to men. Second-wave feminists recognised, however, that this argument that nature or sex needed to be fully overcome in order for all bodies to become human concealed a privileging of masculinity. Was women's association with the body, passions, childbirth and natural reproduction necessarily something to be conquered? Perhaps those familial structures that produced women as embodied, caring, empathetic, conciliatory and concerned with specific others needed to be recognised as alternative and valuable paths to subjectivity, rather than lesser forms of one universal reason. If one followed Chodorow and accepted, and endorsed, a specifically (but not essentially) *different* model of the feminine subject, one would still allow the family to remain as the primary site for the production of gender. This raises two questions. First, if from early social theorists, such as Hobbes, to later feminists, such as Chodorow, the family is used to explain the genesis of gender, thereby avoiding any notion of essential sexual difference, how essential is the family? If the family that comprises caring mother, labouring father and Oedipally structured child were refigured would there still be male and female genders? Second, if it is the mother–father–child structure of the nuclear family that explains a specific ideology of gender, how do we explain the use of male–female mythic polarities in cultures and epochs not dominated by the nuclear family as the basic political unit?

Third-wave feminism, or post-structuralist feminism, took the psychoanalytic interrogation into the fantasy of the family beyond the literal family. The repression of maternal plenitude or *jouissance*, and the submission to paternal law may not be *caused* by familial structures. Rather, there may be a structural dichotomy between presence and absence, law and chaos, language and the body, that the image or figure of the gendered family is used to represent. The mother–father opposition may be expressive of a deeper, even universal, difference.

5 Beyond Sex and Gender

Third-wave feminism

It is common to discuss sexual politics and its competing issues via a distinction among first-, second- and third-wave forms of feminism (Braidotti 1991; Eisenstein 1984; Kristeva 1986; Moi 1985). As we have seen, first-wave feminism emerges in the enlightenment with the rights of man, with its primary value and aim being that of equality and inclusion. It is assumed that there is something like a universal humanity, that this humanity is defined by the power to reason, and that reason takes the form of self-determination. Reason is not, as it had been in pre-enlightenment thought, the recognition of one's proper essence in the divine scheme of things; reason is the refusal of any natural or pre-given determination. The modern feminist demand for inclusion in a common humanity therefore relies upon much broader assumptions about the nature of political being. Politics is the collective, rational and non-coercive expression of right through the interaction of powers; it is not the expression or ordering of distinct and different powers on the basis of genders, potentials or kinds. First-wave feminism relied upon and extended this modern conception of the political, where political order is generated by reasoning subjects who have no determining essence other than their capacity to decide their own being. Subjects did not defer to an order; the political order was structured to allow for the maximisation of subjective freedoms.

First-wave feminism is both a historical category and a conceptual category. Many forms of common-sense feminism today would assume the form of first-wave demands, such as equal rights, universal education, suffrage, and freedom from the particular desires of others. Such feminist demands are extensions of modern democratic principles. The assumption that we are all human, equal and the same 'deep down' – the assumption that sex does not, or should not, matter –

goes well beyond feminism to include the fundamental ideology of Western liberalism or humanism, the belief in a common humanity. Second-wave feminism is also historically bounded, but it did not simply supplant or overtake first-wave feminism; nor was it superseded by third-wave feminisms. Many radical, or second-wave, feminisms still have force today. Various forms of eco-feminism, for example, insist that only with the feminine virtues of care, other-directedness, non-violence and a positive sense of embodiment can 'we' avoid widespread environmental and economic catastrophe. Second-wave feminism challenges the supposed 'equality' of a rational and nature-transcending humanity in order to argue for the value and positive difference of women. Such an insistence can take two forms: essentialist forms, which ground femininity in sex or the body; and constructivist forms, such as Chodorow's or Gilligan's, which explain the specificity of the feminine from the social structure of the family. Both first- and second-wave feminisms assume the difference between sex and gender. First-wave feminisms assert, or aim to achieve, the irrelevance of sex and the dissolution of gender-hierarchy by imagining an ideal humanity in which childbirth and the sexual division of labour no longer impede women's rationality and capacity for political agency. Second-wave feminisms assert that what has been gendered as feminine needs to be refigured, so that sex may express itself appropriately and that gender stereotypes give way to an authentic and autonomous female sex, or a more appropriate balance between masculine and feminine norms and virtues.

Third-wave feminism challenged the sex–gender distinction and did so by drawing on and extending a number of theoretical traditions, including psychoanalysis. There is a common conception of Freudian psychoanalysis as a form of biological determinism: having or not having a penis determines whether one suffers from castration anxiety or penis envy. The psychoanalytic analysis of the genesis of gender can be interpreted as an extreme version of the long-standing cultural assumption that male subjectivity represents the norm or standard and that it is femininity that needs to be explained. Freud, like so many modern thinkers, not only assumes the model of the family; he describes the boy's development within the family as normal. Because women can neither be threatened with castration, nor perceive their mother as lacking what they have, there is no easy way to explain just how women do become cultural subjects. Those who criticise Freud and the Freudian tradition as biologically determinist or essentialist often insist that the family cannot be assumed as a basic and universal structure, that the family is already *gendered* and social, and is not the only form that *sex* or nature may take. Criticisms of Freud, then, have insisted that Freud's description of sexuality is actually a description of gender. Freud takes what is socially and historically specific and presents it as natural and biological.

Difference before sex and gender

The third-wave uses of Freud have, however, defended Freud against the charges of biologism, determinism and essentialism, and have done so by rereading the Oedipus complex, not as a description of a supposedly natural family, but as a mythic structure that explains the very difference between nature and culture. According to Julia Kristeva, for example, the male–female binary is neither natural nor cultural; it is metaphysical (Kristeva 1986, 209). The opposition between male and female is transcendental; only with the difference between male and female, subject and object, presence and absence, self and other, can there be any form of experience at all. Only a revolution in the very nature of experience will liberate us from the boundaries of gender identity. The body, for Kristeva, is not an object with a distinct sex, but that which must be repressed in order for the subject to enter the system of language and become an 'I' (Kristeva 1981, 131). There may be subjects who speak as men and women, but there is also a more radical maternal register of drives, pulsions and rhythms that precedes distinct genders (Kristeva 1981, 136). Kristeva argues that it is this maternal flux, before the division between subject and object, which disrupts the ordered distinction between male and female. Kristeva's quite unique form of feminism challenges both sex and gender. She does not assume two distinct sexual subjects, nor does she see gender as an imposed construction. Rather, she argues that the very notion of reality, our very relation to being, is organised through a complex distinction between bodily desire and language, and that we achieve this distinction through a differentiation from our maternal origin. For this reason, sex is metaphysical; it is bound up with the very emergence of distinct and meaningful experience. Kristeva therefore extended the Oedipal explanation of the subject to consider not just the emergence of the self within the family or society, but the very structure of the subject as a speaking being set over against the flux of bodily life. Kristeva's argument both drew upon and criticised, the linguistic interpretation of Freud inaugurated by Jacques Lacan.

Psychoanalytic theory is not the only tradition to have questioned the distinction between sex and gender, but it does form one of the most significant challenges. It was the French psychoanalyst Jacques Lacan, who reread Freud's theory of sexuality against the Anglo-American interpretation of Freud. If we take Nancy Chodorow's psychoanalysis as typical of the positive feminist reading of Freud we can note that most attention is paid to the development of the ego – the sense we have of ourselves as individuals. Men develop with a sense of autonomy and moral judgement, identifying with their fathers; women develop with less of a sense of distinct ego-boundaries, identifying with, but also feeling ambivalence towards, their already other-directed mothers. Psychoanalysis, in this tradition, sees the self as an ego – a personality – and tries to achieve a healthy balance between this formed aspect of the self and the unconscious drives, including the anti-social drives of desire and the punishing drives of guilt from the super-ego (our internalised moral authority).

Psychoanalysis of this form focussed on familial development, and allowed for a sense of the malleability of gender roles. Ego psychology focussed less on what it saw as Freud's biological prejudices – of penis-envy, castration anxiety and the like – and concentrated on the self's social roles and adjustment. Lacan's 'return' to Freud, by contrast, insisted on the 'phallus' as the cornerstone of psychoanalytic theory and, even more disturbingly, reread the Oedipus complex – with its disturbing negation of femininity – as a universal structure, and not as a social construct (Lacan 1977, 320). Sexual difference, for Lacan, was not located at the level of the ego, or our sense of self and personality. The unconscious itself was structured through sexual difference, and this unconscious was impersonal, inhuman and resistant to interpretation and socialisation. For Lacan sexual difference was *transcendental*: only with the distinction between masculine and feminine could culture, experience, humanity and meaning be possible. In order to make this claim Lacan reread Freud through the insights of structuralism and structural linguistics.

Lacan's structuralism was drawn from two main sources: the linguistics of Ferdinand de Saussure and the anthroplogy of Claude Levi-Strauss. The main insight of Saussure's linguistics lay in his argument that language was a system of mutually produced differences, a structure of differentiation rather than a collection of independent names

(Saussure 1960). On this picture, in order to understand a language we cannot just know one word, as though words were names or labels. We can only understand a word if we understand its relation to the whole. If I pointed to a body and said, 'homme,' you may think that I was uttering a proper name – that this was someone called Homme – or you may think I was making a value judgment – that calling someone 'homme' was expressing approval or disapproval; I could even be pointing out their race, height or age. You could only interpret the word to mean 'man' if I pointed to other bodies in a series, saying 'homme' and 'femme' accordingly. You would build up a system of likenesses and differences, and eventually conclude that I meant 'man' and 'woman' – and that it was *this* relation and difference that the specific word was marking. A language works by division, by distributing the experiences we have into identities and differences.

The differences of a language create the structure of our world. In Saussure's terms, it is the *signifiers* of a language – the words or marks – that create a system of differences that then allow us to have opposed meanings. In order to think differences we do not just need to have different concepts and meanings (or *signifieds*); we also need to have a material and concrete system of marks (the *signifiers* of the alphabet, sounds, physical gestures and so on). Our experience of the world is therefore dependent on an arbitrary structure that, in itself, has no meaning but allows us to experience meaning. We could imagine how impoverished our experience of the world might be if we did not have as many linguistic differences as we do, if our phonetic alphabet had only two sounds; and we could also imagine a language that perceived a world of far more subtle differences. We experience the world meaningfully, and those meanings are created through some differential system. There could be no concept or sense of the difference between one thing and another without a system of marks; we can have the general concepts of male and female only through some structure of signifiers, various material tokens ranging from words and sounds, to gestures and symbols. (And, for psychoanalysis, the human body provides our first basic material marking, with sexually different bodies providing the opposition between presence and absence, self and other, identity and difference.) On Saussure's view, then, language does not have positive terms: it does not begin from meanings that it then labels. We do not simply perceive something under its concept and then find a word or mark for it. Rather, in seeing something *as* something, we have already differentiated it from other things, and recognised some sameness in it that could be likened to something else. To see you as a woman is already to liken you to others of your kind, and this perception of the world as a world of meaningful kinds relies on the structure of (something like) a language.

This is why Jacques Derrida insists that for something to be an identity it must already differ from itself; to see something *as* something is to identify features that could be re-marked, repeated or re-presented (Derrida 1982, 13). This structure of differentiation, which enables specific identities can, itself, never be fully identified: '*Différance* is the non-full, non-simple, structured and differentiating origin of differences. Thus the name "origin" no longer suits it' (Derrida 1982, 11). Further, the system of meaningful difference depends upon material and arbitrary marks, marks that have not been decided or determined meaningfully. Our physical gestures depend on the bodies we are given; the sounds of our language depend on the limits and development of voice; and written signs themselves have a specific technology, with languages varying greatly in terms of the number and types of sounds and marks. Derrida is therefore critical of the 'classically determined structure of the sign in all the banality of its characteristics,' and this is because the very opposition between material signifier and intelligible concept or signified must already have been marked out or traced by a process that itself cannot be brought to presence (Derrida 1982, 9). Further, as we have already seen, the opposition between sensible and intelligible, between materiality and mind, has frequently been determined by images of gender. For this reason many recent feminists have extended Derrida's work to insist that we question the opposition between sign and body, between meaning and materiality (Kirby 1991).

Elizabeth Grosz, for example, has insisted that we rethink the body, not as the material stuff that is organised by mental signs but as itself a process of differing (Grosz 1994, 191). Grosz suggests that instead of seeing the body as a surface upon which language is inscribed, and instead of seeing sex as meaningless stuff that is then ordered by gender, we should think of the body as a process that creates a border or band between inside and outside, that we see the body as *textual* – not because it is an effect of writing but because, like writing, it is never apprehended as fully present but always differs from itself: 'Once the subject is no longer seen as an entity – whether psychical or corporeal – but fundamentally an effect of pure difference that constitutes all modes of materiality, new terms need to be sought by which to think this alterity within and outside the subject' (Grosz 1994, 208). (We will look at Grosz's corporeal feminism more fully in the next chapter.)

The concept of the sign has, however, been crucial to the understanding of sex and gender. If sex is the referent or bodily and pre-linguistic thing to which language refers, then it is differentiated or gendered through signifiers. If, as Saussure argues, the signifier plays its part in organising reality, then we have to forego the idea of the body itself as meaningful or organised into genders, for gender is the social and relational sense of one's body. Saussure argued that the sign consisted of two components: the *signifier* (the noise, gesture or written mark, which is material) and the *signified* (what we take that mark to mean). We could also take a dress, gesture or hairstyle as a signifier. There is nothing meaningful in itself about wearing lipstick, but we do 'read' these marks as signifiers of femininity in a world that is divided between those who do, and do not, wear make-up. Without signifiers or systems of structuring marks we could have no signi-fieds: so we can only speak and mean through *some* material system – whether that be the letters of the alphabet or other conventional oppositions.

Many writers on gender, to this day, follow this insight of Saussure to argue that gender is produced through systems of difference. Fashion, for example, is a way of differentiating some bodies from others. There is nothing essentially feminine about a frilly silk blouse, but such a garment signifies femininity in a culture that ties the femi-nine not just to specific garments but to softness, fluidity, adornment and the frivolous. Our culture has produced a whole series of oppos-itions to produce the difference between male and female and these include the contrasts of fashion, movement, make-up, adornment and language. There could be no meaningful gender opposition without these conventional marks; sense is possible only through an already received system of arbitrary signifiers. Gender is an effect of signifying systems. It is not that I have an inner femininity that I then signify by wearing certain clothes and walking in a certain way. Rather, I can become a social individual only by adopting some gender or another; I become female through the assumption of certain signifiers. Femininity is produced in and through the system of gen-dered signifiers; there is no gender outside this system of differences. Further, as some feminists have insisted, the very experience of a sex lying in wait to be represented is itself an effect, not a cause, of the gender representation system:

> This is not to say that, on the one hand, the body is simply linguistic stuff or, on the other hand, that it has no bearing on language. It bears on language all the time. The materiality of language, indeed, of the of the very sign that attempts to denote 'materiality,' suggests that it is not the case that everything, including materiality, is always already language. On the contrary, the materiality of the signifier (a 'materiality' that comprises both signs and their significatory efficacy) implies that there can be no reference to a pure materiality except via materiality. Hence, it is not that one cannot get outside of language in order to grasp materiality in and of itself; rather, every effort to refer to materiality takes place through a signifying process which, in its phenomenality, is always already material.
>
> (Butler 1993, 68)

Gender is an effect of signification. The signifier divides some bodies from others, and then gives the illusion of a sexual difference that was there all along to be signified. One of the main consequences of Saussure's structuralism was just this insistence on the primacy of the signifier: the capacity for the marks and differences of a system to produce different meanings or signifieds.

Lacan and the subject of signification

Jacques Lacan, however, focussed on both sides of the signifier–signified couplet. He was not just interested in the ways in which maleness and femaleness were produced through opposition, although he did insist upon that. He was also insistent on the condition and structure of signification. In order for a signifier to act as a signifier it must be taken as referring back to a signified, and in order for us to read or interpret a signified behind a signifier we also assume that some subject is addressing us, and that there is a meaning or presence behind that address. To read or interpret is to assume an intent behind the signifier. The signifier is a signifier only in referring beyond itself: 'a signifier is that which represents the subject for another signifier' (Lacan 1977, 316). As Derrida has noted, the very concept of the sign is metaphysical; it necessarily presupposes a sense behind what is seen, a meaning that we aim to render present (Derrida 1981, 281). If I *read* a gesture or a mark then I assume that there was some subject who intended something that is not immediately present, but that can be grasped or represented (Derrida 1988, 18).

This condition of interpretation, this situation of *not* knowing, of 'reading' the immediately present, is what structures subjectivity and our relation to language. We experience the world and others, not immediately, but as something to be interpreted or understood (Felman 1987). We are, according to Lacan, located within a symbolic structure, which orients our relation to the world and others. We are subjected to a system of signs that emanates from elsewhere, a fantasised Other who holds the sense or presence of what is presented to me through the signifier. For Lacan, then, the signifier–signified dyad requires and institutes a complex structure of subjectivity. I can only be a subject if I assume some system of lawful signification, but this lawful system is itself only possible with the assumption of another subject. A sign can speak to me only if it is uttered by *one who speaks*: another subject. These two speakers, upon which signification depends, can only have a subjective relation to each other with the assumption of the Other. I can speak to you, and recognise you as one who speaks, only with the assumption that we share a system within which we are both located. This lawful system through which we recognise others as subjects exceeds and precedes any subject, and is radically Other. That is, in order to relate to you as a specific other who inhabits the same system of signification, I must assume a meaning or law – a third term – that regulates what we say, and allows us to recognise each other as subjects. All our speech, desire and experience is therefore mediated by what is not present. We see others as subjects only by assuming a sense behind what they say; we experience our world as objective only by assuming its existence beyond what we see; we assume a fulfilment beyond all our specific pleasures, a *jouissance* that is not tied to this or that present thing (Lacan 1998, 5). Our lives, in so far as they are oriented by sense and meaning, are structured by what is not present. For Lacan, then, the key question of psychoanalysis is not the ego or self, and its specific sexual and gendered adjustments. What is crucial for psychoanalysis is how absence, non-being or the Other disrupts life (Lacan 1982, 147). How is it that when we look at the world we see it as having a being beyond our immediate perception? Something like an idea of what lies beyond the fully present must have entered our experience.

For Lacan this experience of absence or 'not-all' is both the experience of the signifier and an experience of sexual difference. It is the signifier that enables us to take what we see, hear or feel as the sign of an other (Lacan 1998, 33). If an other offers me food, caresses my arm or utters a sound, then I assume their subjectivity, intent or desire, not by what is actually present, but by what I must interpret. The food, caress, or word may be taken as a sign of love, and in so doing I imagine what I must be for the other, how the other desires me. For Lacan, the human world opens, then, with the enigma of an other. It may be that life begins with the child's experience of all sorts of phenomena and needs but when, for example, the mother fulfils biological need by offering the child food, the child can 'read' this offer as a signifier of the mother's desire, as a sign of love. The other, then, is only given through signification, where signification is the anticipation of what is not present. Further, to assume that what the other says or does has meaning or intent, we must operate within some system. The assumption that what the other says has meaning, can be interpreted, and has a sense that can be brought to presence – the belief that the signifiers of our world are *interpretable* – relies upon the positing of a system within which we are all situated. It is this system, which both allows and precludes desire. Lacan refers to the Symbolic order as radically other or alien, with desire being essentially different from those needs we can articulate, communicate and represent in terms of gender and relations. The system structures desire by allowing us to articulate our demands in relation to an other, thereby taking any demand beyond mere life to the realm of human and meaningful interaction. However, the imagined fulfilment of our desire – the point of *jouissance* beyond subjection to the symbolic system – can only be imagined. Indeed, the signifier of our first demand, the singular point at which we are addressed by or address an other, is *the* ballast point of the unconscious (Laplanche and Leclaire 1972). This 'point of caption' or founding signifer that ties the self to the system, refers back to an imagined point of entry or subjection, and forward to an imagined first or founding Other. That imagined desire beyond the law or Symbolic is what Lacan refers to as *jouissance*, and *jouissance* is necessarily structured by the idea of Woman (Lacan 1982, 144). For it is Woman, Lacan argues – not specific women but an ideal Woman – who is imagined as that original presence and fulfilment beyond all system or structure:

> There isn't the slightest prediscursive reality, for the very fine reason that what constitutes a collectivity – what I called men, women, and

children – means nothing qua prediscursive reality. Men, women, and children are but signifiers.

> A man is nothing but a signifier. A woman seeks out a man qua signifier (*au tire de signifiant*). A man seeks out a woman qua – and this will strike you as odd – that which can only be situated through discourse, since, if what I claim is true – namely that woman is not-whole – there is always something in her that escapes discourse.
>
> (Lacan 1998, 33)

As the post-Lacanian French psychoanalyst Jean Laplanche has argued, the human condition begins with the enigma of signification (Laplanche 1999). The mother who offers the child food does fulfil a biological need, but she also offers the child a signifier, for the offer can always be read as a sign of love, or as a demand – what does the other want from me? The child's dependence on the mother requires that the needs of life be addressed to an other; when the mother responds to that need, or answers the child's cry, the child is given a response. The food is a signifier of the mother's recognition of the child's need. Every look of love, every gesture and every caress is always a message from an other. For Laplanche, we are always subjected to the enigma of the signifier: each act of human communication requires us to ask what the other means. And we answer this question only through the assumption of the Other – that system which subjects us all to the requirements of sense. For Lacan, it is this (phantasmatic) *subjection* to the system of signification that needs to be explained. If it is the case that we can experience our world only through a structure of signifiers that must transcend any specific experience – if our world is always already differentiated and meaningful – how did this structure of meaning and subjection to system emerge? Our subjection to the symbolic or system of signifiers is, Lacan insists, made possible only through a fantasy of sexual difference, the Imaginary.

Despite the fact that the sign – as signifier and signified – appears to be a binary structure, Lacan's explanation of how a signifier can function insists that there must be a third term. For you and I to speak, or recognise each other as subjects, we must inhabit or be subjected to some minimal presupposition of law. Our subjection to the condition of signification is, according to Lacan, lived or experienced as a subjection to law. Our desires are structured by a system that transcends any specific individual, always mediated through the signifier (Lacan 1991, 169). However, we also, as desiring beings, imagine a point beyond all system and mediation – a *jouissance* or presence before all subjection: 'That there must somewhere be *jouissance* of the Other is the only possible check on the endless circulating of significations – but this can only be ensured by a signifier, and this signifier is necessarily lacking' (Lacan 1982, 117). Without the assumption of a presence that exceeds the structure of signifiers, no signification or meaning would be possible. All human desire is therefore ternary in structure. The infant, for example, who demands food from his mother must address an other, must articulate his demands through some sign; he must therefore mediate his address to an other through some system of signs. For Lacan, then, all desire is alienated, for desire must be addressed to an other and articulated in a system or structure of signifiers that transcends both my immediate desire and any specific other. In so far as we address any single other (such as the mother) in language we are subjected to an impersonal or systemic Other, the law or signification.

Given the fact that being human requires our installation in, or subjection to, language, how do we live that subjection? We must, Lacan argues, assume an original lack or not-all; we must assume a beyond or *otherness to life*. Desire goes beyond need or what the organism requires to stay alive, and addresses itself to what is neither present, nor located at the level of life: the desire of the other. For Lacan the very structure of subjectivity is directed to, and produced through, this not-present or not-all; we spend our lives pasting over or repressing the essential gap between the objects we experience and the desire for what lies beyond any possible or experiencable object. This not-all, this absence at the heart of presence, is fantasised as Woman: that which desire strives to gain and which also is other than the letter of the law. The law or signification must be other than the mother, other than mere life. We must both assume that there is a presence beyond the law, that there is an origin, presence or immediate being, which we signify and which lies behind all communication. But we must also recognise that the signifier, which is other than this pure presence, has a lawfulness, value and systematicity that we cannot escape. We must both live the fiction or ideal of a presence beyond signs, and come to terms with our alienation from this presence. We do so, Lacan insists, through the imaginary of sexual difference. The most powerful contemporary defence of sexual difference, as opposed to the idea of two constructed genders that differentiate a single humanity, comes from the Lacanian critic Joan Copjec, who argues that the structures of masculinity and femininity organise our relation and perception to being. Sex, here, has nothing to do with substance or what our bodies are; sexual difference is the way in which we perceive, live and structure our bodies in relation to the real. Whereas man is the 'subject' who must understand himself as set over against a determined material reality, 'woman' is that point beyond all determined perception, as that which cannot be included in our ordered and exchanged objects:

> The universe of men is, then, an illusion fomented by a *prohibition*: do not include everything in your all! Rather than defining a universe of men that is complemented by a universe of women, Lacan defines man as the prohibition against constructing a universe and woman as the impossibility of doing so.
>
> (Copjec 1994, 235)

In her more recent work Copjec has stressed the utopian possibilities of Lacanian sexual difference. As opposed to those who look towards a new genderless humanity, Copjec insists that it is the idea of woman, as that which cannot be included in the recognised world of rational and calculated outcomes that allows for an ethics of singular and exceptional action:

> For this reason Lacan must be understood to be making a claim about ethics in general in his *Encore* seminar, rather than proposing a separate ethics of the feminine. His ethics takes off from the proposal that being is not-all or there is no whole of being. And yet if it is woman who is privileged in Lacan's analysis this is because she remains closer to the truth of being, while man obfuscates this truth through a nostalgic, secondary operation that allows him to maintain a belief in the plenitude of being to come.
>
> (Copjec 2002, 7)

For Copjec it is only by really thinking through Lacan's formulation that woman 'does not exist' that we can get away from the Oedipal fantasy that the band of brotherly love holds humanity together according to a common and really existing object: 'if woman has easier access than man to the God of jouissance, this is because she is less susceptible than he is to the lure of transcendence' (Copjec 2002, 7).

According to Lacan, the Oedipal fantasy is the way in which we live or repress our necessary alienation. Lacan insists that he is neither presenting a system, nor offering an ontology: he is not saying what *being is,* nor offering us *a* truth (Lacan 1982, 142). Indeed, Lacan strictly separates meaning from truth. The world we live as lawful, meaningful and communicable is radically different from the system of signifiers – the meaningless, inhuman, 'machinic' and implacable truth of our being. We think that when we speak we are expressing ourselves, but this is the imaginary illusion of the ego. In fact 'it' or the system 'speaks us,' and it is the task of analysis to confront this truth. Lacan is, then, not offering us the sense, presence or foundation of life; rather, he is demonstrating the fantasy of presence: 'against the being upheld by philosophical tradition, that is, the being residing in thought and taken to be its correlate, I argue that we are played by *jouissance*' (Lacan 1982, 142). We are always, as speaking beings, distanced from presence and installed in the system of the Symbolic, subjected to a law that *has no ground*: the 'Other' does not exist. Lacan analyses our fantasy of being or presence: how we arrive at the idea of that which exists beyond difference and mediation, and how we imagine this presence as a truth beyond the signifier. From the fact that our desire is necessarily not ours – always articulated in language – we assume that we are subjected to law, that law mediates our relation to truth and presence, and that there must be an Other whose authority grounds that law. The father is imagined as the Other who robs me of my immediate enjoyment. The father occupies the position of the signifier, which for Lacan is a phallic signifier precisely because it is imagined as that which the mother does not have, *that which is other than mere life.* The mother, or Woman, is the imagined original plenitude or *jouissance* from which we are forever divorced. Indeed, Woman as such does not exist; she is imagined only as the beyond of the law, the not-all that supplements the system of speech (Lacan 1982, 144).

For Lacan, the Oedipal triangle is an imaginary logic, the way in which we live our alienation. If I am subjected to law then there must be some object that was prohibited – the mother. But this mother must also be other than the law, must lack the power of the law. In fact, only with the imagination of what the fantasised original presence lacks, can I make sense of the transition to law. That which the mother lacks is the phallus. The phallus, then, is never presented; it is imagined as the law that mediates presence, the law whose authority structures our relation to presence. That which the mother – or mere life – does not have is the structure, system or third-term of the law – the signifier, or the name of the father. But Woman is also imagined as that point beyond the subjection to phallic law, for without this imagined 'beyond' the law can have no object, and if any woman objects to the exclusion of this logic she can only do so by mistaking the category of woman as that which is displaced by the law:

> There is woman only as excluded by the nature of things which is the nature of words, and it has to be said that if there is one thing they themselves are complaining about enough at the moment, it is well and truly that – only they don't know what they are saying, which is all the difference between them and me.
>   It none the less remains that if she is excluded by the nature of things, it is precisely that in being not all, she has, in relation to what the phallic function designates of *jouissance*, a supplementary *jouissance*.
>
> (Lacan 1982, 144)

But why is this an Oedipal logic? Why do we imagine the *mother* as the original and pre-linguistic plenitude? Why do we imagine the father as law or culture? And how is it that the phallus – or that which the mother lacks – becomes the transcendental signifier, the value that underpins all language, exchange and subjection to signification? One simple answer to this question would be that our relations to law and logic must begin from our biological and embodied condition, and that it would make sense to assume that the child begins its understanding of the world from the first bodies it encounters. Indeed, late twentieth-century feminists, such as Luce Irigaray, Elizabeth Grosz and Moira Gatens, have drawn upon the notion of *morphology* to defend and criticise the Lacanian tradition. Why are we so hesitant, they ask, to grant the bodies we inhabit a determining role in our relation to the world and others? Our refusal to attribute any force to the body repeats the repression of the body that has marked a Western tradition dominated by the concept of a mind that knows no limit or power other than itself. (They do, however, question Lacan's privileging of the male *phallic* body relating to his 'castrated' mother as the primary negotiating body.) For Grosz, the Lacanian account of the subject displays the ways in which certain bodies, in particular the phallic body, have underpinned the concept of the subject. Grosz accepts the descriptive force of Lacan's Oedipal narrative, but suggests that other morphologies are both possible and desirable (Grosz 1990, 171). Women's bodies are already structured by a different imaginary. So, one answer as to why Lacan interprets our relation to signification through an Oedipal narrative is that this fantasy of the law of the father and its negation of maternal *jouissance* characterises the masculine and dominant cultural imaginary, but that other morphologies are available in the experience of other bodies.

Other feminists, writing before the positive corporeal feminism of Grosz and Gatens, were less keen to attribute positive force to the difference of bodies. Rather, attention was paid to the ways in which sexual difference was determined symbolically and culturally. Juliet Mitchell saw Lacan as offering a diagnosis of 'cultural fantasy,' a fantasy which, up until now, was universal but could be altered once we recognised its force (Mitchell 1974). Here, the force of the Oedipal narrative was to be explained by turning to the other structuralist influence on Lacan, Claude Levi-Strauss and the theory of incest prohibition. Levi-Strauss's structural anthropology explained why it was that the subjection to culture was lived and imagined as the negation of nature – a nature imagined as maternal. One of the reasons why both Levi-Strauss's anthropology and Lacan's psychoanalysis have been important for the theorisation of gender is that both interrogate the distinction between nature and culture. Modern feminists and political theorists have tended to assume that there is a natural and biological *sex* opposed to a cultural and arbitrary *gender*. The former is immutable and beyond argument, while the latter is contestable. For this reason many feminists have resisted attributing powers to this supposedly immutable biology – insisting that femininity is determined culturally as gender. It is just this distinction between nature and culture that Levi-Strauss to some extent, but Lacan and Lacanian feminists more explicitly, sought to challenge. The very idea of a precultural and pre-linguistic nature is always already structured through fantasy, a fantasy that has been unremittingly sexual.

Levi-Strauss and the exchange of women

Levi-Strauss's work on kinship has been influential, not just for Lacan's psychoanalysis but for theories of gender generally (Rubin 1975). According to Levi-Strauss, culture can only emerge in being *other than* nature. It is the negation of nature that allows culture to occur (Levi-Strauss 1969). Most political theorists, from Aristotle to the twentieth century had insisted that there was something 'natural' about culture; the cultural order was grounded in human nature, in the tendency to form families, in the tendency to speak or to be sociable. Against this, Levi-Strauss argues that the submission to the structure or laws of a culture requires the abandonment of nature. To a certain extent, the passage to culture is traumatic, requiring the rejection of immediate pleasure, or what is subsequently imagined to be a moment of immediacy. Nature must be marked as lacking or inadequate. This can only occur, Levi-Strauss argued, through culture and the prohibition of incest. Levi-Strauss therefore imagines the first natural desire to be that of the child for the mother, a desire which is radically anti-cultural for it precludes all development, transcendence of the home and relations to those beyond immediate life.

Levi-Strauss does not assume that culture is continuous with nature, nor that the structures of a culture arise gradually from natural tendencies. Rather, culture begins with prohibition: by imposing a law upon natural tendencies. Culture occurs with the structuring of desire, or the submission of desire to shared norms. The realm of need, nature and immediacy is abandoned. Needs become desires only by being prohibited, for it is through prohibition that biological need is referred to the structure of the social whole, such that the self recognises its needs in relation to others. Sexual difference – our emergence into the world from the body of an other – is neither natural nor culture; it is the point at which culture mediates the natural. Indeed, this is the key difference between sexuality and 'gender.' Whereas gender is the recognition of kinds, forms or identities, sexuality is the condition of differentiation from which kinds emerged. This sexuality is, for both Levi-Strauss and Lacan, neither already formed into masculine and feminine kinds, nor absolutely indifferent. Sexuality, or our 'natural' dependence on the body of an other launches us into culture. Sexuality relates, essentially, to prohibition and law – the submission of the human body to a network of speaking beings. The human condition is one of desire, the articulation of our needs to an other.

For Levi-Strauss *the* founding prohibited and abandoned desire is the desire for incest. The mother's body is the site for the transition from need to desire, for it is the desire for incest that would allow the human body to remain at the level of mere life, never detaching itself from the first desired object of the mother, never regulating its desire by choosing between some bodies and others (Levi-Strauss 1969, 481). By prohibiting certain bodies, such as the body of the mother, from being possible objects of desire, the human body is situated in a structure of kinship: those prohibited bodies who are recognised as one's own, and others who are recognised as possible objects of desire. The prohibition of the natural mother creates the distinction between nature as immediate desire, and culture as mediated desire. Desire for Levi-Strauss is therefore structured originally and primordially through kinship and alliance; the mother is produced as that which is one's own and therefore prohibited, while other bodies are produced as *other* and therefore capable of being related to through marriage. The maternal prohibition creates the condition for social bonds and identities. All social order, identity, law and system begin from the prohibition of the body of the mother. All other laws have to presuppose this law and prohibition, for law is just our difference from immediate and undifferentiated nature. Only with the difference between the prohibited mother and the legitimate kinship structure can there be any order or law at all: 'the rules of kinship and marriage are not made necessary by the social state. They are the social state itself, reshaping biological relationships and natural sentiments, forcing them into structures implying them as well as others, and compelling them to rise above their original characteristics' (Levi-Strauss 1969, 490).

Now, with regard to gender, three key related points need to be noted. First, it is difficult to reduce Levi-Strauss's account to gender in the sense of social overlay, for the very idea of the social and its distinction from nature is an effect of sexual difference, of recognising one's difference from the body of the mother. Gender – the attribution of norms to male and female bodies would require this first and originary difference. Second, it is *kinship* that operates as the original structuring of nature, rather than any other system. Third, this structuring occurs through the exchange of women (Levi-Strauss 1969, 493), with women produced *as women* in this act or institution of exchange. Why this is so is to do with the very (unnatural) nature of human nature. The first object of need is the maternal body; as humans we are born dependent on an other. Only kinship and the incest taboo, which prohibits certain objects of desire can detach desire from need, can orient desire to a deferred, structured and social system of commands. Kinship and the incest taboo must occur, then, as the event that divides nature from culture. The incest taboo is *both* natural and cultural. It is natural, insofar as there is a human tendency towards speech and sociality, which can only be achieved if the human body abandons immediate biological need and orders desires according to some higher end. But kinship is also cultural precisely because it establishes an end or value *other than mere* life, other than need. This is where the exchange of women comes in. In order to abandon the mother and accede to structured desires, such as kinship and culture, some end or value *other than* the mother must be established. There must be that value for which the mother is abandoned – the value of law, which is a value other than mere life and other than the mother. Woman, then, is the first object in the emergence of a structure of subjects, for it is in kinship that woman is no longer desired directly. One must desire this and not that woman, and when one takes one woman rather than another, one establishes ties of alliance to other tribes. To take a woman as one's wife is to submit to the law of kinship and to allow that woman's body to act as a signifier. Marriage between tribes establishes communication and opens a system of exchange. Woman becomes, according to Levi-Strauss, a signifier. She is no longer the thing itself, or that which is valued in itself; she is valued according to the position she occupies. A woman can be married only if she is *not* one's mother, only if some structure of exchange has allowed her to be signified within the law. By being placed in a system of exchange or circulated – one can marry women from other tribes and families – women's bodies become tokens or signifiers, signs of the other's desire:

> The emergence of symbolic thought must have required that women, like words, should be things that were exchanged. In this new case, indeed, this was the only means of overcoming the contradiction by which the same woman was seen under two incompatible aspects: on the one hand, as the object of personal desire, thus exciting sexual and proprietorial instincts; and, on the other, as the subject of the desire of others, and seen as such, i.e., as the means of binding others through alliance with them....In contrast to words, which have become wholly signs, woman has remained at once a sign and a value. This explains why the relations between the sexes have preserved that affective richness, ardour and mystery which doubtless originally permeated the entire universe of human communications.
> (Levi-Strauss 1969, 496)

One does not only exchange women, establishing lines of alliance; one also regards the object of exchange as the sign of some worth, as that for which the process of exchange is undertaken. Woman subtends the relation between communicating subjects. In abandoning the maternal body and recognising an order of culture, or an order other than need, the subject becomes one who recognises others as also occupying the system of exchange. The system uses women to establish relations of exchange and reciprocity. I recognise myself, and you, as human – as *other than nature* – only insofar as we abandon the level of need, and exchange women according to rules and prohibitions. Culture is, therefore, established through prohibition – the object that one must not have. On the one hand, then, the female (maternal) body is established as other than cultural, as that which must be abandoned in order to move from silent and immediate need, to articulated and mediated desire. On the other hand, however, the female body *as signifier* is also the very opening of culture: only when men exchange women and establish an order of relations, recognition and exchange – only when women become signs of the value of culture and mediation – does human life become fully human. Transcending nature is achieved by transcending the maternal body of chaotic fulfilment and plenitude. Establishing culture is achieved by men recognising each other as subjects who freely exchange and choose women as objects.

The fantasy of woman

There are at least five ways in which Levi-Strauss's argument has influenced discussions of gender, and we will deal with these in turn. Indeed, until quite recently, gender debates usually began either from assuming or contesting the prohibition on incest. First, there have been those – such as Gayle Rubin and Sherry Ortner – who have, at least initially accepted Levi-Strauss's argument as an explanation of the universal subordination of women, and the fact that nearly all cultures operate with a gender binary of male–female that parallels culture–nature (Ortner 1996; Rubin 1975). Because woman is the first natural object that fulfils need, the negation of need will be the negation and devaluation of the female/maternal body. One way of dealing with the gender hierarchy today would, therefore, be a dismantling of the imaginary structure that underpins our subjection to the system of signification. We could, for example, recognise the mythic status of Woman as the lost and prohibited other, and then recognise the difference between the bodies of women and the idea of Woman (Cornell 1991), and we could also expose the fictive status of the law – that the Phallus is only imagined as an authority through the fantasy of prohibition. Without recognising the force of the Oedipal fantasy, as that which explains the emergence of culture, we would not be able to restructure the sexual imaginary within which all speaking subjects are located. Lacan's reading of Levi-Strauss needs to be recognised, therefore, as the first step in the deconstruction of gender, where deconstruction takes what *appears* to be originary – the sexual fantasy of prohibition and original plenitude – and exposes it as an imaginary effect. The deconstruction of this imaginary would, then, go beyond Lacan's insistence on the non-existence of Woman, and imagine a point of difference beyond a lost and fantasmatic maternal origin.

Kristeva and the maternal semiotic

In contrast with the criticism of the imagined status of the maternal origin, there have been those who affirm the pre-cultural mythic status of the maternal body. Rather than trying to overcome the sexual binary that allows us to imagine our relation to law, a number of feminists have accepted that the maternal body is, indeed, necessarily repressed in our submission to law. Indeed, whereas Lacan argues that Woman does not exist and that we can only know the 'beyond' of the law from within the law, some feminists have insisted that one can, and should, disrupt the phallic law, through a writing of the body. Here, the body would be that which precedes and exceeds exchange. One may not be able to represent and signify this body in a lawful, translatable, systemic and coherent manner, but the body could nevertheless function as the disruption or negation of system. The law as we know it has been structured around the self-presence of the male body, with the phallus operating as the body part that signifies value, a body part that becomes a signifier of the power to signify. Lacan referred to the phallus as the 'transcendental signifier': those who claim to possess the phallus are those who can exchange women and stand outside the system of exchange. The phallus is established as that which will be lost in any Oedipal return to the mother; its very being occurs through threat and prohibition (Lacan 1977, 317).

If the incest taboo prohibits the maternal body in order to establish culture, then the transgression of this prohibition and the disruption of the body that is other than signification will be revolutionary. Julia Kristeva cites a series of authors, ranging from James Joyce to Louis-Ferdinand Celine, who present the desire for the maternal body as a disruption of language and order (Kristeva 1981, 142). For Kristeva, incest is revolutionary and poetic language is incest. Poetic language is a dimension of speech – those aspects of sound, metre, rhythm and sonority that enable meaning but are themselves not meaningful. Unlike Derrida who regards the 'trace' as a purely graphic, inhuman and machinic process of difference, Kristeva argues that language and subjectivity are produced from traces, marks or 'semioses' of the body (Kristeva 1984, 142). Derrida, she insists, can only see what is other than 'thetic' – other than the judging thesis of the subject – as negative, but Kristeva insists that there is a 'before' of the law that is on its way to becoming a subject, a subject-in-process, before all regulated exchange and external relations. That is, language does not emerge from the systemic difference of a set of signs, but from zones and borders of the body and these bodily differences – in the form of sounds, rhythms and pulsions – can always re-emerge to disrupt the 'paternal' position of language. There is some regularity or repetition at this level – it is not undifferentiated chaos – but the marked out rhythms do not yet have the referential order of a system. Think of the rhyme schemes or metrical tendencies of a poem (without the specific words or sense) which form something like a recognisable form but do not necessarily refer beyond themselves, athough reference and meaning are certainly potential:

> The notion of *heterogeneity* is indispensable for though articulate, precise, organized, and complying with constraints and rules (especially, like the rule of *repetition*, which articulates the units of a particular rhythm or intonation), this signifying disposition is not that of meaning or signification: no sign, no predication, no signified object and therefore no operating consciousness of a transcendental ego. We shall call this disposition *semiotic* (*le sémiotique*) meaning, according to the etymology of the Greek *sémeion* (δημειον), a distinctive mark, trace, index, the premonitory sign, the proof, engraved mark, imprint – in short, a *distinctiveness* admitting of an uncertain and indeterminate articulation because it does not yet refer (for young children) or no longer refers (in psychotic discourse) to a signified object for a thetic consciousness (this side of, or through, both object and cosnciousness). Plato's *Timaeus* speaks of a *chora* (χωρα), receptacle (υποδοχειον), unnameable, improbable, hybrid, anterior to naming, to the One, to the father, and consequently, maternally connoted to such an extent that it merits "not even the rank of syllable".
>
> (Kristeva 1981, 133)

Consider the significance of Kristeva's refiguring of gender here: she both draws upon and radicalises one of the most significant figures of

Western thought. Thought has always been determined as a One that departs from itself, gives itself specific form through the imprinting of a matter which has no positive being, and then recognises and returns to itself (Kristeva 1989). But the matter or body, Kristeva insists is *not* reducible to the meaning and form given to it; we may always be within a system of meaning, but that does not stop the matter or body that enables meaning from pressing in upon meaning. The body and matter, the maternal ground or birth of the subject, is not reducible to the images we have of it; it exercises a force of its own, albeit a force without will, intent, object or consciousness. The feminine, then, is not just the ground imagined as other to paternal law; it has a positivity of its own. Kristeva accepts the traditional form–matter gender binary, but allows neither term to explain or subsume the other. There is no meaning, judgement or law without some material differentiation of sounds and rhythms, but there is no direct grasp of this materiality; it is felt and lived only in its relation to law. We could also say that for Kristeva the male–female binary of gender – the way in which we conceptualise the opposition between form and matter, meaning and non-meaning, identity and difference – do have their basis in sex, but this 'sex' is not a blank biological body. Rather, sexuality is just that process of desire from which both male and female subject positions are formed.

From a faithfully Lacanian point of view, the pre-Oedipal is radically other than language; the minute one speaks one is within the law and has already abandoned the immediacy of life. There is only one logic of sexual difference. For Kristeva, however, there is a point between pure immediacy and the full structure of the law, between sex and gender. Borrowing from Plato she refers to this as the *chora*, which is the receptacle or ground from which distinct identity and lawful difference emerge. But the *chora* can only be an *analogy* for this pre-symbolic register, for its very nature is to be other than any positive name: 'Neither model nor copy, the *chora* precedes and underlies figuration and thus specularization, and is analogous only to vocal and kinetic rhythm' (Kristeva 1984, 26). This ambivalent position, she argues, is not left behind when we become speaking beings. Indeed, in order to speak we must also rely upon bodily and sensual differences, such as the rhythms and sounds of a language. This 'poetic' dimension is, of course, played down in scientific discourses, which seek to establish a strict distinction between the speaking subject and the object posited (what Kristeva refers to as the 'thetic' position). But in certain forms of literature the poetic dimension is foregrounded. Meaning or system is still at work, but there is also a dimension not reducible to meaning. If one were to 'speak' without any system at all, then one would not be a speaking subject, one would not occupy a position. Mere noise or pure sound would result in psychosis, or fascism – the loss of all difference and judgement. But poetic language occupies a fragile subject position, a subject in process who bears the primary differentiations that will enable meaning but are not yet fully systematised. Unlike Lacan's speaking subject who is nothing more than a position within the law, Kristeva's speaking subject has a body; the sounds enjoyed by this body recall that pre-Oedipal moment of 'semiosis,' where the body must begin to differentiate various sounds in order that it might, subsequently, become a lawful speaking subject.

Kristeva's feminism was, not surprisingly, extremely important for understanding the gender of literature in third-wave feminism. She did not assume, as earlier feminists had done, that women's literature would be a way of exposing prejudice, producing a female subject or entering the canon of great voices and authority. Nor did she assume that there was a different women's subjectivity, awaiting literary expression. Rather, she insisted that great literature needed to play with the borders between subjectivity and femininity. On the one hand, literature must adopt a voice and speak. On the other, literature is only literature, or poetic, if it explores those mobile, feminine and incestuous moments of a language, where the sound of the voice, the materiality of the text, recalls the body of the mother, and a bodily *jouissance* before system and the law.

Kristeva's work was both hailed as a 'deconstruction' of sexual difference that provided a way of overcoming the strictures of Lacan's essentialism (Jones 1986; Moi 1985), and was itself condemned as a form of essentialism (Stanton 1986). Those literary critics who saw hope in Kristeva's work emphasised her declaration that we needed to see the gender binary as 'metaphysical.' The opposition between male and female was not given in the body but was produced in the process of taking up the system of speech. In poetic language, furthermore, we could see this subject in process (Minow-Pinkney 1987). Unlike Lacan, who regarded Woman as a *fantasy* of what is other than the law, Kristeva insisted that the body and its expression in language disrupted the border between the speaking subject of law and the repressed maternal body. Poetic language puts the subject on trial, exposing both the subject and the law as having a tie to the body.

If the masculine speaking position is created by adopting the signifying system in opposition to the vagaries and pulsations of the body,
and if the feminine position is produced as that which lies outside the
law, then any literary experience that explores the border between
meaning and non-meaning will also be revolutionary. Indeed, revolution in its full political sense needed to begin with sexuality at this
fundamental level.

Judith Butler and the heterosexual matrix

Whereas Kristeva saw the masculine subject as one who represses the
maternal body, other feminists drew upon her work to argue that the
body and sexuality could not be reduced to the male–female binary.
Judith Butler is one of the most prominent theorists of gender to have
questioned what she refers to as the 'heterosexual matrix,' which
establishes the father as other than the mother, and the mother or
feminine as the position opposed to the cultural masculine. Butler
accepts that kinship, or the break from an unrepresentable nature,
establishes culture and order; but goes on to question why kinship
should take the form of a prohibition of the *mother* and the exchange
of women by men. She also challenges the Platonic representation of
physis (or nature) as *chora* (the ground for forms and representation).
For, she insists, the male–female and form–matter binaries do not
exhaust possibilities or potential for being (Butler 1993, 41). Far from
accepting and problematising the binary, Butler insists that we think
difference outside the heterosexual organisation of male–female as
emblematic of all relations (Butler 2001, 627).

   Like Levi-Strauss, Butler agrees that it is *prohibition* that is constitutive of the position of the subject (Butler 1997). However, she rejects the
idea that there was a desire *for* the mother that law comes along to prohibit. Rather, it is the act of prohibition itself that produces its 'before.'
In arguing that the mother *not* be desired, the law produces the difference between mother and culture, and creates the mother *as mother* by
producing a system of familial relations. The problem with psychoanalysis and its uptake of Levi-Strauss, according to Butler, is that it
assumes the sexual binary – the difference between men's and women's
bodies, and assumes that these bodies are ordered from the 'natural'
relation of mother and father (Butler 1990). Both Levi-Strauss and
psychoanalysis begin their explanation of gender positions from the

opposition between bodies sexed as male and female, and assume a heterosexual structure of desire. To negate the mother is, they assume, to adopt the position of desiring father. Against this 'heterosexual matrix' Butler insists that there is no 'natural' mother–father–child relation; such relations are effects of social structures. The supposedly 'female' body that was prohibited is sexed as female and maternal, or other than the male subject, only through the intervention of law.

Those psychoanalytic feminists who accept the Levi-Strauss/Lacan story, Butler argues, fail to realise that such explanations repeat, rather than explain, the structure of the law (Butler 2000, 15). We need to avoid the idea that the female sex can be used as a radical voice beyond the law. Nor should we imagine that we can strategically occupy the position of woman to oppose the law. As long as one speaks as a man or woman one speaks from within the system. It is the very idea of a natural sexual desire – the idea of an original plenitude that is fully and immediately sexual – that the law assumes, creates and prohibits. Butler's account is, therefore, critical of any attempt to retrieve or radicalise sexual difference. And she certainly does not want to articulate another system or a point beyond the law: for the idea of a sexuality or embodiment before all law is precisely the fantasy that the law installs. We should not see the law as a structure that is imposed on a disruptive, pre-cultural and anti-social (female) chaos. To do so, Butler argues, would be to situate women in a position of impossible speech. Butler therefore also attacks all those who insist that without the sexual binary, without the mother–father structure, the subject would fall back into psychosis, lacking all structure and socialisation. The supposed chaos that the law comes along to order, the fantasised anti-cultural incestuous desire, is a creation and *effect* of the law. By *prohibiting* the chaotic fusion with the mother, the law creates a fantasy of a threatening chaos, and creates us as subjects who *must have* desired such a lawlessness. Rather than accept this point of pre-symbolic transgression and feminine otherness, Butler argues that the law must continually re-inscribe or 'perform' the very otherness it seems to order. It is only through repeated injunctions and prohibitions that the border between culture and nature is maintained, and it is this very need for repetition that also installs the possibility of change. The need for the law to repeat itself, to prohibit and negate the 'maternal origin' allows for the possibility for the law to be quoted, perverted, distorted and displayed as the performance, rather than description, of the border between nature and culture. The maternal-feminine does not exist outside acts of prohibition. Adopting the voice of the feminine *as feminine* only sustains the gender binary. The law or the difference between male and female has no existence beyond its specific performances.

Rather than find a point beyond the law one needs to perform the law against itself. Butler insists, against those queer theorists who try to imagine a sexuality that is outside the male–female structures of kinship, that *some* system of positions and identities will always structure sexual relations; but these positions are social, rather than timeless, and can therefore be transformed (Butler 1997, 17). Instead of an attempt to imagine desire outside the system, one needs to refigure the system. Those gay men who create 'families,' or lesbian sisterhoods that produce different relations and identities, still occupy a social structure, and still recall the traditional roles of the heterosexual family. However, in repeating the roles of heterosexual kinship *outside* the heterosexual community, the norm is rendered different. Only a counter-performance can challenge the seemingly natural heterosexual system: 'Consider that in the situation of blended families, a child says "mother" and might expect more than one individual to respond to the call' (Butler 2000, 69). If one speaks as a man but also desires another man, or if one has a body that has been culturally sexed as male, but then acts as a woman, one exposes the law itself as a performance. Instead of finding a position outside the performance of law, one performs the law itself *as* an explicit performance. When, for example, a woman takes on the voice of the law, and when that voice expresses a desire for a prohibited other (such as another woman, or, as in Butler's reading of *Antigone*, the brother), then the position of law as other than feminine and as other than incest is overturned (Butler 2000, 82). There is no law outside its continued performance, and no sexuality outside its constant prescription, prohibition and performance. All those acts of speech – from the tragedy of *Antigone* to contemporary drag – which expose sexed subjectivity as constituted through signifiers, show the ways in which natural sexuality is produced as a fantasy upon which the law supposedly takes hold: 'the very description of the symbolic as intractable law takes place within a fantasy of law as unsurpassable authority' (Butler 2000, 30). There is no sexual binary outside its inscription in a kinship structure, and if kinship produces the very sexuality it seems to order, there is no reason why alternative sexual imaginaries might not structure desire.

Deconstruction

Deconstruction has been highly influential in arguments regarding gender and sexuality, with both feminists and queer theorists extending the implications of Jacques Derrida's deconstruction of logocentrism. Here, we will consider Derrida's specific criticism of Levi-Strauss's attempt to explain the origin of culture. Derrida situates his critique of Levi-Strauss within a broader project, which inquires into the possibility of breaking with Western metaphysics. Metaphysics has always, necessarily, been a form of logocentrism. Logocentrism assumes that there is a single logic or law and that our experiences in all their difference can ultimately be accounted for through some single point of truth – that all differences refer back to some grounding and originating presence, which can always be brought to light. In terms of language, this would mean that various systems or structures could be compared *as different* from some over-arching position of explanation. In terms of sexual difference, this would assume that however different bodies or cultures are, there would be an underlying or primary humanity, reason or human nature, which then expressed itself in differing kinds.

On this picture, the logic of the sex–gender distinction would partake of the metaphysics of presence, for gender – different kinds – could be seen as constructions or organisations of an underlying sexuality that is of the same substance – one biological matter organising itself into distinct kinds. Reason, or the *logos*, is always capable of recognising, incorporating and making sense of, what is other than itself. Differing kinds can be explained and comprehended by a preceding ground of sameness, and this ground or foundation is the truth of life. Deconstruction, according to Derrida, is not a 'method,' for this would suggest that there is a clear and stable difference between presence (or what is) and its way of being known; but Derrida insists that the very idea of being or presence is achieved through the differential structures of experience. There is not a nature or sexuality that is then known and differentiated; rather it is through processes of marking and tracing that one imagines an original and natural 'before.' The idea of a sex that precedes gender, where sex is the truth or reality before gender takes part in the logic of metaphysics and truth. Such a logic cannot simply be abandoned, for even if one were to accept that gender were merely a construction with no underlying reality one would still be relying on a distinction between the true and the constructed. When Butler insists

that 'sex' is produced as a 'before' through the process of social performance, law and inscription she makes a distinction between the reality of performance, act and law, and the fictive sex that is its effect. It is
just this distinction that is both necessary and impossible, according to
Derrida. All speech and experience is intentional – directed to some
truth or presence that is deferred. This truth must, by its very nature, be
capable of being re-presented, brought to light and rendered independent of any particular utterance or speaker. Recent criticisms of the
sex–gender distinction have, if anything, intensified this opposition
between the ground of truth and the secondariness of inscription.
Butler's demystification of 'sex' relies on attributing force and reality
only to the acts and performances of signification, rejecting the natural
body as an effect of law; what she cannot acknowledge is a body or
nature outside iteration or inscription, a body that does not perform or
actualise itself. Butler sees negation, otherness and the outside as
effected *from* law, as different *from* identity. Derrida, by contrast, inter-
rogates how such oppositions between a before and after, a positive
and negative, are effects of a field of pure and anarchic difference. The
contemporary sex–gender debate – in which the 'reality' of sex and
gender is disputed – assumes that one term is the origin of the other.
Butler argues that sex – the illusion of a pre-linguistic body – is produced
from a process or legalising prohibitions. She therefore grants one
term – inscripton, performance, marking, law – a greater reality. Criticisms
of Butler have merely taken the opposite turn and assumed the reality of
sex and the secondariness of gender. In *Beyond Sex and Gender*, Wendy
Cealey Harrison and John Hood-Williams criticise Butler for imposing
the 'sociological' categories of gender – masculine and feminine – on her
explanation of sexuality (Harrison and Hood-Williams 2002, 207). By
describing gender norms through the prohibition of the mother, Butler
loses sight of the multivalence of sexuality, its polymorphous structure
that only subsequently gets organised through the object positions of
mother, father and child (Harrison and Hood-Williams 2002, 212). It is
sex, not gender, that's real and primary; 'identities as such do not exist'
(Harrison and Hood-Williams 2002, 218).

Against the attack on one or other term of an opposition, Derrida
insists that we look to the ways in which oppositions 'decide' a border
between first and second, real and parasitic, present and absent. When
Derrida uses the language of sex and gender he does so in a self-
consciously deferred manner. One can think of life through the figure
of sex, as Derrida does in his essay on Freud, but he uses Freud's writings

on sexuality to demonstrate the impossibility of grasping life *as such* (Derrida 1981, 214). One can use various figures, textual marks or oppositions to think about the differences within which we think and speak, but no opposition – whether that be nature–culture, sex–gender or male–female – can organise and transcend difference in general.

How is life determined as *that which is*, as a substance that bears an identity which thought can re-present? Truth has been established, Derrida argues, as that which remains the same above and beyond any particular utterance or sign; the ideal of truth is the ideal of presence. Truth is what grounds, precedes and underlies difference. If something is true then it must be capable of being retrieved and rendered self-evident by any subject whatever (Derrida 1989). The 'logos' of logocentrism is just this ideal of a metaphysics that could arrive at self-present truth without having to rely on anything other than itself. Logocentrism is also, therefore, a form of *phallo*gocentrism, for the figure of the father as pure insemination and form that gives reality to matter has dominated metaphysics. Not only is the ideal of a self-generating unity that gives form to itself analogous to the traditional image of the active male body, it is also the case that the disembodied, single and universal status of truth is associated with a reason that has always distanced itself from the 'feminine' qualities of physicality, difference, plurality and affect (Protevi 2001). Indeed, the phallus has always functioned as that body part which allows us to imagine a body that masters and overcomes itself; a phallic body transcends itself and gives form to itself, independent of natural, accidental or contingent differences (Derrida 1986, 222). Metaphysics is established with the ideal of pure self-presence, without mediation by any body or materiality: the ideal of that which is true and lawful above and beyond any body or difference. Phallogocentrism is just this ideal of self-fathering, a thought that can give birth to itself without mediation, difference or loss. But Derrida does not argue that the figure of the father is a privileged metaphor, for that would imply some true origin outside all analogies and relations. Rather, the concept of the 'original' or properly philosophical cannot be untied from metaphors of fathering and forming:

> The family never ceases to occupy the stage, and yet there is the impression that there is never any question of that. The philosophical object named 'family' seems ceaselessly to slip away. The ontotheological premises, the infinite kernel of the family structure, of nomination, of filiation to be sure, are visible. But the whole fundamental

syllogistic is controlled by the father/son relation about which we can ask ourselves whether it opens or closes the possibility of the family.
(Derrida 1986, 97)

For Derrida, reading through Hegel, the natural figure of sexual difference is already determined by a metaphysical decision, but such a decision cannot be thought without these figures – which are, therefore, no longer 'mere' figures in the everyday sense:

> But the difference is not so simple. To say that one element dominates here, the other there, is not enough: in the female the essence consists of indifference – rather the indifferent (*das Indifferente*), in the male the essence consists in the difference, the divided-in-two, rather, the opposition (*das Entzweite, der Gengensatz*). Male and female are not opposed as two differents, two terms of the opposition, but as indifference and difference (opposition, division). The sexual difference is the difference between indifference and difference. But each time, in order to *relieve* itself, *difference* must be determined in/as *opposition*.
> (Derrida 1986, 111–112)

Derrida begins his essay on Levi-Strauss by arguing that structuralism appears to provide a radical break with the Western tradition of logocentrism. Levi-Strauss himself argues that he is not going to establish a metaphysical foundation or origin; he is not going to uncover the ultimate truth of life and being. Structuralism does not present itself as the self-present truth or logic of life. Rather, structuralism merely looks at how specific cultures form different systems (Derrida 1981, 284). The structural anthropologist therefore steps back from making any universal truth claims and merely looks at how each particular culture establishes its own truth. Furthermore, Levi-Strauss also acknowledges that his own discourse is not one he holds to be ultimately true; his method is nothing more than an explicitly acknowledged set of tools that one can use to analyse various cultures, and is not itself established as a foundation beyond all culture. Instead of seeking some ultimate metaphysical truth, Levi-Strauss insists that his method will look at the comparison of cultures, affirm their difference, and desist from any ultimate truth claims. In this regard, then, it might appear that all those Western discourses that had established truth, being and foundations in opposition to difference would be overturned with the advent of structuralism. If this were so – if structuralism really were capable of providing a break with foundationalism – then it might also provide a way of surmounting the implicit gender hierarchy of Western thought. For, as we have already noted, it is the elevation of truth, the light of reason and a single logic of pure thought that has been defined in opposition to the chaos of matter, difference, flux and embodiment. And this opposition has always been figured as gendered. The active light of reason is masculine, defined in opposition to feminine embodiment and sensual difference. If structuralism were to break with the ideal of presence it would also provide a way beyond the implicit gender hierarchies of logocentrism.

As we have already noted, many gender theorists have seen structuralism in just such a liberating light. If the difference between male and female, and nature and culture, is seen to be constructed through culturally specific systems of signs, then we might affirm the positivity of difference and abandon the notion of supposedly self-evident and present sexual subjects who have an identity before all representation. Derrida, however, reads Levi-Strauss, and structuralism generally, as reaffirming the metaphysics of presence. First, Levi-Strauss's claim that he will not make truth claims, that he will simply present various cultural systems of difference, can only provide one more foundation. Indeed, the ideal of *not* adopting a position, of situating oneself above and beyond any specific culture is one more example of the disembodied, general and surveying voice that disowns its own locatedness. The very idea that one might inhabit a discourse, such as that of anthropology, and *not* commit oneself to its truth-claims is, Derrida insists, one more version of a Western reason that claims to detach itself from all specificity (Derrida 1981, 285). Second, Levi-Strauss's assertion that he is only presenting various cultural systems, and that each system is relative, with no ultimate truth, is itself an ultimate truth claim, for all these cultures and differences are located within the general condition of culture. The claim that all truth is produced through cultural systems establishes 'culture' as the ultimate explanatory horizon. Finally, Derrida argues that Levi-Strauss's structuralism becomes one more instance of empiricism (Derrida 1981, 288). Levi-Strauss will gather a collection of cultural systems, analyse their condition, establish their inner logic and refrain from positing anything other than what he has simply found. Empiricism is just this effacement or disavowal of the position of the knower in the face of the 'data' under examination. But this ideal of empiricism is, Derrida insists, thoroughly metaphysical, for it seeks to discover the truth of what it finds. Empiricism merely presents *what is*, without supplement, deviation or difference.

Against Levi-Strauss's claims for a structuralist liberation from metaphysics, Derrida argues that there must be some 'supplement' in any discourse: some point upon which the structure relies but which itself cannot be accounted for from within the structure. In the case of Levi-Strauss's argument, it is incest prohibition that explains the emergence of law and structure. Incest functions as a point of explanation; it allows one to think the emergence of all structure, culture and difference, but is itself accepted as a point before all difference, as a structuring principle. But in order to offer this account of cultures and structures, Levi-Strauss himself must adopt a structured position, must assume the idea of incest prohibition and its particular way of inscribing the border between nature and culture, the unstructured and the structured. The idea, then, that sexual difference can be explained by the transition from nature to culture must itself be located within a structure – the discourse of structuralism, anthropology, kinship, cultural systems and so on.

How, Derrida asks, can the incest taboo be used to explain the emergence of structure and culture, when the very story of this taboo is itself expressed from a structure and culture? For Derrida, then, there can be *no* originating story of gender, no maternal origin, whose loss can be explained. Any such pre-cultural origin or feminine is always described as original and lost *from* culture and structure. The feminine cannot be described as that which exists *before* difference, structure and culture, for the idea of the 'feminine' is always already cultural, already differentiated. Derrida concludes his essay on Levi-Strauss by imagining a different notion of difference. Here, difference would not be that which is imposed upon an otherwise undifferentiated nature; difference would not be reduced to various structures which are all located within, and can be surveyed from, the field of anthropology. Derrida uses the metaphor of childbearing to overturn the privileging of an intellectual labour which can always master itself. This new form of difference would not be the differentiation of some substance into different kinds. Rather, if we think *birth* radically, not as man giving form to himself, but as the emergence of what is *not* oneself, not reducible to a single substance, then we will take gendered and generating metaphors far more literally. Derrida asks whether we can decide between the notion of structure as that which differentiates some unknowable ground, or structure as that which produces difference without ground or commonality:

> …we must first try to conceive of the common ground, and the *dif-férance* of this irreducible difference. Here there is a kind of question,

let us call it historical, whose *conception, formation, gestation,* and *labor* we are only catching a glimpse of today. I employ these words, I admit, with a glance toward the operations of chilbearing – but also towards those who, in a society from which I do not exclude myself, turn their eyes away when faced by the as yet unnamable which is proclaiming itself and which can do so, as is necessary whenever a birth is in the offing, only under the species of the nonspecies, in the formless, mute, infant and terrifying form of monstrosity.

(Derrida 1981, 293)

Difference would not be the *differentiation of* a present and unstructured nature. Derrida's imagined difference would be *positive*: not the differentiation of some ungraspable presence, but a difference that has no ground, no centre, no origin, and no sense of a lost foundation. This would then yield a more radical concept of play. Whereas structuralism can only think difference and play within systems, Derrida asks us to think about a play or difference which cannot be comprehended and explained, for it is this radical difference from which any system of explanation emerges:

There are thus two interpretations of interpretation, or structure, of sign, of play. The one seeks to decipher, dreams of deciphering a truth or an origin which escapes play and the order of the sign, and which lives the necessity of interpretation as an exile. The other, which is no longer turned toward the origin, affirms play and tries to pass beyond man and humanism, the name of man being the the name of that being who, throughout the history of metaphysics or of ontotheology – in other words, throughout his entire history – has dreamed of full presence, the reassuring foundation, the origin and the end of play.

(Derrida 1981, 292)

In his later work Derrida begins to draw out the sexual implications of this positive notion of difference. Here, the feminine would, contra Levi-Strauss, not be that imagined lost origin before all culture, law and difference. Rather, if we imagine difference beyond the phallogocentric ideal of a difference that merely mediates presence, then we will have to think of a difference freed from sexual binaries. This would not be a difference *between* male and female bodies; it would be a positive process of differentiation freed of all notions of origin. Such a difference would be 'feminine,' not because it is located in women's bodies, but because it is other than the ideal of phallic man, an ideal of reason that returns to and gives birth to itself. The feminine would, from a deconstructive viewpoint, have no essence in itself; we could use the word 'feminine' to think or mark that process of difference that has usually been set against the self-present subject or man of reason. The 'feminine' would only be one more way of thinking this other difference; there could be nothing essentially feminine about positive difference. The aim of deconstruction would be to arrive at 'choreographies' of difference that are no longer located on a sexual or gendered binary. Even if there is something necessary or implacable about the sexual binary, the very thought or dream of a non-binary sexuality produces a positive otherness:

> The relationship would not be a-sexual, far from it, but would be sexual otherwise: beyond the binary difference that governs the decorum of all codes, beyond the opposition feminine/masculine, beyond bisexuality as well, beyond homosexuality and heterosexuality, which come to the same thing. As I dream of saving the chance that this question offers I would like to believe in the multiplicity of sexually marked voices. I would like to believe in the masses, this indeterminable number of blended voices, this mobile of non-identified sexual marks whose choreography can carry, divide, multiply the body of each 'individual,' whether he be classified as 'man' or as 'woman' according to the criteria of usage. Of course, it is not impossible that desire for a sexuality without number can still protect us, like a dream, from an implacable destiny which immures everything for life in the number 2.... But where would the 'dream' of the innumerable come from, if it is indeed a dream? Does the dream itself not prove that what is dreamt of must be there in order for it to provide the dream.... the desire to escape the combinatory itself, to invent incalculable choreographies, would remain.
>
> (Derrida 1995, 108)

Deleuze and Guattari: Alliance before filiation

Gilles Deleuze and Félix Guattari accept Levi-Strauss's emphasis on kinship or the ordering of bodies and relations as the origin of human culture, but they insist that Levi-Strauss's story begins far too late in the picture. Their *Anti-Oedipus: Capitalism and Schizophrenia* ([1972] 1983) had two main targets: Lacanian psychoanalysis, and its assertion that it is absence, lack or what is *not* present that structures desire; and the modern concept of the subject, which they see as crucial to the workings of capitalism. Their 'universal history' seeks to expand the concept of sexuality beyond the self, beyond gender and beyond humanity.

All life is sexual, and all life is difference, insofar as life *is* desire. Life just is the power to create, differentiate and further itself. And this process of difference is sexual, because creation and expansion are only achieved, not by something remaining what it simply is, but through connections with other desires. A plant can live only by connecting with light and moisture; a human body can live only by connecting with other bodies. Sexual difference is the very becoming of life. Sexually differentiated bodies, or sexual beings and identities are productions of life. We cannot, therefore, try to explain sexuality by beginning from already gendered terms. Genders – the relatively stable kinds of male and female – are effects of a sexual process of change, creation and flux that transcends any specific body.

Deleuze and Guattari, like Derrida, criticise Levi-Strauss for explaining the emergence of culture from already differentiated terms. Levi-Strauss assumes both sexual difference – the opposition between male and female bodies – and the distinction between nature and culture (Deleuze and Guattari 1983, 155). Against this, Deleuze and Guattari want to give a history of the genesis of sexual difference. One of the key notions of their history is that genetic tribal difference precedes sexual difference (Deleuze and Guattari 1983, 85), and that the idea of a single human 'subject' is the oppressive motif of Western thought. Before gender binaries – which is how we currently understand sexual difference – sexual difference was tribal and racial; bodies were grouped or 'territorialised' according to marks and differences that were not as general as 'male' and 'female.' Without the organisation of bodies into genetic units of sameness or tribes, there could be no familial relations (Deleuze and Guattari 1987, 379). Racial difference is what must be repressed in order to produce a general binary of 'man' and 'woman.' The assertion of race, of a difference that cannot be reduced to the subject in general, is necessarily radical or 'nomadic':

> The classical image of thought, and the striating of mental space it effects, aspires to universality. It in effect operates with two 'universals,' the Whole as the final ground of being or all-encompassing horizon and the Subject as the principle that converts being into being-for-us....It is now easy for us to characterize the nomad thought that rejects this image and does things differently. It does not ally itself with a universal thinking subject but, on the contrary, with a singular race....
>
> (Deleuze and Guattari 1987, 379)

They establish this point by arguing that before we can have Levi-Strauss's argument about prohibition, before we can have relations among mothers, fathers and children (or lines of filiation), there have to be structures of alliance (Deleuze and Guattari 1987, 238). Levi-Strauss begins his analysis from families or tribes, who then form alliances by marrying or forming kinship ties. But how, Deleuze and Guattari ask, are these tribes or territories formed? How did we arrive at the unit of mother–father–child? Before there can be a mother or father, they argue, there must have been differentiation among groups of bodies; from an undifferentiated flow of genetic material, the 'intense germinal influx,' one group of bodies is marked off as different from another. A tribe, territory or alliance is formed. *Then* after this difference, and within this group, certain familial relations may be formed. In general terms they therefore argue that racial difference precedes gender difference, and that racial difference is sexual in the broadest sense. Tribes are produced through the alliance of bodies with similar – but never the same – genetic marks; these first identities or territories are formed by taking a complex flow of difference and producing a relative stability. Once the tribe or assemblage is formed it is *then* possible to produce sexual positions within the tribe, but these would not in the earliest stages be the minimal mother–father–child roles so much as relations among chieftains and sexually subordinate bodies (Deleuze and Guattari 1983, 165). Indeed, the despot is one who, before the nuclear family, is allowed to *enjoy* all bodies, who can take any woman. It is the enjoyment of incest – not its prohibition – that is primary, and this incest is not a negation of 'the mother' so much as the production of a group of women's bodies that is exclusively available to one violent and imposing body (the despot).

So, against the miserable 'family' story of Oedipal gender, Deleuze and Guattari want to argue that the modern male–female binary is produced from a complex history, which begins from a much more differentiated and multiple sexuality. First, they argue, is a process of territorialisation. This occurs, they insist, not by life being differentiated through an imposed structure, as in the Lacanian notion of a law imposed upon life, but by the vast difference of life *organising itself* to form relatively identical bodies. We begin from the intense germinal influx – a flow of bodies, each with their specific and different genetic make-up. Some features, however, can mark these bodies as the same. If, for example, we took skin-colour as a mark, we might differentiate one group from another, but each body in each group would be different, and choosing another mark, such as hair colour, would have formed a different territory. In this process of territorialisation, then, difference is reduced, and this is achieved by marking: some specific difference is *selected* as a way of assembling or gathering bodies together to form a territory. The primitive body was, Deleuze and Guattari note, literally marked by tattooing, scarring or painting in order to gather one assemblage of different bodies and establish it as the same. This marking was not the repression of desire but itself an act of desire; bodies assemble and produce themselves as different in order to act and further life. The key question, then, is how this historical process of productive difference and desire eventually produced the identity of universal 'man,' and how this identity enslaves difference and desire.

Deleuze and Guattari's entire history of man is premised upon an understanding of sexuality that is irreducible to gender; as long as we understand sexuality as the relation between men's and women's bodies we have missed and belied its very nature. Sexuality may produce relatively stable kinds – such as the species and sexes that we can identify – but these points of sameness are merely the ways in which sexuality, in general, achieves ceaseless change and production. Identity is not imposed upon an undifferentiated matter; physical life is self-differentiating life, with forms being moments of perceptible change. Sameness emerges from difference. We do not begin from a group of bodies marked as the same – say, human in general, that are then differentiated into male and female. Rather, from bodies that are radically and singularly different, certain samenesses are formed. The identities that we take for granted today, such as male and female, depend upon the assemblage of different bodies into territories.

For Deleuze and Guattari, it is not the prohibition of the mother that is original. The Oedipal story of lack and prohibition applied only to the modern subject, and can only be understood and overcome if we undertake a genealogy of its emergence. How is it that we think of ourselves as a subject who has given up a desired maternal object, and what set of interests and desires are produced by this story? For Deleuze and Guattari, the story of sex and gender is the story of capital. Life as such is inherently revolutionary, sexual and desiring; it is a striving that cannot be reduced to fixed forms. All social systems therefore bear a potential for increased flows of desire and the production of difference, but can also turn back and produce moments of stability or 'anti-production.' Capitalism, they argue, has both a radical and conservative tendency. Radically, the flow of goods, actions, objects and products would free life from imposed systems. This 'decoding' is how modern capitalism proceeds, and, indeed, all societies have this tendency towards flow which is 'warded off' by methods of 'coding.' Conservatively, however, one of those productions comes to order and define the whole. One of those points of relative stability – say, captivation by a notion of 'man' – can slow down desire, production and change. In contemporary capitalism it is the Oedipal understanding of sexual difference that reduces desire to sexuality in the narrow sense – sexuality as a family story, as a relation between fathers, mothers and children. Only if we see the political nature of sexuality – that sexuality is production and desire as such, beyond its human forms – will we be able to challenge a fully blown capitalism that has reduced all desire and production to the figuring of the subject and his private desires. In order to expand our understanding of the sexual we need to see its productive and social nature, beyond the idea of incest prohibition.

> When we relate desire to Oedipus, we are condemned to ignore the productive nature of desire: we condemn desire to vague dreams or imaginations that are merely conscious expressions of it; we relate it to independent existences – the father, the mother, begetters – that do not yet comprise their elements as internal elements of desire. The question of the father is like that of God: born of an abstraction, it assumes the link to be already broken between man and nature, man and the world, so that man must be produced as man by something exterior to nature and man.
>
> (Deleuze and Guattari 1983, 107)

According to Deleuze and Guattari, before prohibition and lack – before desire submits itself to a law of the father – there is force and excess. A group of bodies produces more than it needs for life; the body that seizes this excess creates itself as a governing body. We do not form societies because of scarcity and submission, but through excessive production which then enables mastery and enjoyment. We do not submit to incest prohibition in order to leave the family and become productive workers; it is only when one body – the despot – enjoys every body of the tribe that certain bodies are placed outside enjoyment. It is not our slavery and submission to life that forces us to produce a master; it is one body's desire that produces itself as masterful. Forceful mastery, assertion, excess and enjoyment precede prohibition, loss and the unthinkable maternal origin. Within a territory or assemblage of bodies, the despot enjoys the sexuality of all bodies without restriction; it is his excessive enjoyment that creates him *as* a distinct, governing or 'deterritorialised' power – a point produced from within a body that extends and gives new identity to that body (Deleuze and Guattari 1983, 194). With the excess of enjoyment one body (the despot) becomes a power controlling other bodies.

When the bodies of the tribe overthrow the despot, and seize power and enjoyment for themselves, and do so by distributing women among the tribe, then the deterritorialised power of the despot is *reterritorialised*; each body takes the law into itself. Man is not subject to an external body, but obeys his humanity, recognises his desire as essentially repressed: 'Oedipus is always colonization pursued by other means, it is the interior colony, and we shall see that even here at home, where we Europeans are concerned, it is our intimate colonial education' (Deleuze and Guattari 1983, 168).

'Man' is produced as a being who relates to 'woman' under the rubric of being 'human.' Instead of the force of law being imposed from without – the enjoying authority of the despot – 'man' is produced as a being who is differentiated from 'woman,' and 'woman' is defined as that denied maternal object that one must have wanted. 'Sexuality' is produced in modernity as the underlying truth of our being, as the difference which produces social life and structures. But the reverse is the case; the sexual self is a modern ideology, a way of masking the historical and forceful production of 'man' as an enslaving authority: 'To the degree that there is oedipalization, it is due to colonization' (Deleuze and Guattari 1983, 169).

The modern father – the authority of the family – is an effect of this political history, whereby the male body of law and force is gradually accepted as the body of 'humanity' and identity *per se.* In the beginning is the tyrannical despot, who becomes through time the recognised authority of the male leader or king, and who is overthrown only to be replaced by 'man' or the father-figure of humanity within us all. 'Man,' therefore is produced as a political fiction or affect to which we are enslaved, and the difference between male and female reduces a polit-ical and historical story into a private and 'familial' narrative. The idea that subjectivity emerges from the negation of the mother's body takes a social category – the mother of the modern family – and presents it as timeless and universal. To use gender as an explanatory rubric is, there-fore, to miss the positive production of differentiated categories from the forces and flows of life. Deleuze and Guattari insist that there can be no desired mother's body that is *then* prohibited. Rather, it is only with the injunction *not* to have sexual relations with certain bodies, that these bodies are then marked as members of one's family. It is the prohibition that produces the mother; and the prohibition is an effect of excess: the enjoying despot who has originally possessed all bodies produces another body – the tribe – as an ordered body. Against Levi-Strauss, the cultural structure of the family does not organise an otherwise chaotic and immediate nature that lacks all law and relation; the family is the effect of a history of creations of difference. Deleuze and Guattari want to insist that differences, such as the genetic differences of bodies, are actually far more complex than cultural structures. There is no underlying sameness, such as humanity, which is then divided into tribes; rather the modern notion of the 'human' is the result of the production of one single tribe in the network of capitalism. Culture does not differentiate life; culture takes an infinitely differing life and reduces it, first, to territorial relations among tribes and then to relations within tribes.

Levi-Strauss had argued that women become the first signifiers; it is through the exchange of women that a body of men can establish themselves as *other than* mere life, with women then acting as tokens of exchange or signifiers in the network of cultural recognition. Deleuze and Guattari want to challenge both the image of the mother as the first prohibited object, and the idea of the 'signifier' as the token of exchange that establishes cultural meaning and relations. To begin with, Deleuze and Guattari criticise the notion that difference occurs at the level of the signifier. And they do this by challenging the Oedipal explanation of difference. Recall that for both Lacan and Levi-Strauss 'woman' is established as that mere immediate life which must be negated and abandoned in order to take up the position of law. The signifier is what is *other than* immediate presence; it is the systemic, lawful and recognised differentiation of presence. But Deleuze and Guattari argue that before difference is thought of as a lawful system that signifies nature, there are positive and excessive differences that have no meaning. The marks of tattooing, scarring and body-painting are not *signs of* some law; they are ways in which bodies assemble. The marks do not *represent* an identity; there is no assemblage or sameness outside of the marking. Of course, much later in human history, such bodily markings *do* become signs. In the case of slavery, for example, the bodies that were overpowered shared a common feature of skin-colour, and blackness then became a sign of slaves as a natural kind. Even more importantly, as Deleuze and Guattari note, certain body parts, such as the phallus, which were once simply elevated as totems to mark out a tribe, became signs of man in general. But this 'phallic signifier,' occurs only with a specific historical epoch. In the first stage of history, bodies are marked as different, but this difference has no reference or meaning beyond itself. In the second stage, the marks are deterritorialised. The markings on the body refer to some despot or authority who appears as one body of the tribe who has power over the tribe: 'It is perhaps at this juncture that the question "What does it mean?" begins to be heard, and that problems of exegesis prevail over problems of use and efficacy. The emperor, the god – what did he mean?' (Deleuze and Guattari 1983, 206). In the third stage of civilisation the marked body *signifies*; the body is the sign of an underlying subject or 'man.'

> For what is the signifier in the first instance? What is it in relation to the nonsignifying territorial signs, when it jumps outside their chains and imposes – superimposes – a plane of subordination on their plane of immanent connotation? The signifier is the sign that has become a sign of the sign, the despotic sign having replaced the territorial sign, having crossed the threshold of deterritorialization; *the signifier is merely the deterritorialized sign itself.* The sign made *letter*. Desire no longer dares to desire, having become a desire of desire, a desire of the despot's desire.
>
> (Deleuze and Guattari 1983, 206)

It is the third stage that Deleuze and Guattari define as both Oedipal and capitalist. In the Oedipal understanding, bodies are marked according to having or not having the phallus, and this feature is seen as the 'sign' of one's sexuality – one must 'be' masculine or feminine in relation to having or not having the phallus. The child supposedly sees the mother as lacking the phallus and interprets that lack as the sign of some phallic law. Further, this signification is established through prohibition: the mother's lack of a phallus produces her as other than the law, as the desire prohibited by the law, and – therefore – as that which one *must have* desired: 'The law tells us: You will not marry your mother, and you will not kill your father. And we docile subjects say to ourselves: so *that's* what I wanted!' (Deleuze and Guattari 1983, 114).

This marked phallic body that is the supposed sign of one's humanity is, Deleuze and Guattari point out, the effect of a historical and economic development. In order for societies to expand and increase production they must create ever greater lines of alliance: all bodies must be included, eventually, within the one tribe of 'man' – one single and undifferentiated humanity: 'Oedipus, the incomparable instrument of gregariousness, is the ultimate private and subjugated territoriality of European man' (Deleuze and Guattari 1983, 102). The feature that now marks the body is that of the phallus: that of the man who has no feature apart from being other than his (prohibited) mother. We interpret the phallus as the sign of law, paternity and the prohibition of sexual chaos *because* of the Oedipal narrative. It is only by being told that we must have desired the maternal body that the paternal body is established as an inevitable law.

Freud's Oedipal narrative and Levi-Strauss's explanation of incest both repeat, rather than challenge, the structure of capitalism that presents all desire as structured by the family and gender. But sexual desire is *not*, according to Deleuze and Guattari, gendered. Desire begins, not by desiring the sameness and stasis of the maternal body, but by seeking the radical change, flux and difference that recognises no bounding identities or stabilities. It is only by prohibiting the mother's body, that the maternal is produced as what one desires. And it is only with this story of prohibition that social relations, which are actually economic and derived from the capitalist expansion that produces one family of man, are presented as sexual and familial. Sexual difference is *the* ideology of capitalism. By explaining desire and identity from the relations between mothers, fathers and children, capitalism presents a specific social formation as universal. It accepts that one's identity is male or female, that one is 'man' or 'woman,' when in historical reality the notion of 'man' is formed by all the genetic differences of bodies being subsumed under the image of the subject. This subject who we all recognise as our own unique selfhood is an internalised despot. Instead of being marked and subjected from without, by another body – such as the king or the despot – we recognise ourselves as human. In so doing we both internalise an Oedipal story, and identify with the body of white, bourgeois, familial and neurotic man.

Deleuze and Guattari are therefore critical of the *subjectification* of sexuality – the idea that sex is something that 'we' have, and that our gender or subjectivity is the truth of our personal being. Against this idea they insist that sexuality is directly political. The image of 'man' or the 'subject' is assembled from a series of invested qualities (Deleuze and Guattari 1983, 104). Whereas bodies were originally assembled through explicit markings, and then governed by an external body – the marked and sanctified body of the king – we have now taken certain political qualities as the sign of humanity in general: white skin, the aggressive phallic body, the voice of reason and the body organised by mind. 'Humanity' is not, Deleuze and Guattari argue, an underlying, sexless essence that is then parcelled out into different bodies. On the contrary, difference is repressed by the notion of a common humanity, and in the notion of two sexes, who are different kinds or instances of an otherwise human substance.

Deleuze and Guattari therefore reverse the psychoanalytic relation between sex and politics. On a Freudian understanding, we submit to external authorities, such as the king, despot, or fascist leader, because we have an original investment and desire for the image of the father. For Deleuze and Guattari the opposite is the case: we now believe in a necessary father figure because we have taken all those politically and historically formed images of male power such as the tyrant and the despot, and internalised them as the judging father within us all. Their project of 'schizoanalysis' therefore shows how the supposedly private and sexual psyche is composed from politically sexualised body parts and other intensities: the humanity within us all that governs our morality must rely on some image of the human – the private bourgeois individual of the Oedipal narrative. Referring to non-capitalist societies, Deleuze and Guattari draw attention to the political, rather than sexual, points of identity from which the gendered matrix of Oedipus emerges:

> Rather than everything being reduced to the name of the father, or that of the maternal grandfather, the latter opened onto all the names of history. Instead of everything being projected onto a grotesque hiatus of castration, everything was scattered in the thousand breaks-flows of the chieftainships, the lineages, the relations of colonization. The whole interplay of races, clans, alliances, and filiations, this entire historical and collective drift: exactly the opposite of the Oedipal analysis, when it stubbornly crushes the content of a delirium, when it stuffs it with all its might into 'the symbolic void of the father'.
> (Deleuze and Guattari 1983, 168)

'Schizonanalysis' is also, then, critical of a personal sexuality. It does not analyse the psyche of psychoanalysis – the sexual self or identity that then relates to others. Rather, schizoanalysis looks at the various 'schizzes' or forces of bodies and affects from which selves are composed (Deleuze and Guattari 1983, 274). Man is made of the thinking brain, white skin, ruling hand, threatened phallus, voice of reason (Deleuze and Guattari 1987, 292). Deleuze and Guattari step back from gender – the constituted terms of male and female, to the processes of sexual difference from which these terms emerge. This difference is creative, positive and productive. To use Elizabeth Grosz's expression, it is *pure difference*: not the differentiation *of* some grounding identity (humanity), nor difference *between* male and female identities (Grosz 1990, 124). Sexuality is the power to differ, to create differences – a power that has been reduced by binary concepts of gender. Sexuality is the desire of life that flows through and across bodies. We need to see specific bodies as points through which desire passes.

Deleuze and Guattari draw upon evolutionary theory in their reversal of the relation between sexuality and genders. Sexuality is not something that species *do* in order to maintain themselves as the same, in order to reproduce. Rather, a species or perceived sameness is really the result of the observer's incapacity to see life as a proliferation of difference, creating ever-different bodies, with each body being an affirmation of difference, not the repetition of the same. Genders, the supposed male and female kinds that underlie reproduction, are also an illusion. The reduction of sexuality to maleness and femaleness both belies the multiplicity of sexual difference and imposes one particular political structure – the nuclear family – on a human history that has yielded far greater assemblages.

The only way of depersonalising sexuality, for Deleuze and Guattari, is to destroy the gender binary, realising the 'thousand tiny sexes' that cannot be reduced to the Oedipal triangle (Deleuze and Guattari 1987, 213). This also requires abandoning the Levi-Straussian theory of kinship and incest. Life does not emerge from the family, and culture does not emerge from the negation of the mother. The 'mother' is the result of a history of political formations, formations that restrict the creative and revolutionary powers of difference.

Instead of affirming the rights of 'man' or humanity, Deleuze and Guattari refer to 'becoming-animal' – becoming other than human – and to 'becoming-imperceptible,' which would require having no perceivable kind or type, nothing to differentiate oneself from the flow of life (Deleuze and Guattari 1987, 294). They also refer to 'becoming-woman,' which, they argue, is the *beginning* of all becomings. If becoming-imperceptible is the goal of life this is because life, as creation and difference, is always radically other than any recognisable or perceived form; it is certainly *other than* any fixed gender identity. Becoming-woman is the beginning or key to this process because it is only in refusing the subject of 'man,' only in refusing the white, western, rational, acquisitive, voice-governed, world-surveying 'man' of good sense, that life can be freed from the internalised authority of 'the

subject.' Becoming-woman is, for Deleuze and Guattari, an affirmation of positive difference: not the differentiation of man from
woman, but difference that is not grounded on humanity (Deleuze and
Guattari 1987, 276). In their theorisation of 'becoming-woman,'
Deleuze and Guattari draw on the literature of Virginia Woolf (Deleuze
and Guattari 1987, 277). They insist that it is literature, and its creation
of specific *styles* – rather than some representative rational voice – that
will free us from our subjection to the myth of a general and universal
'humanity.' The radical task of feminism, then, would be *micro*political: it would not be a demand to include women within humanity, nor
to establish Woman as an alternative humanity. Rather, becoming-
woman would be the creation of voices, bodies and styles that affirm
difference.

Woman, here would not be different *from* man. Becoming-woman
would not be the affirmation of qualities that 'man' has defined as
'other.' Deleuze and Guattari's 'becoming-woman' would not be a feminism that affirmed care, nurturing, the passions, sympathy or ecological empathy. Micropolitics, they insist, is a form of non-recognition,
refusing any fixed kind. Whereas pre-modern societies had been
structured by binaries, such binaries were always recognised as emerging from a field of interacting forces and differences (Deleuze and
Guattari 1987, 212). In modernity, however, difference is reduced to
a single binary that explains all difference: the difference between
subject and object, also figured as man and woman:

> ...every politics is simultaneously a *macropolitics* and a *micropol-
> itics*. Take aggregates of the perception or feeling type: their molar
> organization, their rigid segmentarity, does not preclude the exist-
> ence of an entire world of unconscious micropercepts, unconscious
> affects, fine segmentations that grasp or experience different things,
> are distributed and operate differently. There is a micropolitics of
> perception, affection, conversation and so forth. If we consider the
> great binary aggregates, such as the sexes or classes, it is evident that
> they also cross over into molecular assemblages of a different
> nature, and that there is a double reciprocal dependency between
> them. For the two sexes imply a multiplicity of molecular combina-
> tions bringing into play not only the man in the woman and the
> woman in the man, but the relation of each to the animal, the plant,
> etc.: a thousand tiny sexes.
>
> (Deleuze and Guattari 1987, 213)

On the one hand, Deleuze and Guattari's work relies heavily on Levi-Strauss and Lacan, for they accept that the *modern* subject is constituted through the prohibition of incest. On the other hand, they insist that this Oedipal narrative, which supposedly explains repression, *is* repression. It is only by accepting that we are sexed subjects, subjected to the law of the phallus and forever alienated from the imagined and unattainable maternal plenitude, that we fail to see the politics of sexuality. All desire, they insist, is revolutionary, precisely because desire has no structure or identity (Deleuze and Guattari 1983, 379). Desire is just the expansion and differentiation of life that flows, connects and destroys any bounded identity. Desire is fully active not when its recognises itself – 'this is what I want because I am a woman' – but when it refuses all recognition:

> The revolutionary unconscious investment is such that desire, still in its own mode, cuts across the interest of the dominated, exploited classes, and causes flows to move that are capable of breaking apart both the segregations and their Oedipal applications – flows capable of hallucinating history, of reanimating the races in delirium, of setting continents ablaze. No, I am not of your kind, I am the outsider and the deterritorialized, 'I am of a race inferior for all eternity... I am a beast, a Negro.'
>
> (Deleuze and Guattari 1983, 105 [quoting Arthur Rimbaud's *Une Saison en Enfer*])

Deleuze and Guattari's extension and criticism of Levi-Strauss's anthropology raises the question of the limits of thinking of gender critically. Should we accept the historical story of the formation of man and woman from biological life, or should we go beyond this limited story to think of the emergence of the very ideal of anthropology, as a discipline that already assumes the being of 'man' as a signifying and cultural animal. In the next chapter we will return briefly to Lacan and Freud in order to negotiate the very problem of the anthropological and historical: how is it that we describe the origins of human beings from mere life, and does this story already require an image of sexuality? Is the idea of gender, as the human meaning 'we' give to our bodies, itself sexed – dependent upon the image of a body that is able to transcend itself?

6   Sexual Difference and Embodiment

Lacan, negativity and desire

Levi-Strauss's argument was anthropological. He sought to explain the emergence of culture, the seeming universality of gender binaries and the prohibition of incest. Why is incest always prohibited, and why is the law that prohibits always masculine? Anthropologists have both taken up and critically extended Levi-Strauss's insights, referring to the real conditions of culture that might explain why, despite historical, geographical and religious differences, there seems to be some differentiation, hierarchy and mythic figuration of male and female. Some anthropologists have also been critical of the assumed universality of the binary, insisting that there is often a third, in-between or neuter gender (Herdt 1993; Parker 2001, 326). But even if this is so, even if there were a frequency of third genders across cultures, one would still have to ask why such a term is situated between male and female. For many anthropologists, such cultural universals refer us back to our biological dependence (although Vicki Kirby and Pheng Cheah have recently challenged the idea of a static and self-present biology that precedes cultural inscription [Kirby 1997; Cheah 1996]). Culture and gender are the ways in which we organise natural sexual conditions. One can therefore bracket or preclude discussion of a supposedly natural sexuality and focus on gender as representation and mediation. Sexuality provides a minimal biological sense, which culture deploys for the purposes of power, ideology or domination. It is this idea of gender as the social reproduction of sexual facts that dominates Pierre Bourdieu's recent work on masculine domination (Bourdieu 2001). The anthropological problem is, therefore, concerned with how bodily life is rendered meaningful. Now it is just this idea of gender that is problematised by Lacan. Lacan is less concerned with the meaning we supposedly impose on our bodies – gender – and more concerned with the ways in which we imagine the relation between meaning, law, speech and sense on the one hand and our irreducible bodily life on the other. It is the fiction of imposition that produces the sexual body as an object of law, as that which speech must both regulate and desire. The story adopted by anthropologists – that there was a time before speech and law – is just the fantasy of origins that Lacan sets out to diagnose. Lacan's work therefore paves the way for recent criticisms of the anthropological paradigm: the idea that it is the human subject who is the origin of meaning, law and inscription.

Lacan does not rely upon biology so much as investigate how it is that we cope with the trauma of our detachment from the biological. For no story based on the needs of life, on the interests or striving of the organism, can explain why we subject ourselves to law or why our sexuality is structured by the desire to be loved by another. Like Deleuze and Guattari, Lacan begins from *the* political question: how is it that desire turns against itself? Again like Deleuze and Guattari, Lacan refuses to accept that there simply *is* something like, humanity, human nature, morality or human interest. Rather, he is interested in how the idea of such notions emerges. Lacan also agrees that the Oedipal structure has a history, and that the imagination of Woman as the barred object that would fulfil our *jouissance* has, in modernity, become increasingly privatised and dependent on fantasies of an object that stands in the way of our fulfilment (Lacan 1992, 176).

For Lacan, the prohibition of the mother, the image of the law of the father and the imagined lost object that has been abandoned for the sake of culture is a fantasy. Its truth can be verified not by looking at whether there really was some stage or origin of maternal plenitude that was subsequently prohibited or structured. The truth of the Oedipal fantasy is imaginary – that is, it is the fantasy that structures our relation to being. Insofar as we speak, our desires are subjected to a law of language. We therefore imagine: (a) that there was some moment of fulfilment beyond the law and prohibition; (b) that there was one – the Other – who exercised that prohibition and who holds the power or force that we lack; and (c) that the origin must lack that law and power, must lack that which we all recognise to be lawful. If the origin is imagined as maternal, then the law must be *other than* maternal, and must hold that which the mother lacks – the phallus. The phallus is, therefore, not an object or thing so much as that value which is held by the law that structures our relation to all things, including the original barred thing (*das Ding*, or the mother).

For Lacan, then, no desire is immediate. Desire is not need. Desire is structured and articulated in relation not just to others but through the Other of language. We imagine a point of joy or fulfilment beyond this submission, a desire that would not be structured and mediated through culture. This would be *jouissance*, a pleasure beyond the law that we only imagine from the law, and that we also assume to be other than the punishing father (Lacan 1992, 189).

Sexual difference, in this respect, is transcendental. We can only have a world or presence – something that is real and exists and remains the same – if we imagine a presence behind differences and language. Language only works as signification if it is the sign of some presence beyond the signifier, and so the signifier is also desire. The striving towards the not present, the anticipation of what the other wants to say to me is also an aiming at what will be presented. Only if we assume that the structures we inhabit and exchange – everything from language, fashion and gestures to commodities and artworks – relate to some underlying presence can any item in these structures make *sense*. When you speak to me I assume that your words signify some intent, that there is a *subject* behind what is said. I also assume that there is a world or presence beyond the mere flux of appearances. Without this assumption of presence, being or reality, speech would not be possible, nor would experience be experience *of* some world. We assume then, Lacan insists, that there is a truth or presence beyond the signifier (Lacan 1992, 150). More importantly, though, this necessary relation to a presence from which we are necessarily distanced or alienated is lived through a sexual imaginary. That which lies behind culture, signification, structure and the law is imagined as Woman. The prohibiting law is imagined as the law of the father. Lacan therefore provides an analysis of the sexual imaginary. What is *necessary* is that we assume some ultimate being or presence; what Lacan explains is the (embodied and sexual) way in which we think this highly metaphysical and abstract relation.

The body

Freud frequently insisted that the child is not simply born as a subject or already formed ego. Indeed, Freud, like Lacan after him, assumes mobile drives or processes *from which* points of relative stability, such as the ego emerge. Indeed, in *Beyond the Pleasure Principle* Freud describes life as having two tendencies. First, there is the erotic tendency to connect and form wholes (which he describes, metaphorically, through the image of male and female halves reuniting to achieve identity). Second is the tendency towards death or dissolution of all closed identities in order to return to some ultimate unity or origin (Freud 1991, 276). In order to have a self who orders and recognises his own experiences over and against a world that is assumed to be outside and other, something like an 'ego' or self as object needs to be formed from the chaotic drives of life. For both Freud and Lacan this genesis of the human self is *sexual* precisely because the boundary between self and other, or self and world, is produced through desire and fantasy, and in relation not just to other bodies but to desired body parts. I become a subject or 'I' only through my relation to an other who addresses me, only when I am installed in a system of signifiers – only when something interrupts my life with a sense that is beyond what is immediately present.

To begin with, Freud insisted on the ways in which biological need organises the body, and relates the body to other bodies. The relation between self and other, for example, begins with the mouth of the child and the breast of the mother. When the child is deprived of the breast it feels need and separation; when the child then *imagines* that breast in order to deal with need, something like a rudimentary self as object is formed. The ego or self begins with the internalisation and fantasy of an external object; the self begins by incorporating an aspect of the other, and so the self begins with a complex narcissism. The self is gradually built up of these bordering experiences: all the signifiers addressed to me from the other, all the looks, touches and sounds of the mother address me from a world that I must make sense of, and that then constitutes me as a subject. Furthermore, the rudimentary relation between self and other has also to be formed through body boundaries, where experience gradually differentiates an inside self from an outside world. The ego, Freud insists, is first and foremost a bodily ego; the idea I have of my 'self' comes about both from the image of the other's body as some type of wholeness and the image of myself as seen by the other.

Many feminists have drawn on this insight to insist on the importance of the body and bodily difference. It is not the case, for example, that we have a human psyche that happens to be in a body. Rather, the self or 'I' in language can only function if some primary formation of a bodily boundary allows us to establish a surface of the self in relation to an outside world. Perhaps the most influential and groundbreaking work in this area was undertaken by Elizabeth Grosz. Grosz's early work drew on the Lacanian notion of the imaginary (Grosz 1990). But she also extended the insights of French feminist critics, such as Julia Kristeva and Luce Irigaray, to radicalise Lacan and the politics of sexual difference (Grosz 1989). We have already seen how Kristeva argues that the speaking subject must also have its ground in the body, that the differences of language are formed from sound and rhythmic differences traced by the child's voice in a quite physical way. Kristeva did, though, accept the account of the subject as emerging from a feminine and maternal pre-symbolic. Grosz went further and insisted that taking the body seriously would require an entirely different understanding of sexual difference. If it is the case that the abstract 'I' of speech and embodiment must be formed from some physical image, then different bodies may well have different modes of subjectivity (Grosz 1994). This yields two possibilities. First, one might imagine an alternative, non-phallic and autonomous imaginary that would be thought from the female body. If the mother is not seen as lacking a phallus, then the structure within which we speak and relate to others might take on a different morphology. Second, if the ego is formed by incorporating an image of the self, then subjectivity will depend upon, and be created through bodily comportment.

For Lacan, however, there has only been one imaginary, that which constitutes the self in opposition to the maternal body, that which divides a subject of speech and law, from a body beyond the law. In Lacan's defence we might note that he is analysing, and not justifying, a cultural imaginary. Anyone who consumes literature would have to admit that Western literature, at least in its canonical form, does seem to operate with just such an imaginary. English Romantic poetry, for example, presents the 'I' of the poem as lamentably detached from an original maternal plenitude; it also imagines this plenitude as necessarily other than speech and sociality. Further, and more importantly, the desire to regain this plenitude is abandoned in favour of the active poetic representation of the origin, and – in a final moment of resolution – the origin is imagined as given only through its poetic presentation *as lost*. One way of approaching this structure of the Romantic lyric is to say that it confirms Lacan's account of the way in which we imagine our relation to reality. Another approach is to suggest that the dominance of such a myth can be explained by the fact that we read male writers, and that women authors of the time did not see nature and the subject in such dichotomous terms. Even so, to read Romanticism requires that one sees gender, not as a metaphor used here and there, but as a structuring principle. Without the opposition between speaking subject and a material/maternal nature the lyric would have no dynamic. The question is whether this dynamic is transcendental, as Lacan suggests, or whether one should strive to find, or establish, alternative imaginaries. If we accept, as Grosz insists, that there is necessarily *some* imaginary, or shape within which thought and vision takes place, and that this imaginary begins from the body, then art and literature and their distribution of sexual difference gain a significance well beyond concerns once confined to feminism or 'women's liberation.' For the character and structure of the body – morphology – would have a determining role in judgement and reason.

What unites Lacan, his feminist critics and theorists of the body, such as Grosz, is the insistence that our logical, rational and subjective being is made possible through the imagination of a body, and that this body has a sex. As Lacan insists, the one necessary and transcendental opposition that underlies all experience is that between presence and absence. We must have a notion of 'not-all,' that the world we see is the signifier of some fuller presence which is not yet presented. We establish this original border, between presence and absence, between the fullness of being and the 'not-all,' through bodily relations. Without the imagination of a presence that is other than what is presented we could have neither language nor experience. I must imagine both the other's subjectivity beyond presented signifiers in order to have meaningful speech, and I must also imagine a presence beyond my perceptions, an absent present, in order to have experience. This relation between presence and absence emerges, Freud had insisted, through the mastery of one's relation to the maternal body. In *Beyond the Pleasure Principle* Freud describes his grandson throwing a cotton-reel to and from his cradle, to the alternate chanting of 'there/gone.' Freud explains that the infant is mastering his relation to his mother. The cotton reel represents the mother he has lost, and in this act of representation the infant establishes a border between himself and the world he signifies. The first lost object is imagined as the lost mother, and the ego is the self that can master and represent that object (Freud [1920] 1984).

Lacan insists, following Freud's description of the production of self and presence, that he is not offering an ontology. Lacan is not giving us a theory of *what is* or Being, but how we think or relate to Being: that in addition to the 'One' of Being there is the 'not-One' of human questions and desire. Lacan is describing the way in which we imagine Being, the fantasy of that which lies behind all the differences and signs we are presented with. We imagine this lost presence as maternal, and the law that separates us from that origin as paternal. Our imaginary is structured this way because of our embodiment. We use the body, its parts and morphology, to construct a metaphysical fantasy. The phallus is the transcendental signifier, the value that inaugurates the system of exchange or the Symbolic order. Only with the fantasy of a value that is other than immediate life can one live the submission to culture. The phallus is, therefore, not a presence but the signification of presence; the law that controls the relation to presence. The phallic signifier mediates our relation to lack.

Understandably, there have been a large number of feminists, anthropologists and theorists of gender who have argued that the law need not necessarily be represented as paternal, and that the opposition between nature and culture need not be figured as the negation of that which lacks the phallus. Juliet Mitchell, in *Psychoanalysis and Feminism*, originally argued that the incest prohibition was universal and helped to explain the subordination of women across cultures (Mitchell 1974). The only way in which one can challenge gender binaries is to go deeper than arguments about rights and equalities, and confront the very construction of sexual difference that emerges with all culture and system. This would mean confronting the cultural fantasy of an original, lost and negated feminine, and it would also mean restructuring the relations of the unconscious. One of the key questions for the analysis of gender is whether another imaginary is possible: is the relation between presence and absence, or nature and culture necessarily figured by the Oedipal triangle? And can there be other morphologies; could a non-phallic body produce a different logic?

Luce Irigaray and the positive feminine

One way of moving beyond the seeming Oedipal deadlock of Lacan's insistence on the transcendental status of sexual difference has been to deconstruct the relation between the imaginary and the symbolic. According to Lacan, the symbolic as language, system or law is radically formal and impersonal. It is the experience of system – any system – that creates the illusion or 'imaginary' of an originally lost presence. And we imagine our loss of this presence as castration, as the imposition of a value which the mother does not have, but whose integrity the law holds. Whereas the Symbolic is the pure system of signifiers – our necessary submission to language, culture or the Other – the Imaginary is the fantasy through which we live that system. We imagine what is other than the law as maternal, and imagine the Other as paternal. The very idea of the imaginary is based on the dependence of thought or ideas on some figure or signifier; we do not just think abstract relations and logic; our thought is located within and dependent upon concrete images, such that body parts are our first significa-tion of basic relations such as presence and absence.

One of the challenges to the Lacanian Imaginary is that *other* bodies might allow for a different logic. Lacan assumes that the Imaginary is structured by the relation between self and other, presence and absence. Now there are two ways of challenging this imaginary. The first is to establish alternative imaginaries. Why should what is other than culture be presented as feminine? And why should the feminine subject's position be maternal? The second, and related challenge, would aim for a different logic: not a subject–object logic, where what is other than the self is absent and negative, but where the self becomes what it is only by relating to and recognising the positive difference of an other. Lacan and Freud base their account of the emergence of the ego in relation to the mother as the first object. Lacan then argues that the feminine, or woman, can never herself be a subject who signifies; she will always be imagined as that which is abandoned in order to accede to the system of signification: 'A woman is a symptom' (Lacan 1982, 168).

One of the most challenging criticisms of Lacan has come from the French feminist psychoanalyst, Luce Irigaray. Irigaray accepts that the self or subject is constructed through a sexual imaginary, that the speaking self or 'I' position must both relate to an other, and have some bodily image of that relation. Irigaray also concedes that the Lacanian theory of the subject is an accurate description of the subject of Western metaphysics. For the subject has always been defined as that which represents, gives order to, actively forms, and creates itself in opposition to a matter that has no being, existence or force outside of its subjective representation (Irigaray 1985, 136). For Irigaray, Plato establishes philosophy as the true idea or form of matter (Irigaray 1985, 151). The subject of philosophy is produced as the negation and mastery of mere appearance in favour of a logic and truth that remains present and lawful above and beyond the body. Freud, similarly, assumes that one becomes a subject by imagining a law and presence, a system and logic, other than the opacity of matter; it is the ego's image of itself as the master of absence and difference that allows a self to be formed in opposition to the mother (Irigaray 1985, 33). Lacan's emphasis on the signifier as the system within which sex and gender are constituted repeats and affirms a Western logic that has always privileged knowledge and representation.

Irigaray accuses this picture of being sexed. This self-constituting subject of philosophy is created through the repression and negation of the feminine. Furthermore, the feminine is, at present, thought of as nothing more than an effect of this negation. The feminine, the maternal and the material, have always been defined as that which is given form, truth and logic by the male subject. Indeed, it is not that there are sexually different bodies – male and female – with Western thought privileging the male over the female. Rather, there has according to Irigaray been *no* sexual difference (Irigaray 1985, 28). The feminine is nothing more than a fantasy of the (male) subject. The male–female binary is, in fact, a polarity or hierarchy with only *one* term: the phallic subject. To be a subject is to be other than matter, to be that which forms, represents and systematises a matter which in itself is formless, inert, passive and *other*. There can be only one system, to which we are all subjected, and matter is merely the outside, negation or effect of that system.

> Matter – feebler far than the Soul for any exercise of power, and possessing no phase of the Authentic Existents, not even in possession of its own falsity – lacks the very means of manifesting itself, utter void as it is; it becomes the means by which other things appear, but it cannot announce its own presence.
>
> (Irigaray 1985, 176)

Irigaray, however, does not accept the argument that the imagined feminine passive ground before all system and law is an effect or mythic 'otherness' to all law; she wants to see sexual difference positively. Indeed, any position which sees gender as nothing more than the social or cultural representation and differentiation of an otherwise undifferentiated matter repeats the Western phallic binary which opposes self-present and self-constructing thought to a matter which is nothing more than that which awaits formation. Despite the fact that she was often accused of essentialism (Moi 1985), Irigaray actually works against the standard logic of essence; her work is *materialist* rather than essentialist because she is concerned with the genesis of relations and kinds from physicality (Schor 1994). Conventionally, essence is what makes something what it is, in itself, before all relations. On this picture, there could be an essential sex or femininity, and then the way we relate to that femininity in culture and history. To say that there are essences, in this sense, is to argue that there simply are identities, which then bear a relation to each other. Truth and subjectivity are notions grounded on the logic of essence. The subject is he who can represent and discover the essence of the thing, and can do so without contributing or altering anything of his own being, and without being affected by the object he knows and represents (Irigaray 1985, 291).

Irigaray's *Speculum of the Other Woman* reads the history of philosophy and psychoanalysis to look at the ways in which the 'subject' has been formed as a fantasy of a certain type of body. A body that is nothing more than a power to represent, order and give form to the world must present itself as other than matter – a matter that remains the same, and whose essence or form can only be brought to light and actuality through the subject. Other subjects are also, therefore, similarly set over against this unchanging matter, and are therefore mirror images of this one universal subject. The subject has always been, Irigaray insists, the negation of matter. The subject produces and differentiates itself from that which, in itself, is without thought, act, force, difference, or power. The matter that is other than the subject is non-being, merely the potential to be represented. What is other than the subject, particularly when that subject is seen as active construction, representation and signification, is merely the subject turning back upon itself. What is other than the subject ultimately serves as a medium for the subject's own self-reflection and self-recognition. The subject cannot acknowledge a *different subject*, for subjectivity is established as that power which differentiates, and brings distinct essences to form and actuality:

> Now, if this ego is to be valuable, some 'mirror' is needed to reassure it and re-insure it of its value. Woman will be the foundation for this specular duplication, giving man back 'his' image and repeating it as the 'same.' If an *other* image, an *other* mirror were to intervene, this inevitably would entail the risk of mortal crisis. Woman will therefore be this sameness – or at least its mirror image – and, in her role of mother, she will facilitate the repetition of the same, in contempt for her difference. Her own sexual difference.
>
> (Irigaray 1985, 54)

Irigaray's autonomous and positive feminine tries to overcome this non-relation by using the traditionally negated feminine as the beginning of a new mode of subjectivity. She begins by accepting Lacan's notion that there is no sexual relation and that the feminine occurs only as the fantasy of the unrepresentable, but she then goes on to imagine what this unrepresentable otherness might itself enable us to imagine. The male subject becomes a self by being other than mere life. Through the negation of life, birth and generation, the male subject establishes a logic of being and truth that remains essentially the same and re-presentable. To imagine a subject who is different from this logic of self-recognition is to imagine a subject who realises herself through difference. Whereas as the logic of male subjectivity is tied up with essences, for the male subject's being remains the same regardless of its encounters and relations, another logic would recognise that the subject can achieve its identity only through its relation to an other. The female subject can be imagined as the thought of one who relates to the other through generation, life, otherness, and the body. If the male body has been imagined as that which gives form to and determines matter, the female body can be imagined as fecundity, difference, becoming and relation before form and determination – as an openness to otherness, as the relation to a world that is not determined in advance as representable, quantifiable and a mirror of the self. The female subject would become other than itself, take on its own mode of becoming, only in *not* knowing what is other than itself.

Instead of assuming that subjectivity is the representation and bringing to light of an inert objectivity, Irigaray asks how we might imagine two *genres* of subjectivity (Irigaray 1993a, 61). Whereas gender (on its usual understanding) is the differentiation of an otherwise homogenous matter, Irigaray's *genres* are really distinct kinds that must form a relation and that have no proper relation – such as the Oedipal triangle – that organises their being:

> Sexed desire, sexual desire, should not have its end, its effectivity, in the family as such, nor in the State, nor in religion, for then it perverts the truth and spirit of the community. Sexual desire demands a realization appropriate to its matter, its nature. This realization takes place in the body proper and in the couple that man forms with the other sex – woman. This couple forms the elementary social community. It is where sensible desire must become potentially universal culture, where the gender of the man and of the woman may become the model of male human kind or of

female human kind while keeping to the singular task of being
this man or *this* woman. In realizing the transition from nature to
culture, from singular to the universal, from sexual attraction to
actualizing gender, the couple formed by the man and woman
ensures the salvation of the community and the conservation of
nature as macro- and microcosm, as human species and gender.

(Irigaray 1996, 28)

A subject who *related to* another subject would no longer assume
a ground of consensus or law within which we are located. Irigaray
tries to imagine sexual difference as a productive relation; the relation
to a different body allows me to recognise the specificity of my body,
allows me to feel the specificity of my way of relating to what is not
myself. If two bodies were to relate as two modalities of subjectivity
then the address to the other would not be able to determine, in
advance, a common norm of thought and logic; it would be the
constitution of community from singular bodies, not the determination
of bodies from the point of one logic.

As an example, we might think of a practical problem in feminist
politics. On the one hand, women need to work against their exclusion
from the domain of rights, reason and subjective recognition. On the
other hand, any demand for inclusion risks subsuming women within
the already constituted norm of the subject. If this subject has been
formed through a phallic imaginary, as a pure and universal reason
detached from the body and partiality, then how can the bodies of
women really be recognised? A body capable of pregnancy, for
example, can neither regard her body as a fully free expression of itself,
nor regard the body to which it will give birth as definitively other
(Diprose 1994, 115). Indeed, if the masculine imaginary has established the subject as pure self-transcendence, freed from all natural
determination, then the recognition of an *other* subjectivity would not
be the passive maternal body beyond all culture and thought, but a
subject who has being and specificity only through the force and
potential of its body. Here, Irigaray's work challenges a trend in social
theory, literary theory and cultural studies. Why are words like 'essentialism,' 'biologism,' 'determinism' or even 'sexism' pejoratives? They
are because to see oneself as affected by the body is to see oneself as
deprived of autonomy, where autonomy refers to active self-creation,
freed from all otherness. If however, one can only think or have a self
because one has a body, and because this body is different from
another body, then we might need to reassess the relation between

subjects and embodiment. Irigaray's positive and autonomous feminine defines autonomy, not as the capacity to give a law to oneself, but as a capacity to become aware of the difference and potential of one's sex. Being a subject requires recognising one's difference, and difference requires relating to an other. Subjectivity is not the disembodied mind's representation of the world; it is an ongoing negotiation between a body as a series of encounters, affects, sensations and images, and other bodies who relate to that world differently. The world is not an object for the subject to encounter; the world is always given to me as a world with others, others who have different bodies and therefore a different world.

For Irigaray, then, we must begin from *at least* two sexes. The male–female binary of Western thought emerges from *one* body and *one* fantasy, the body that is other than a maternal body. To create another sex would be to imagine the feminine, not as that which is given value through the exchange and representation of men, but as *a body that becomes*. Embodiment would be neither that which is *represented* as gendered, nor some neutral matter that a subject inhabits. To affirm the feminine positively is to affirm a positive experience of the body, where the body allows one to relate to others, to have a world of touch and sensation, to realise the difference of other subjects, and to acknowledge that thinking is never pure act and representation but is grounded in a specific way of relating to the world (Irigaray 1996, 37).

One of the questions and objections directed to Irigaray's work has been her sustained reliance upon the male–female binary that she also criticises. On the one hand, Irigaray recognises that Western thought has only acknowledged one sexual subject, with the 'feminine' being an otherness constructed from the myth of masculine self-fathering. On the other hand, Irigaray argues that only by establishing the *feminine* sexed subject can this logic be undone. One way of defending Irigaray here would be to say that if Western thought has always produced the feminine as its imagined other, then it would be radical, and perhaps necessary, to begin another voice precisely from this negated otherness. If it is the gender binary that has been metaphysical thought's primary trope, then only the radicalisation of *this* binary can begin a rethinking of oppositional logics. Irigaray's work has often been read as a 'mime' of philosophy (Whitford 1991). One cannot appeal to an essential and already existing feminine, but one can adopt all those positions and voices repressed by the philosophical tradition *as feminine* in order to expose its supposed rationality. One

cannot write as a woman, as though femininity were already an independent and autonomous essence. One can, though, write *through* the
voice of the male fantasy, exposing it as a fantasy, and thereby create
the feminine speaking position as that which relates to, plays with, and
differs from its masculine other.

This is, indeed, what Irigaray's *Speculum of the Other Woman* does.
She adopts the voice of Plato, of Descartes, of Freud and of Heidegger,
showing the ways in which that voice produces itself as other than
feminine. The voice of reason that presents itself as the disembodied
voice from nowhere is exposed as masculine through its dependence
on an imagined feminine. The feminine is, here, just that capacity to
think the body and difference of the other, just that refusal of the
universal voice of man.

Irigaray's positive femininity raises two general questions. As already
indicated, some critics have questioned her commitment to the
feminine as the other of the masculine voice of reason (Butler 1993, 49;
Hope 1997, 208). Ethics, she argues, requires two genders, for only if
the other subject is of a different sex am I capable of recognising a
different opening to the world, a different modality of experience, and
a different passage from the immanence of the body to the transcendence of what is other than the body. However, one could ask whether
Irigaray's appeal to *sex* as the defining difference closes down the
possible modes of otherness. Why should these two genres be male
and female? We will consider this problem of the primacy of gender
and the sexual binary in the following chapter on queer theory.

7 Sexuality and Queer Theory

Michel Foucault and the history of sexuality

We have already seen that for Deleuze and Guattari the notion of a personal and private sexuality that is defined within the Oedipal triangle of mother–father–child is a historical and political phenomenon. Michel Foucault's *History of Sexuality* also explores the way in which the discourse of sexuality from the nineteenth century onwards provides new ways for power to operate upon bodies. Like Deleuze and Guattari, Foucault reverses the Freudian concept of repression. Whereas conventional readings of Freud stress that sexuality is repressed *because* it disrupts social order and constraint, Foucault argues that the idea of repression produces a sexuality that allows the social order to operate. It is by talking about, and studying, a sexuality that is there to be revealed that discourses, such as psychoanalysis, produce a whole range of perversions and norms (Foucault 1981, 36–37). The idea that there is a radically disruptive sexual energy that would threaten sociality is precisely what allows the practices of psychiatry, sociology, sexology and criminology to take hold on bodies. The concept of repression produces a particular mode of subjectivity and interiority. Whereas sexual relations were at one time explicitly political – say, in epochs dominated by kinship and models of restriction on alliance – sexuality is now defined as *other than* political, and thereby creates a border between the inner, sexual and pre-social subject on the one hand, and a law that must regulate that anti-social sexuality on the other (Foucault 1981, 109). The supposed liberation of sexuality is therefore one more way of confirming the modern construction of the self as a sexual subject, a subject whose desire, gender and orientation are essential and determining. We have produced sexuality as a substance to be known, rather than as a series of practices whose force and relations we might question.

According to Foucault, we usually understand the discovery, explor-
ation, affirmation and liberation of our personal sexuality as the lifting
of social repression. We assume, he argues, a *negative* notion of power:
that we have a sexual subjectivity that morality *then* represses. For
Foucault however the contrary is the case. Power is positive and
we only have an inner sexual subjectivity *because* of the discourses of
sexuality, such as psychoanalysis, therapy and – we might add, following Foucault – certain forms of feminism, new age philosophy and
popular self-help manuals which enable us to 'find' ourselves
(Foucault 1981, 131).

Crucial to Foucault's criticism of the concept of repression and the
negative understanding of power is his critique of normalisation. It
is the thought of power as something that comes along to repress,
misrepresent or conceal our *real sexual selves*, that produces that very
self we supposedly uncover and interpret. And, as in the discourses of
psychoanalysis, this real self we uncover is determined beforehand
through its way of being known. By analysing the self through the
Oedipal triangle the self is produced as that which must have wanted,
but abandoned, an original maternal plenitude. It is, therefore, not the
prohibition of incest that produces the self and divides it from its
maternal ground. The self is produced through the discourses of
knowledge, such as those of Levi-Strauss, Freud and Lacan, who
believe they can uncover and interpret the ground from which the self
emerges. In contrast, Foucault insists that there is no self, nature, subjectivity, or humanity, *before* the discourses and relations of knowledge
and power. Further, different modes of knowledge and power produce
different modes of self (Foucault 1981, 100).

Foucault's history of sexuality therefore looks at different epochs or
'historical apriori': different ways in which the relation between
knowledge and power was configured. For example, we have already
seen that for pre-modern accounts of gender, the different kinds and
orders of the world were discovered by 'man' who was one being
among others. The ground of knowledge, or the space across which
distinctions were drawn and understood, was the order of nature. By
contrast, modern knowledge produces the subject as the substratum
of knowledge and power; it is the subject – the subject of language,
sexuality, consciousness or culture – who is the ground and origin of all
distinction and difference. Human life, in ancient times, understood
itself as part of a general system of order and regulation. Self-knowledge
for the Stoics, for example, was not concerned with discovering one's

personal and inner self. Self-examination was a way of ordering one's body and desires in order to create oneself as a harmonious whole. Knowledge was a form of self-creation, of recognising what can and cannot be altered, of realising one's position in a broader political and natural order. Crucial to this ancient relation between what was said in the name of knowledge, and the self who spoke with the authority of knowledge, was a radically different mode of sexual discourse. One discussed sexuality, not in order to discover an inner self before all relations of power and sociality; regulation of one's sexual self, and the discussion of this regulation, was itself a political practice, a way of ordering oneself and presenting oneself *as ordered*. Sexuality was part of a larger concern with political order (Foucault 1986, 84). One should control one's desires, regulate one's passions and reflect on relations among bodies; sexuality was as much about managing slaves and one's household as it was about forming one's self.

More importantly, one's sexuality was not defined according to sexual difference or sexual orientation: whether one favoured sex with boys or women was not a defining feature. The self in this discourse did not 'have' a gender, nor did he 'have' *a* sexuality – bisexual, heterosexual or homosexual. Rather, the way in which sexuality was governed was connected with discourses of mastery, self-government and social relations. It was assumed that this self was male, but this had nothing to do with gender, sexual difference or intrinsic properties; men were political masters, and neither women nor slaves, by virtue of their political position, could occupy this discourse of mastery. Men could be either active and penetrating agents, or passive and receptive objects – with the latter being a clearly devalued position, precluding one from being an ideal citizen (Parker 2001, 321). Not only was the gender of one's partner not a defining feature, and so there was no homosexual/heterosexual divide, it was also the case that sexuality was not *explained* by one's body. Sexuality, like other political relations, was about power and governance, about those who could form themselves and master others. If one was a slave by nature, or if – as for women – one was excluded from the mastery and self-management of ideal citizen-ship, this had to do with relations among bodies, about who could take up active positions, about who could form themselves and their bodies with a sense of the whole of life. Today, we do not, or not often, regard *political* identity and persuasion as something expres-sive of one's natural and given self; we do not think of ourselves as conservative or liberal by nature. We may see all sorts of factors, intentional or otherwise, going in to how we vote; but these do not *precede, cause and underlie our social being, for they are our social being*. The same was the case for ancient sexuality; sexuality was something someone did; it was neither caused by biological being, nor constructed and imposed as some mandatory social identity. Sexuality was a practice, not a substance:

> The relation to truth was a structural, instrumental, and ontological condition for establishing the individual as a moderate subject leading a life of moderation; it was not an epistemological condition enabling the individual to recognize himself in his singularity as a desiring subject and to purify himself of the desire that was brought to life...
>
> Through the *logos*, through reason and the relation to truth that governed it, such a life was committed to the maintenance and reproduction of an ontological order....
>
> (Foucault 1988, 89)

Foucault's history is a complex account of the ways in which sexuality intersected with other discourses in order to create new subjects of knowledge. Christianity, for example, with all its modes of confession, its notion of the corruption of the flesh, and its emphasis on one's personal *soul*, was crucial in the formation of modern 'man.' One of the key shifts of modes of knowledge in the production of 'man' was the gradual and uneven move from knowledge as active, as a way of managing and forming the self, to knowledge as reactive, a way of uncovering and discovering the self. Foucault saw medical discourses, criminology and the human sciences as contributing to the production of man as an object to be known, and once this subject of 'man' was produced through *knowledge* it would also become possible to establish a normal humanity, with its natural sexuality, as a moral authority (Foucault 1981, 144). The ancient production of the masculine subject of mastery was explicitly political, with relations between the self and others presented as the outcome of acts, decisions and an operating power. By contrast, the modern production of 'man' as a political animal situates sexuality before knowledge and power, as that which needs to be known and regulated.

Foucault situates the production of the subject through the discourses of sexuality in a much broader history that relates modes of knowledge to power. The discourses of sexuality, such as psychoanalysis, therapy, sexology and fertility control, are part of a much broader *episteme* (or network of knowledges), which produces 'man' as an object to be known. Recall that for Deleuze and Guattari, power, prior to modernity, was explicit and positive: bodies were literally marked and manifestly subject to all forms of force and cruelty. The law was clearly an external body, a body that acted positively – operating, often with an open enjoyment of terror – on the bodies it governed. In modernity, however, bodies are not controlled by external and explicit forces but subject themselves to an authority that they seemingly recognise as their own: I do this because I am human. Now in this movement inward, power shifts from being explicit, active and positive force – an obvious contest among desiring bodies – to a reactive inter-pretation of *who we are*. By creating an underlying sexuality that we must recognise, uncover and obey, we are, according to Foucault, normalised. There have always been, and must always be, operations of power on bodies. For bodies are just powers to do and be in certain ways, and bodies achieve identity and specificity only in relation with other powers. Indeed, the idea of a human world that is *then* subjected to power – the idea of bodies before all power – is not only an idea that Foucault rejects, it is also the idea that underpins normalisation: 'Through the themes of health, progeny, race, the future of the species, the vitality of the social body, power spoke *of* sexuality and *to* sexual-ity; the latter was not a mark and a symbol, it was an object and a target' (Foucault 1981, 147).

Against this, Foucault insists that bodies become through power. Bodies are what they do, and *who we are* is always produced through the way we manage, regulate and order our selves. Man or humanity is not something lying in wait to be known; it is through knowledge practices and the problems that we set ourselves that we take on a particular form of selfhood. Today, for example, we could see sexu-ality as a mode of knowledge and a style of problems that creates who we are and the power relations that determine our polity: is there a genetic homosexuality; is sexual difference essential; is bisexuality normal; is there a female brain? We see sexuality as something we have, something we can know, something that tells us who we are, *and* something that can be medically managed. Sexuality, Foucault argues, has shifted from being an explicit form of self-management and regulation, to being a form of self-interpretation and public management. By producing sexuality as a substance – as that which precedes relations of power and discourse – we also establish sexuality as something to be known.

One of the main consequences of Foucault's history of sexuality is the challenge it presents to what Judith Butler has referred to as the 'heterosexual matrix.' The explanation of one's gender as emerging from familial relations assumes that sexuality is sexual identity, a gender or orientation, and not what one does. Such an explanation also assumes that gender identity is defined by the objects towards which desire is directed. One becomes a male sexual subject by abandoning the mother and identifying with the father. To be a subject one must be other than natural/maternal and the negation of the maternal is the paternal. Not only does Foucault show that sexuality was once thought of, not as defined by the object of desire but as given through the management of desire, he also challenges the very mode of psychoanalytic and anthropological knowledge that explains the emergence of subjectivity. Discourses of anthropology, ethnography, psychoanalysis and other human sciences are, Foucault insists, ways of producing the 'subject' as some distinct substance – as other than nature. By interpreting subjectivity as the underlying condition for language, culture, knowledge and discourse we refuse the positivity of power; we imagine that underlying the various structures and differences of various cultures and epochs there is some underlying condition. The sexual explanation of the subject in both psychoanalysis and ethnography – that the subject emerges from the negation of the mother – establishes the explanation of subjectivity and the condition of sexuality as the ultimate interpretive horizon (Foucault 1981, 113). Against this, Foucault argues that we should look at discourse and power positively. How do the discourses of sexuality produce the subjects they supposedly reveal? If sexuality is not something that is lying in wait to be interpreted, behind all culture and history, and if there is no position outside the relations and forces of knowledge, discourse and action, what sort of force does the concept of the sexual subject produce?

Performativity

One consequence of the modern discourse of sexuality is that sex is produced both as a natural biological phenomenon of 'life,' and as a substance that precedes actions and relations. Judith Butler has tried to deconstruct this supposedly underlying sexual substance by pointing out that the self is nothing more than a series of actions – a performance – and that we then retroactively imagine that one performed this way *because* one was male, female, homosexual and so on. Butler's own project differs from that of Foucault, for whereas Foucault turned back to ancient thought to insist that one need not posit a subject and sexuality behind action, Butler argues that the we cannot avoid the logic of subjection (Butler 1997, 9). All we can do is work critically with the systems that produce us as subjects. There can be no historical point, for Butler, outside the logic of the signifier that creates its 'before' or outside. Our very existence as speaking subjects locates us within a system to which we are subjected; we cannot step outside this system but we can destabilise it from within (Butler 1993, 98). We can do so, by disrupting the heterosexual matrix. If it is the case that we necessarily posit a subject behind the speech-act, and a sexuality behind one's social gender, then one needs to expose this supposedly underlying ground *as an effect*. If, for example, one takes the conventional signifi- cation of femininity – all the clothes, movements and comportments of the constructed female body – and acts them out from a male body, then the performance of gender is exposed *as a performance* and is thereby disengaged from any imagined underlying sexuality:

> The parodic repetition of gender exposes as well the illusion of gender identity as an intractable depth and inner substance. As the effects of a subtle and politically enforced performativity, gender is an 'act,' as it were, that is open to splittings, self-parody, self-criticism, and those hyperbolic exhibitions of 'the natural' that, in their very exaggeration, reveal its fundamentally phantasmatic status.
>
> (Butler 1999, 187)

For Butler, then, the exemplary body – the body that presents sexual politics in its true workings – is the body of the drag-queen, a body that at once performs and creates a gender quite explicitly, but also does so from a body that is sexed as *other than* the signifiers or actions it carries out. Whereas heterosexual 'man' presents his actions and performances as effects of his humanity, as an expression of *who he is*, the drag-queen disrupts this causal relation, exposing gender to be that signifier which leads us to assume an underlying sexuality:

> ...drag is not unproblematically subversive. It serves a subversive function to the extent that it reflects the mundane impersonations by which heterosexually ideal genders are performed and naturalized and undermines their power by virtue of effecting that exposure....
>
> (Butler 1993, 231)

Butler's insistence that natural sexuality is an effect of signification, not its cause, aims to be strictly immanent. Butler refuses the idea of sex as a prior substance, refuses a matter that achieves its expression in social relations and language; she also refuses the axis of interpretation – that the dress and actions of a body are signs of its sexuality. It is not that the body acts and performs in order to signify what it is; the body itself is nothing outside its actions and significations. Sexuality, accordingly, is an effect of a system that reads bodies as effects of their underlying matter. Matter is not, according to Butler, that which precedes action. *Matter acts.* From these actions and performances we imagine, falsely, some underlying inert materiality – some subjective ground or essence – that is the distinct cause of action.

> Insofar as matter appears in these cases to be invested with a certain capacity to originate and to compose that for which it also supplies the principle of intelligibility, then matter is clearly defined by a certain power of creation and rationality that is for the most part divested from the more modern empirical deployments of the term. To speak within these classical contexts of *bodies that matter* is not an idle pun, for to be material means to materialize, where the principle of that materialization is precisely what 'matters' about that body, its very intelligibility. In this sense, to know the significance of something is to know how and why it matters, where 'to matter' means at once 'to materialize and 'to mean'.
>
> (Butler 1993, 32)

One of the main problems of Butler's approach lies in her rigorous insistence that what we interpret as the ground of the action – the natural sexual body – is a fantasmatic effect. For if it is the case that the body's matter is nothing more than its act, produced through its signifiers – if sex is an effect of gender – how does the drag-queen perform or display a disjunction between the performed or signified gender and the preceding body? One way to answer this question is through Butler's own reference to parody. All sexuality is produced through performance, but for the most part this performance is not seen as performance but as expression – as the sign of an underlying body. In drag, however, it is not that there is some ground – the natural body – from which the performance differs; it is that the exaggeration of performance exposes performance as performance. Excessive make-up, overly emphasised breasts, impossibly high heels, ridiculously long eye-lashes and outrageously lavish evening gowns: all these gestures take the marks of femininity and extend them to the point where they can be noticed *as* marked. In addition to parody, one might also think of the techniques of pastiche, or the layering of incongruent styles. If it is the case that our current social structure performs bodies as the expression of two distinct sexes, then a drag act that combined masculine and feminine signifiers would destroy the supposedly natural ground of sexuality – a diva with a moustache, a ball-gown over a hairy chest, an Elvis costume over an hour-glass figure, all these would disrupt the conventions that pass 'naturally' from body to gender. To defend Butler, then, we would have to differentiate those instances of drag that emphasise the *disjunction* between sex and signified gender, or that emphasise the difference between natural body and clothed gender, from drag that takes over and plays upon the body it adorns. Films like *Tootsie, Mrs Doubtfire* or *What Women Want* show male characters adopting female garb only to struggle with the extreme and incongruent difference of the female world – thus emphasising the conflict between the tokens of gender and one's underlying sex. Films like *Some Like it Hot*, by contrast, as no shortage of critics have argued, expose the malleability of gender, the inability to determine just when the gender impersonator is acting in or out of character – thereby suggesting that the assumption of a gendered persona can constitute, and not just mask, subjectivity.

One of the key problems, however, of Butler's strong insistence on performativity, act, signification and force is her refusal of a positive outside to the gender system. Butler continually refers to a constitutive outside, that what is other than, or prior to, enacted gender is produced only through the act: 'To posit by way of language a materiality outside of language is still to posit that materiality, and the materiality so posited will retain that positing as its constitutive condition' (Butler 1993, 30). It is not that I am a subject who then signifies; it is only through speech and subject that an 'I' is produced as one who was there to be recognised. The body, then, is not a natural bearer of sexuality that then expresses itself in, or is gendered through, signification. The body is just its performance and act. What Butler insistently refuses is an embodiment, matter or physicality that precedes act and relations; she therefore differs from recent arguments in feminism that want to think embodiment as a power to produce relations, as a power *not* reducible to the images we have of it. Now while we may want to agree with Butler that the body can only be seen as naturally sexed, as male and female, through the performance of gender, does this mean that the body is exhausted by or reducible to its performance? Why are we so hesitant to acknowledge powers that have force and precede the act, but which cannot be known, recognised and reduced to the act? If it is the case that Western metaphysics can be regarded as masculinist because it refuses any forces or powers that remain outside consciousness and comprehension, then Butler's insistent refusal of the *body itself* – her repeated rejection of that which lies outside performance and effect – may repeat the rationalist emphasis on activity and incorporation that has also constituted a female, inert, inactive and material body as its unthinkable remainder. It may be illegitimate to think the outside of gender as a natural and causal sexuality, but is this the only way in which one can think the body?

Volatile bodies

One way of interpreting Foucault has been to take his argument regarding the constitution of the subject through the discourses of sexuality as a social construction argument. Here the self would be nothing more than an effect of the discourses through which it speaks and through which it is represented. There could, then, be no natural sexuality, certainly no natural self; both self and world would be effects of an all encompassing power which has no 'real' outside. Such a 'discursive' understanding of Foucault (Macdonell 1986), despite its wide appeal, is just the type of argument Foucault's work on power and knowledge seeks to overturn. To begin with, Foucault's argument for 'historical a priori' insists that there is no single explanation or form of the relation between subjects and power. In modernity, for example, we imagine the self as that which constitutes itself and its world through language and structure, but prior to modernity it was not the subject that was regarded as the ground of knowledge so much as the order of the world. In antiquity, truth was not regarded as some underlying foundation but as an ongoing and avowedly political practice of self-formation. The history of sexuality, for Foucault, is also therefore a history of truth. Whereas sexuality was once regulated according to the ways in which bodies ordered their pleasures for explicitly practical reasons, sexuality has now become our 'truth,' a truth that is lying in wait, there to be disclosed.

By writing a history of sexuality, Foucault wanted to contest the seeming naturalness, both of sexuality and of the ways in which we know sexuality. His work is, then, not just compatible with and useful for queer theory, it also suggests that the queer body, by challenging the normal concept of the subject as produced through the family, also challenges the establishment of sexuality as an explanatory horizon. The idea that the body is constructed in discourse and that one's being is the effect of an imposed system is, according to Foucault, a peculiarly modern mode of knowledge (Foucault 1981, 102). Far from seeing language as *the* sole condition for subject formation, Foucault's work looks at the ways in which bodies (and other powers, such as spatial systems, technologies and disciplinary procedures) also create conditions and relations. Forms of architecture, such as the modern prison, enable the criminal to be produced as an object to be studied, and therefore have as much to do with the formation of 'man' and the human sciences as do certain conceptual and linguistic changes. Medical practices, such as dissection and new technologies of examination, also determine the ways in which the subject is produced in relation to its world. There is no single constituting system. Neither language, nor consciousness, nor ideology, determine the world; rather, power is multiple and operates through overlapping and sometimes conflicting relations, 'a mutliplicity of discursive elements that can come into play in various strategies' (Foucault 1981, 100). One cannot say that bodies are produced through discourse, but one can look at the way certain discourses, such as sexuality, intersect with other powers – medical, legal and social procedures. One needs to see the body, its actions and its comportment as one power among others, and not as some underlying substance.

The idea that there is 'a' power, and that this power takes the form of one system, such as discourse, and that this system then determines all bodies and relations is precisely what Foucault criticises in his analysis of modern modes of knowledge, such as structuralism. Foucault tries to create a distance from modern modes of knowledge, which produce various transcendental conditions for existence, such as sexuality, ideology, consciousness or language, and which establish human life as the ground of all relations. One of the aims of Foucault's project is to form a notion of power as that which cannot be reduced to thought and intention. Consider his ideal of ancient sexuality and the body. Here, the body was not the essence of one's identity, an identity that was ultimately sexual; the body was a power, something with which one worked. Indeed, one way of thinking the positivity of power is to consider power as plural: not as a system that determines, organises and produces the world as some sort of construction, but as powers or potentials that may or may not be actualised or brought to present. It is the modern understanding of power, as a single, determining and repressive system, that conceals all the inhuman, contingent, unthought and unintentional forces that operate across our being. Foucault sees sexuality as a power, a potential for the body to act or be in a certain way. The regulation of sexuality is an encounter with other powers, the power to know, to master others, to form oneself. To see power as positive is to see it as having a specificity. Power is not just a quantitative force; it is a capacity to do or be in a certain way. To interpret the body through power, then, is not to see the body as an effect or construction, but as something whose force requires work, requires us to think, and may well resist thought and action. The idea that there is some single conditioning logic, system or order of existence, such as ideology, discourse or structure, precludes us from understanding the positivity of power: all those forces that act on thought, that mobilise bodies, that remain opaque to analysis and that disturb self-consciousness.

In contrast to many of the readings of Foucault that focus on discourse and language, Elizabeth Grosz saw a more radical potential in Foucault's concept of power (Grosz 1987). Grosz's *Volatile Bodies* draws on a number of psychoanalytic, feminist psychoanalytic and anti-psychoanalytic accounts, including the works of Foucault, Deleuze and Guattari, and Irigaray. The body, Grosz argues, has always been repressed, marginalised and subordinated in Western thought: 'Since the inception of philosophy as a separate and self-contained discipline in ancient Greece, philosophy has established itself on the foundations of a profound somatophobia' (Grosz 1994, 5). Philosophers, for example, have seen the body as a vehicle for mind, as that which ought to be governed by mind, or as that which is an imaginary effect of mind. Grosz does not want a simple reversal of this opposition. To say, for example, that it is the body that is the primary principle – that, say, consciousness can be explained physically, or that the mind is reducible to the biological brain – still leaves the traditional notion of body in place. Body would still be that given, immutable and underlying substance that can then be explained mechanistically. Grosz refuses both a dualistic account, which would establish mind or body as a causal principle, and a monistic account, which would explain body as a fiction of the mind – as a construction – or would explain mind by body – reducing consciousness to calculable interactions of matter. Her work therefore

reacts strongly against a tradition of feminism that sees the body or sexuality as an effect of, or determined by, political forces. Both Monique
Wittig and Judith Butler, for example, argue that the natural sex that is
supposedly referred to by discourse is produced through discourse. But
why, Grosz asks, do we feel the need to abandon the sex of bodies? Why
do we so adamantly refuse the notion of different genres of body, and
why do we insist that the difference of bodies is reducible to differences
effected through language? The body in Western thought has always
been an undifferentiated and sexless body, made sense of and differentiated by one reason and one subject. The body has always been different *from* the mind, not that which may be caught up in the very image
that mind has of itself. Grosz places her own position between, or
beyond, Foucault and Butler. Against Foucault, she insists that there is
a sex *of different bodies* that cannot be reduced to the knowledge and
mobilisation of 'sexuality.' Even if the construction of 'our' natural
sexuality has been normalising, this does not mean that attention to
differently sexed bodies might not open up new ways of thinking. But
Grosz does not want to use Butler's term gender – the norm that marks
bodies as male and female. To think of *sex* would be to think of the
difference, power and potential of a body beyond both sexuality – the
social practices of that body – and gender – the norms that mark that
body as male or female. Sex, for Grosz, is the potential to differ and
express, a power that is more than, and irreducible, to its expressions
in either the gender system or regimes of sexuality. There is a positive
sexual difference before norms of male and female, and before the
oppositions between 'queer' and 'straight':

> While not wishing to deny this range of variations in the cross-
> cultural and historical scope of sex, nor the performative and self-
> productive notion of 'identity' Butler develops, I am reluctant to see
> gender regarded even as the expression of sex, as Butler suggests,
> insofar as sex is itself always already expression, which in itself does
> not require (or forbid) second order expression...
>   In my understanding, the term 'sex' refers, not to sexual impulses,
> desires, wishes, hopes, bodies, pleasures, behaviours, and practices:
> this I refer to the term 'sexuality.' 'Sex' refers to the domain of sexual dif-
> ference, to the question of the *morphologies of bodies.*
>   (Grosz 1995, 213)

Note that Grosz refers here to the 'question' of the morphologies of
bodies. The body is not a ground or answer, something that we would

find at the end of knowledge and questioning, but a power to provoke the ways in which we think. The thought of a body, physicality and materiality beyond the terms of our language and practices might lead us to think and act differently. It is this idea of positive difference that Grosz draws from Deleuze and Guattari, against a dominant tendency in Foucault, even though 'Foucault does in fact distinguish between the functioning of power (the deployment of sexuality) and a somehow pre-power real, a real' (Grosz 1995, 217). Whereas Foucault locates this 'real' in the once-upon-a-time ancient experience of 'bodies and pleasures,' Grosz argues that the question, not the ontology, of lesbian desire is more radical, for it is this desire that opens a new way of thinking about *what a body can do*, not what a body is (Grosz 1995, 222).

Grosz draws upon Foucault's history of bodies to argue that we should not just imagine Western culture as a history of ideas; we should also consider the ways in which different bodily practices – everything from imprisonment, punishment, medical technologies, architecture and sexuality – organise relations and the powers of bodies. Power is not, then, an *idea*. Power is what a body can do. If a body is docile or subjects itself to certain norms then this may be because of certain spatial relations. The most obvious example is Foucault's discussion of the panopticon, where the construction of a central viewing tower in a prison produces a certain self-regard in the prisoner (Foucault 1979, 201). The body acts in a certain way, not through beliefs or ideology, but because it is placed in a certain relation. One might also imagine, as Grosz does in her later work, an examination of the power of 'queer' spaces (Grosz 2001, 8). Gay saunas, cruising areas, bars and clubs are not just places where certain bodies with less power and recognition assemble. Rather, the production of space and the division of certain sexual orientations from each other are coterminous. A family presents, constitutes and displays its acceptability by occupying open and public spaces – everything from literal spaces such as parklands, to the virtual spaces of representation, with the images of family life dominating shared space. Queer or gay culture is marked as queer through its occupation of concealed, closeted and anonymous space. Distribution of bodies in space is not an effect of power, where the idea of the homosexual is used to create spatial borders; rather, it is through the practices and distribution of bodies that identities and relations of power are effected. One could argue, for example, that the idea of a distinct, positive and specific queer culture was achieved through complex developments in urbanisation, medicalisation and legislation, which enabled gay areas in cities.

Grosz goes further than this to consider not just the power that operates through bodies, but also the power of bodies. Foucault's work already argues that the focus on language as the way in which the world is constructed merely produces one more way of reducing the complexity of power and forces to some ultimately human and transcendental condition. According to Grosz, the body is neither a simple causal power and condition, nor that which is determined by power. The body forms itself through power, achieving both its specificity and its sex through actions and relations to other bodies. Western thought has always represented itself through one body, with the female body being defined as different *from* the morphology of the male body. The body of 'man' has always been a phallic body: a body with distinct boundaries, characterised by active self-command, a body that masters itself and knows no corruption, fluidity or plurality. The feminist turn to a sexually different body would not, then, retrieve some essential female body lying in wait, nor seize upon the feminine as that which has been defined as different *from* man. Sexual difference, Grosz argues, needs to be thought as positive or 'pure difference.' A body has a power to differ, to *not* be reduced to a paradigm of *the* body, and to bear an autonomy precisely in its resistance to already given notions of what is essentially human. The pure difference of sexual difference begins with a question rather than the statement as to what the feminine *is*. How might we imagine space and time if we did not assume *one* body as the ground of reason, thought and subjectivity?

Whereas the body has always been imagined as the passive other of a self-determining reason, Grosz suggests looking at the ways different bodies might yield different modes of relation between self and world, inside and outside, sameness and identity, or normality and perversion. Grosz does not privilege the female body as essentially radical, but she does see her work as feminist in that she directs herself against the supposedly neutral and sexless subject who has always been the subject of a male body. Grosz's notion of a *volatile* body is designed to destroy the notion of disembodied mind, for the mind is produced through the body's encounter with space, while space is produced through the action of a body. Grosz uses a number of metaphors, but her most lucid is the idea of the body as a moebius strip, with inside–outside relations produced from one *differentiating* medium (Grosz 1994, 209–210); the body is an achieved surface, an in-between. The body is neither fully one's own and intentional – for embodiment orients the sense we make of the world – nor is the body simply determined by outside; for each body has its specific power to relate to other bodies and powers:

> ...sexual difference is a framework or horizon that must disappear as such in the codings that constitute sexual identity and the relations between the sexes. Sexual difference is the horizon that cannot appear in its own terms but is implied in the very possibility of an entity, and identity, a subject, an other and their relations.

> This notion of sexual difference, a difference that is originary and constitutive, is not, strictly speaking, ontological; if anything it occupies a preontological – certainly a preepistemological – terrain insofar as it makes possible what things or entities, what beings, exist (the ontological question) and insofar as it must preexist and condition what we can know (the epistemological question).
>
> (Grosz 1994, 209)

When Deleuze and Guattari talk about desire and sexuality as fully real and yet also claim that, historically, tribal and racial differences precede 'man' and 'woman' they also have this positive understanding of sexual difference as pure difference. There is one desiring life that connects, differs, becomes according to its really distinct powers. The formation of identities is 'sexual' because a body becomes what it is through what it desires and what it can do. One could imagine, for example, different spatial comportments depending on different bodies, and this would require understanding sexuality *not* in terms of male and female genders, nor in terms of sexual orientation. Blind, disabled and ageing bodies, would experience space at different speeds, and would work with different modes of orientation. If someone, for example, says that a certain place is '5 minutes away,' this already assumes a space oriented by bodily capacity. There are of course generalisations and regularities to collections of bodies – we can speak about morphologies, or the ways in which we have made sense of bodily potential – but there is no direct causal relation between what a body is and its already given expressions; other relations are possible. If one refers to oneself as 'man' or 'woman,' one does so because one occupies a cultural, historical and political locale. Gender – man and woman, male and female – is an impoverished expression of a sexual difference reduced to an opposition.

Drawing on the work of Luce Irigaray, Grosz extends this notion of bodies and powers to raise the possibility of sexed bodies and morphologies. If it is the case that space is given from the orientation, capacity and potential of one's body – if we accept that our lived world is not constructed through a disembodied mind or language – then it may well be that our relation to the world is sexed. Luce Irigaray's *Speculum of the Other Woman* reads the history of Western philosophy as the history of a certain bodily morphology. It is the phallic body, for example, that orders other bodies as male–female, as having or lacking the phallus, as present or absent, as within or before the law. Irigaray draws on the psychoanalytic insight that our most abstract notions – such as presence, negation or truth – must be formed from one's body, and that the idea of one's own body is formed through a relation to a sexed other. Irigaray both draws upon, and contests, one of the fundamental concepts of psychoanalysis. She accepts that the formation of the subject is bodily, but she challenges the psychoanalytic premise that there is a single (Oedipal) pattern of formation in which the body that is other than oneself is nothing more than a negated object.

Freud had argued that the idea of judgement – acceptance or rejection, affirmation or negation – must be built up from the borders of the body: I take this in; I spit this out (Freud 1984, 441). The dualisms that govern Western thought, with emphasis on non-contradiction, presence–absence, active–passive or male–female, are grounded on a certain bodily imaginary. The phallic body, for example, negates what is other than itself, establishes a strict border between subject and object, assumes a single law and a single universal subjectivity. The very logic through which we think the world is formed is through a certain morphology of body. Irigaray's insistence on morphology is not a form of sexual determinism; it does not, for example, insist that one's sex *causes* one's thinking. For such a position already sees body and thought as two distinct terms. Rather, one's sex, the way one thinks of oneself *as sexed*, is achieved through the way one differentiates self and world, the bodily surface one imagines as foundational to the 'I.' A non-phallic body whose sexuality was not located in a single visible organ, Irigaray argues, would relate to its world in less rigidly dichotomous terms. A body capable of pregnancy, of breast-feeding, of multiple pleasures, might not have a strict boundary, and might relate to what is other than itself, not as a negated and inert object, but as a positive other. Whereas Western thought has presented itself as pure reason that uses the body and gender as a metaphor or figure, Irigaray suggests that we need to think of life in concrete terms, as the creative interaction of male and female genres. Grosz goes beyond this notion of two sexes to think of lesbian desire as that which could not be represented in already gendered terms. Grosz remains faithful to the challenge or questioning power of Irigaray's concept of sexual difference, a concept that has a capacity to exceed the thought of genders, genres and representable kinds:

> Here we must be careful not to erect a new ontology based on what woman *is*, in and of herself. Irigaray, and other theorists of female sexuality have not provided an account of female sexuality in its essence or fixed form, but rather have worked on the paradoxes and consequences generated for female sexuality by a culture, a value system, forms of knowledge and systems of representation that can only ever take female sexuality as object, as external, and as alien to the only set of perspectives presenting themselves as true – men's. Female sexuality, lesbian desire, is that which eludes and escapes, that which functions as an excess, a remainder uncontained by and unrepresentable within the terms provided by a sexuality that takes itself straightforwardly as being what it is.
>
> (Grosz 1995, 222)

Irigaray's challenge to Western thought and gender binaries raises more questions than it answers, but these have been some of the most fruitful and provocative questions of the last few decades. To begin with we need to ask to what extent body morphologies are binary, whether the difference between male and female bodies is the way in which human life necessarily figures itself. Second, if it is the case that Western logic has been dualist, operating from a rigid binary system of self–other, presence–absence, male–female, and so on, can we go beyond Irigaray's project of demanding *genuine* sexual difference – a truly other and autonomous sex – and overcome binarism altogether?

Queer theorists have objected to the heterosexism of the privileging of gender, insisting that the difference between male and female, and its psychoanalytic explanation from the Oedipal family has repressed and prohibited those modes of bodily comportment that 'fail' to line up on either side of the heterosexual divide (Weed and Schor 1997). I think the best way to approach this problem is to see it as a *problem*. Irigaray has raised the question of whether the narcissistic fantasy of woman might be adopted in order to think of (at least one) different morphology. Once we think of bodies as constitutive to our notions of identity, time and space – once we see the specificity of the body as crucial to our sense of locatedness in the world and our relation to others – then we might go on to think other non-heterosexual bodily comportments. Elizabeth

Grosz has taken Irigaray's insistence on bodily morphology to put forward the idea, not only of an 'autonomous feminine' liberated from the phallic logic of lack; she has also insisted that sexuality and embodiment cannot be limited to the gender binary. Where Grosz differs from Irigaray is that while Irigaray stresses that there need to be two genders, or two different and relating modes of sexual subjectivity, Grosz moves from pure difference, defined non-relationally, to liberation from genders, binaries and subjective norms. Irigaray is insistent that one's autonomy or specificity is achieved through relation, and that one can recognise who one is only through the recognition of a different other. One can only have an identity through *some* genre, from seeing oneself *as some kind*, and so there cannot be a pure self who then has a different body. Rather, bodily difference gives the self specific form, and this form is recognised only in relation to another form. Irigaray insists that gender is the mode of 'concrete universal' that allows for self-formation (Irigaray 1994, 19, 25). One can only *be someone* if one takes on a universal, if one can recognise oneself as *this* kind of identity; this universal cannot be an abstract 'I,' a mere point of identity with no difference. The universal must be a form or genre, a kind that is given concretion in a body, a body that defines itself through another body:

> Transcendence is thus no longer ecstasy, leaving the self behind toward an inaccessible total-other, beyond sensibility, beyond the earth. It is respect for the other whom I will never be, who is transcendent to me and to whom I am transcendent. Neither simple nature nor common spirit beyond nature, this transcendence exists in the difference of body and culture that continues to nourish our energy, its movement, its generation and its creation.
>
> (Irigaray 1996, 104)

It is this emphasis on relation and the giving of form or genre to one's body that leads Irigaray (1996, 12) to remain with the male–female relation:

> The existence of two subjects is probably the only thing that can bring the masculine subject back to his being, and this thanks to woman's access to her own being.

Both Elizabeth Grosz and Moira Gatens, who were heavily influenced by Irigaray's stress on morphology have, in quite different ways, produced a less relational model of difference. Grosz argues for pure difference: a body's power to become and give form to itself has a force that goes beyond the difference between male and female, and beyond the idea of *gender* or bounded kinds. Just as Irigaray's notion of an autonomous feminine remains problematic, for it leaves the question of whether going beyond phallic logic only allows for one other genre, so Grosz's pure difference allows for two interpretations. At one point, Grosz defines pure difference in radically relational terms. The differences of a field or system have no identity outside their relation, and the system itself is neither organised nor grounded on any single term (Grosz 1990, 93). On other occasions, and this is stressed in her later work, Grosz suggests a positive, non-relational pure difference, where a distinct differential power might be granted to a body, and that this power persists and insists, and creates relations from itself (Grosz 1995, 129). On such an understanding, matter itself would have differential force, and bodies would not be reducible to the ideas we have of them; there would be a sexuality beyond relations of gender.

Moira Gatens has also raised the problem of sexual difference as positive. Why, she asks, do we feel so hesitant to attribute force to physical powers; why do we think of matter as only having the power to give form through mind? Gatens rejects both the appeal to the body *per se* and the rejection of the body as a blank slate for sexual inscription. For Gatens, the idea that the West has evidenced somatophobia should not lead us to affirm the body, but to question the very concept of the body as that which is substantively distinct from gender, power, mind or ideas (Gatens 1996, 68). Rather, we can go beyond the sex–gender distinction, which repeats the distinction between biology and culture, and see our ideas as dependent upon the capacities of our body, and our discourses of the body as determined by various operations of power:

> By abandoning the dualist ontology of mind versus body, nature versus culture, we can circumvent the either/or impasse of contemporary feminist theory between affirming an essential mental equality, which the progress of civilization can be entrusted to expose, and affirming an essential bodily difference.... The mind is constituted by the affirmation of the actual existence of the body, and reason is active and embodied precisely because it is the affirmation of a *particular* bodily existence.
>
> (Gatens 1996, 57)

Gatens draws upon Spinoza's definition of mind 'as an idea of the body' (Gatens and Lloyd 1999, 12). Her work is part of a much broader political retrieval of the seventeenth-century philosopher Baruch de Spinoza, whose thought is deemed to be valuable precisely because it works against the Cartesian tradition of mind and body as two distinct substances, and instead sees life as one substance that expresses itself in different modes, so that mind and bodies are different ways in which one differing life acts and expresses itself (Deleuze 1992).

However, Gatens' work differs markedly from the recent uses of Spinoza by the Marxist critics Michael Hardt and Antonio Negri, who insist that liberation can only be achieved if humanity is no longer divided from itself by distinct images of 'man' but instead affirms one immanent, self-producing and active humanity of living labour: 'homo-homo, *humanity squared*' (Hardt and Negri 2000, 204). Here, humanity is defined through a process of work, production, activity and self-expansion – values that have always defined a male body. If we thought of a body that could give birth, a body whose mode of production went beyond its own self to produce other bodies, and whose relation to 'biology' could not so easily be transcended then we might stress the different processes by which different bodies imagine their common humanity. Gatens argues that the body politic – the idea and image we have of the community – is imagined from a lived, acting and desiring body, a body that thinks of itself through what it can do, but that this is also determined through a relation to *other* bodies: 'The psychical image of the body is necessary in order for us to have motility in the world, without which we could not be intentional subjects. The imaginary body is developed, learnt, connected to the body image of others, and is not static' (Gatens 1996, 12). Gatens does not affirm a single self-producing humanity but is aware of the tensions that different bodies with different capacities may produce in any community relation: 'the polarization between men and woman is a part of our sociopolitical histories which cannot be ignored' (Gatens 1996, 56). Gatens stresses the *bodily production* of our images and ideas, that the concept of humanity within which we think and move is made possible by the powers of our bodies. This allows for an expanded concept of the sexual body, for the desires of the body that imagine a 'collective humanity' would be inflected both by the sexual capacities and the distinct cultural histories of bodies. For this reason, Gatens is critical of the emphasis on, and conceptual structure of, gender. Even if we were to move to a gender-neutral society, where the same norms governed each body – if, say, we were all accepted as rational, active and self-defining – these norms would have a different force depending upon which body they related to:

Concerning the neutrality of the body, let me be explicit, there is no neutral body, there are at least two kinds of bodies: the male body and the female body. If we locate social practices and behaviours as embedded in the subject, as we have with perception, rather than 'in consciousness' or 'in the body' then this has the important repercussion that the subject is always a *sexed* subject. If one accepts the notion of the sexually specific subject, that is, the male or female subject, then one must dismiss the notion that patriarchy can be characterized as a system of social organization that valorizes the masculine *gender* over the feminine gender. Gender is not the issue; sexual difference is. The very same behaviours (whether they be masculine or feminine) have quite different personal and social significances when acted out by the male subject on the one hand and the female subject on the other.

(Gatens 1996, 9)

Grosz's idea of the sexed body and Gatens' concept of specific sexual difference challenges a dominant trend in feminism, some versions of queer theory and liberal political theory. Sex and embodiment, they suggest, have a power to differ that cannot be reduced to, or explained, by social impositions of gender. Both Grosz's and Gatens' readings of Irigaray refuse to accept the accusation of 'essentialism' either as a term of abuse, or as a relevant way of approaching the question of sexual difference. The very logic of essentialism assumes that something can be what it is, and then relate to other terms. A sexual essentialism would begin from a difference between male and female, and then explain how those bodies related to each other and were constitutive of gender. But this is already a 'sexed' picture. The idea that a body takes on its social meaning through gender divides mind from body; and it is the disembodied mind that has always defined man – man as an imaging and self-transcending or 'performative' being who gives himself his own body.

If it is the case that the very way in which the border between self and world depends upon the morphology of one's body, then there could not be *one* sexual relation, one axis of difference, but two genres. The feminine might be imagined, in contrast to phallic logic, not as that pure act of thought that is other than body, not as a mind that is constituted through the detached representation of its world, but as that which is directed to *another possible world*. For if the feminine recognises another morphology, another way of living the border between self and world, then its primary relation is not that of subject–object, but subject–subject, where the other subject raises the question of a world and experience that is other than my own, an entirely different morphology (Gatens and Lloyd 1999, 101).

Grosz suggests that we can go beyond Irigaray's project of defining this other sex; we can explore multiple sexualities, incongruent and divergent (or perverse) mappings of space and time, and the possibility of futures that are not just refigurations or parodies of already existing models (Grosz 1995). Whereas Irigaray's *genres* of sex are two positively different ways of conceiving the relation to the world – and not two kinds within the world – and whereas Judith Butler sees all performance as located within a gender system that it must both repeat and also subvert, Grosz's concept of pure difference aims at the disruption of already given kinds, the disruption of logics of relation, with the passage to a future that breaks with all notions of ground, presence and the already given (Grosz 1999). This can only be achieved when the body is more than that which is presupposed by discourse, and where the body is more than the figure through which thinking conceives its world.

Queer theory and the critique of gender: Butler, Sedgwick, Edelman and Bersani

One of the common ways of approaching sexuality in feminism and queer theory has been to adopt a primarily linguistic or textualist terminology. We have already seen that for Judith Butler, sex is produced as an effect of interpretation. From the performances of bodies, we assume that there was some natural sexual subject who preceded the performance. The subject is produced as that which was there to be read, as the signified of the signifying body. The value of the queer body, for many queer theorists, is that this seamless transition or event of interpretation that produces the sexed body is, in the body of the homosexual, exposed as production. According to Eve Kosofsky Sedgwick, the metaphor of the closet that has traditionally been confined to gay identities is typical of subjectivity *per se*. Sedgwick's key notion of an *epistemology* of the closet, of the self as that which is both hidden and must come to be known, emphasises the ways in which subjectivity is produced and maintained through practices of knowledge, monitoring, naming and identifying. Sedgwick acknowledges that the very modern concept of being 'gay' relies on recent assumptions that one's sexuality is determined by object choice. Instead of emphasising this supposed paradigm shift, she insists that the inability to secure sexuality – either through biology or culture – is precisely what enables queer theory to intervene in readings of texts and their descriptions of desire. Sedgwick suggests that it is precisely the historical and cultural difficulty of establishing any such thing as a 'queer' identity that allows us to open debates of sexuality:

> The most dramatic difference between gender and sexual orientation – that virtually all people are publicly and unalterably assigned to one or other gender, and from birth – seems if anything to mean that it is, rather, sexual orientation with its far greater potential for rearrangement, ambiguity, and representational doubleness, that would offer the apter deconstructive object.
>
> (Sedgwick 1990, 34)

Sedgwick tries to negotiate the difficult relation between gender and sexuality, aware that the axis of gender – man–woman – has tended to assume a heterosexual norm. Even though the very notion of heterosexuality relies on a modern understanding of sex as sexual orientation, Sedgwick argues that we need to understand definitions of gender alongside norms about sexuality (Sedgwick 1990, 31). For Sedgwick, then, gender binaries are produced through broader cultural, historical and sexual systems of norms. It may well be, however, that the twentieth-century stress on knowing, interpreting and revealing sexual identity produces a '*special* centrality of homophobic oppression' (Sedgwick 1990, 33). So, while gender remains a legitimate concern, it is the undecidability and interpretability of the homosexual body that requires an overthrow of the sex–gender distinction, for one's sexual identity has at least as much to do with one's behaviours and orientation as it does with one's chromosomal body (Sedgwick 1990, 28). Sedgwick presents her work within the tradition of deconstruction, which would emphasise the textual, unstable and *incoherent* nature of binaries. Reading should move beyond constructivist or essentialist understandings of homosexuality, and move beyond the either/or of sexuality and gender to explore the textual negotiation, contamination and production of various binarisms.

Like many 'queer' theorists, Sedgwick problematises the very concept of 'queerness' by focusing on discursive and textual strategies; she does not accept either a constructed or natural identity from which her theory takes place. Her argument is, therefore, part of a larger movement that wants to move beyond the questions and problems of sexual difference through an attention to its textual conditions of both coherence and incoherence. Queer theory is not, then, a supplement to feminist theory – a claim that gay men and lesbians also require recognition. It complicates the very notion of identity and recognition by lacing the sexual binary of male and female in more complex networks of object choice, behaviours and prohibited desires. This attention to the inscription of binaries within multiple textual fields is made even more explicit in Lee Edelman's *Homographesis*. For Lee Edelman, the natural assignment of gender binaries is disrupted by 'homographesis,' – the fact that the male body of the homosexual must be interpreted as other than the seemingly same body of the straight man. The body is not a self-present substance, an essential nature, but a text to be read:

> ... a recognition of the cultural inscription of the gay body as writing or text suggests that a necessary project for gay critics and for the expanding field of gay theory must be the study of the historically variable rhetorics, the discursive strategies and tropological formations, in which sexuality is embedded and conceived; it suggests that the differing psychologies of figuration in different places and at different times bear crucially on the textual articulations and cultural constructions of sexuality; and it suggests that the sphere of gay criticism need not be restricted to the examination of texts that either thematize homosexual relations or dramatize the vicissitudes of homosexual/homosocial desire.
>
> (Edelman 1994, 20)

This can take us back to Butler and her insistence that gender as the expression of a sexual dichotomy produces the fictive naturalness of its 'original' opposition. For Butler, lesbian and gay bodies should not demand straightforward recognition for what they are – for the coherence of their identity – but should expose the ways in which the queer body disrupts all the norms of gender identity. Butler's understanding of the performative – of the action or signifier that produces the self it supposedly represents – insists on an understanding of textuality as positive force. We should not see the text or speech-act as the effect or expression of some preceding agent or subject; the speech-act produces the self it supposedly names. There is no being behind the act, no potential that comes to expression through speech. Speech is pure, self-realising potential that then creates the illusion of its outside or 'before.' The act or performance is productive rather than expressive. It is not that there is a body that then proceeds to be represented; it is in and through actions and events that one differentiates the visible body from some supposedly underlying self. The body, like all material signifiers that demand to be read, differentiates itself, and produces the effect of some subjectivity or sexuality that gives the body its gender.

> In this sense, what constitutes the fixity of the body, its contours, its movements, will be fully material, but materiality will be rethought as the effect of power, as power's most productive effect. And there will be no way to understand 'gender' as a cultural construct which is imposed upon the surface of matter, understood either as 'the body' or its given sex. Rather, once 'sex' itself is understood in its normativity, the materiality of the body will not be thinkable apart from the materialization of that regulatory norm. 'Sex' is, thus, not simply what one has, or a static description of what one is: it will be one of the norms by which the 'one' becomes viable at all, that which qualifies a body for life within the domain of cultural intelligibility.
>
> (Butler 1993, 2)

For Sedgwick, Butler and Edelman, any appeal to a subject before the act – any notion of a self somehow hidden or concealed behind signification, but that can express itself fully in the visible body – reinforces the logic and law of natural sexuality. Such a logic posits a ground behind actions, forces and events. This logic of sexuality or 'metaphor' (where the body functions as sign of some underlying but naturally joined identity) allows for the prohibition, marginalisation and repression of supposedly unnatural sexualities. It is assumed that the male body is expressive of a sexuality oriented towards desire for the feminine. Any body that conceals *another* meaning – such as the homosexual body – disrupts the supposedly natural relation between body and sex. The queer body can therefore be seen to have an exemplary critical, because relational and non-essential, force in the disruption of the ideology of gender.

Butler's work can be distinguished from a body of queer and feminist politics that relies upon liberating or emancipatory notions of uncovering, outing, recognition, self-discovery and revelation. The queer body is not some essential identity outside gender relations; it is a capacity to repeat and destabilise gender identity from within.

Leo Bersani has provided the most trenchant criticism of Butler's celebration of parody and the explicit non-identity of the queer body. To begin with, Bersani argues, parody is not the happy celebration of a queer identity that has freed itself from all demands of coherence, identity and recognition. On the contrary, it is because our only socially constituted models of subjectivity, gender and normality are heterosexual, that the bodies in drag, mime and pastiche submit to images of the family. It is because there is no value placed on same-sex relations that male bodies in drag, as objects of male desire, take on the signs of female gender: 'in their pathetically minute attention to the styles of a power from which they have been permanently excluded, the oppressed perform nothing more subversive than their own sub-mission to being brainwashed, safely sequestered, and, if necessary, readied for annihilation' (Bersani 1995, 48). Bersani argues that what needs to be radically refigured is the model of difference as such, espe-cially the idea that gendered identity is produced through processes of negation and distancing from the other.

Recall that for Levi-Strauss it is through the negation of the mother as mere immediacy and non-differentiated chaos that the masculine subject must locate himself in a system of differences, placing himself in a relation of *identity* to other male subjects who similarly distance themselves from the natural and maternal feminine as other. Recall that for Simone de Beauvoir it is the structure of self-versus-other that has produced 'woman' as the object against which the subject defines himself as actively different, as always in a process of self-becoming. One might say, then, that Butler's celebration of the body that is never identical to itself, that is always other than any supposedly natural gender – a body that refuses any specific or determined sex – is thoroughly compatible with the logic of self-constituting identity that has underpinned the male subject. What Butler wants to reject is any sexuality, any bodily or specific difference, that might determine the acts and performance of the self as signifier. What if there were a form of difference that could not be reduced to the body as it acts out its gender? What if the self were more than performance, if selves demanded to be recognised for who they were in their bodily specificity? How might we think a subject who demanded, not that he always be different from any natural body or sex (Butler's parodic body), but who demanded recognition?

In *Homos*, Bersani argues for a revaluation of sameness. In the back-ground we need to note, as Irigaray has so insistently argued, that male identity – the image of the self-constituting subject that dominates Western philosophy – is defined as the pure act of self-distancing and becoming, which defines itself against a nature that does not present itself. The female body is therefore produced in Western thought as that inert, passive and un-self-conscious matter, against which the act, representation and self-projection of the male subject is defined. If there is a masculine privileging of *identity*, this is an identity that can measure itself as the same, only by relating to itself, presenting itself to itself, actively creating itself as a self to be contemplated and recognised. And this production of the self as the same to itself, requires a process of self-distancing and reflection. Gender difference is crucial to the production of this sameness, for the self-reflecting body that gathers itself to itself, is defined as that which is *other than* any merely passive, natural or immediate body. It is only by distancing himself from the merely given, from that which remains in itself, that the masculine subject produces himself. The disembodied mind that is unencumbered by anything that cannot be reduced to thought and self-determination is defined against the physical and material body, *borrowing* bodily and sexual figures only to be *other than* any determinate body.

Butler's matter is freed from the usual notions of matter as unthinking, unreflected and inhuman stuff, and becomes remarkably man-like: dividing from itself in order to signify what is other than itself. For Butler, matter signifies, performs and differentiates itself. Matter is *not* the unreflected other of mind. When Butler privileges parody and the *performance* of gender, she wants to free gender from fixity and biology. By contrast, Bersani is critical of a process of 'de-gaying' of which Butler's celebration of parody is typical. Bersani argues for new forms of sociality where the self does not just *play* with the already given norms of gender, power and domination but enables relations to the other that do not associate the phallus with having and the passive other with not-having. Crucial to Bersani's criticism of Butler and Foucault, and their dream that sexuality might be pure play freed of all bodily determination and identification, is a certain reading of Freud. Freud sees sexuality in general as an oscillation between mastery and submission, between the pleasure of control and boundedness and the pleasure of dissolution, or the *jouissance* of self-loss. Rather than associating mastery with the masculine and loss of self with the feminine, two gay male bodies would have to allow the *same* body to be both same and other, both masterful and submissive. Sociality would, then, no longer be structured around the dichotomy that negates otherness, but would see the same–other, active–passive, self–non-self relations as irreducible to one gender or another.

> There is a more radical possibility: *homo-ness itself necessitates a
> massive redefining of relationality.* More fundamental than a resist-
> ance to normalizing methodologies is a potentially revolutionary
> inaptitude – perhaps inherent in gay desire – for sociality as it is
> known....we may discover, within the very ambiguities of being gay,
> a path of resistance far more threatening to dominant social orders
> than vestimentary blurrings of sexual difference and possibly sub-
> versive separations of sex from gender.
>
> (Bersani 1995, 76)

To claim an identity and specificity of the homosexual body is not,
then, to appeal to an essence, but it is to say that if gender relations
have deployed different bodies to map out relations between self and
other, then the affirmation of same-sex relations would move beyond
the *parody* of heterosexuality to relations no longer figured through
the gender binary – a binary that has always been deployed to give a
proper and marked relation between active and passive, public and
private, form and matter, self and non-self. Bersani suggests that the
project of de-gaying, the project that would include gay men in a
general humanity that refuses to define itself through any specific
norm or body, merely repeats the naïve liberal commitment to unimpeded self-creation. If Bersani is critical of gender it is because, as it is
defined by Butler, gender works with the heterosexual matrix of negation, identification and melancholy, and does not explore the ways in
which bodies might relate to each other differently. Bersani's argument
only works, however, if we hold on to sexual difference. His two male
bodies must both recognise each other as the same and as different,
and they can do so only by being male. Unlike the man of reason,
Bersani's man is embodied, sexed and dependent on an other body
that is more than a medium for active self-recognition.

Moira Gatens and the critique of gender

We may want to agree with both Butler and Foucault that any reference
to a prior sexual subject, as an actual, determined and essential
ground, commits the error of locating some substance outside all
power and relations. But can the self be explained as nothing more
than the performance of its own power, as nothing more than the,
albeit unstable, repetition of already constituted systems? Moira
Gatens wrote a trenchant and sophisticated criticism of the concept of

gender in 1983, well before Butler's *Gender Trouble* of 1990 used the concept of gender to demystify sex (reprinted in Gatens 1996). For Butler it is gender – social performance, acts and forces – that produces the sexual body as a 'before' to be represented. It is this notion of gender as a radically undetermined and *neutral* process that Gatens sets out to criticise, and she does so from two directions. First, as we have already seen, she is critical of the assumptions about both mind and body that are crucial to the very concept of gender. The idea that one is gendered through social process, and that such gender roles can be adopted by *any* body presents the body as a passive and neutral blank slate upon which the active forces of society and ideology might work. This picture is rationalist in its denial of any force to the body, and in its presentation of the body as sexless, as acquiring sex only through the imposed actions of language and culture. And if the body is presented as passive and neutral, as awaiting social inscription, the mind is no less undetermined: the mere receptacle of social norms and roles, thoroughly undetermined by bodily sex.

In this sense, Gatens' work anticipates that of Butler, for Gatens is highly critical of the dualism presupposed by the sex–gender distinction and the idea that gender forms and determines a prior and passive body. However, and this is the second and more important dimension of Gatens' work, she is also critical of the concept of gender and its refusal of sexual difference. Butler intensifies the force of gender. Gender is not just an overlay of the sexual body; the acts and expressions of gender *produce* the sexed body as some supposedly pre-existing ground. By contrast, Gatens emphasises the sexuality of bodies, and does so in a way that contests both terms of the modern distinction between sex and gender, a distinction that reinforces traditional binaries and hierarchies. To make sense of Gatens' notion of sexual difference, which she describes as contingent but not arbitrary, we can return to the concept of essence.

There are, as a number of contemporary feminists noted, two strands to the definition of essence (Grosz 1994; de Lauretis 1994). First, following Aristotle, we can define essence as the essential properties of a thing: that which makes a thing what it is; the specific power or potential that characterises a thing. This first strand is crucial to Gatens' work as a whole, for she draws on the notion of a body as a power, as a specific potential or capacity to become. Such a notion of essence is defined against a modern tendency to reduce what something is to its constituted relations or to its way of being known. There may well be powers or potentials, capacities for striving and becoming, that are not yet realised in knowledge, and that can have a force to disrupt or produce knowledges. In this sense, essence is also not that which remains the same – some static property that thought might simply lay hold of; rather, essence is a power to become or unfold itself in a certain way. Such a becoming would be different depending upon the other powers it encountered, but it would not be reduced to its already established relation to other powers. It is this notion of essence that could be set against a modern accusation of 'essentialism' and modern constructivism. For we can think essence or, in Gatens' terminology, powers, as capacities to produce relations, with relations differing according to the powers in question. Instead of one single set of relations – say, the relations of scientific laws, the relations of language, or relations of one field of force – we would need to think the relations between minds and bodies, the relations among bodies, the relations between language and historical forces, between language and biology, between genetics and environment. Thought would be placed within this cosmos of relations, and would not be some privileged and elevated point that could reduce all relations to an overarching logic or system:

> A micropolitical feminism is able to imagine alternative possible forms of sociability. This power of imagining things otherwise, in concert with the imaginings of compatible others, has the creative power to decompose and recompose the social field, bit by bit, molecule by molecule.
>
> (Gatens 2000, 72)

In this regard, to think of bodily essence would be to think of that which cannot be reduced to thought. To think of sexuality essentially would be to entertain the idea that different bodies might relate to the world differently. A body capable of menstruation, reproduction, breast-feeding and menopause might have a different relation to time, space and other bodies than a male body.

In addition to the Aristotelian notion of an essence, being the form that a being takes in order to be what it is, an essence is also how we know, define or experience something. Following John Locke, we can distinguish the first sense of essence from the second. A *real* essence refers to those intrinsic qualities that give each thing its specific or different power. A *nominal* essence is the way in which those qualities are known by us, that is in relation to knowledge, experience and other bodies. Now it follows that we can never *know* or *experience* a real essence; for what something is, in itself, before all relation, lies outside the relation of knowledge and experience. We only know intrinsic powers or potentials in our own relations and experience. This means, also, that our nominal essences bear a relation to real essence, but that this relation will vary through experience. To make sense of this we can return to Gatens. Our thoughts, experiences and understandings of the world always proceed from and make sense of bodily experience; how could we have a world of spatial relations, others, a sense of identity, without some image of our own bodies? We never know a body in itself, but only in its *lived* and *imagined* form. Menstruation, Gatens argues, will be a forceful and significant event, which we will imagine in *some* form, but this form will also vary culturally (Gatens 1996). Sexual difference cannot just be seen as an effect of social ideology, as an act of thought. Rather, our thoughts respond to, make sense of, and imagine, our sexual bodies. As we have already seen, most cultures imagine life and identity – not just personal identity, but the very emergence of any bounded thing – in terms of the figures of male and female. The way in which we imagine the sexually different body may vary, and we will only know and experience that body through its lived relations, but this does not mean that the body itself has no force prior to the imagination.

Indeed, the privileging of a human society that has only one self-determining body and that is unimpeded by biology, otherness and the imagination takes the imagined anatomy of one body – the male, phallic and unified body that has separated itself from maternal confusion – as the body of all (Gatens 1996, 22). The concept of gender is the concept that there are different kinds *of* some identity, such that gender differentiates and gives form to an otherwise undifferentiated matter. Against this, Gatens looks at sexual difference, not as different versions or forms of one underlying humanity, but as distinct powers or potentials. Our very concept of humanity has always been defined through figures of a body that makes, invents and gives form to itself, in opposition to an unthinking and unbecoming nature. The body politic has, similarly, been understood according to an implicitly masculine morphology of a self-forming, independent, bounded and rationally motivated organism. Gatens' project for the recognition of sexual difference does not appeal to what the female body *is* – hers is not an essentialism that would step outside already constituted relations – but she does insist that bodies are not reducible to constituted relations.

If gender is understood as the social or ideal form added on to an inessential body, then gender takes on all the Cartesian aspects of disembodied mind in opposition to a matter that has no intrinsic differentiating properties. We imagine and figure the male body as that which invents and gives form to itself, in opposition to a female body mired in biology. While it may be the case that our image of biology is always an image – for we always relate to biology and never know it in itself – this does not mean that biology is reducible to an idea. On the contrary, by looking at the ways our imagined anatomy inflects our understanding of mind we can recognise the peculiarly masculine construction of reason. If reason has always been understood as unimpeded, transparent and disembodied self-determination, then this can only be because a certain image of the male body, as detached and liberated from anatomy, has been both borrowed and then disavowed.

The body needs to be revalued from two directions and liberated both from the ideology of gender and the gender of ideology. The sexual body as power, potential or striving is not (as it is for Butler) an effect that can be known only in its actualisation as gender, for the body has powers and potentials that cannot be reduced to the already constituted norms of gender. The body is always more than the images we have of it, and to demand recognition of this positive striving body is to contest the current notion of the image, as something purely mental, rational and thoroughly malleable. Second, not only is the body more than the passive site upon which gender is inscribed, the very opposition between mind and body – our very fantasy of the brute body of biology prior to all discourse and engendering – is the fantasy of a male body. It is the male anatomy that is imagined capable of detaching itself from passions, affects, otherness and determination, in order to represent itself. The body of biology can only be fantasised or imagined as pre-social, pre-linguistic and pre-political if we imagine the political as an act of pure creation liberated from all determination – liberated from women and nature. A bodily fantasy underpins the disembodied subject. The gendered subject – the subject who has no body other than that which is created and assumed by human and rational culture – is a subject liberated from sexuality.

Conclusion: Reading Gender

How does a gendered reading differ from a feminist reading? Feminist readings can obviously take a number of forms, which we can sketch here briefly by way of a reference back to the often-noted three stages of feminism.

First-wave feminist and humanist reading

A first-wave feminist approach is in line with a humanist mode of reading. We accept that women are equal to men, and that fears, anxieties and judgments about women's biology are prejudices that ought to be eliminated. A liberal feminist reading would either expose the ways in which texts maintained a sexist or determinist connection between women's biology and social inferiority, or would affirm the ways in which texts challenged sexist ideology. As a woman writer, Mary Shelley would have been attentive to the ways in which the male world of Romantic poetry had excluded women from creation and expression. Victor Frankenstein not only sees himself as a God-like figure of creation who has circumvented the need for women's bodies, he is also emblematic of a scientific will to power that cannot acknowledge human limits.

If we read *Frankenstein* as a moral and cautionary tale, then the feminist and humanist readings coincide. Victor's over-reaching and ambition not only takes over the role of God; it also remains closed to nature, women's bodies and otherness in general. Victor is incapable of seeing anything outside his own imagination, an imagination that lacks receptivity, passion, concern and any sense of limit. On this reading, the novel sets up an opposition between the scientifically driven Victor, who can only see the world as so much manipulable matter, and feminine characters – not just his sister who is represented as being closer to nature, but his more feminine male friend Clerval, who reads

romances, studies other cultures, communes with nature and has concern for others.

Like Walton, who recounts Victor's tale, Victor is drawn to first causes;
he cannot perceive nature's forms and beauty, only forces. Indeed, the
novel is dominated both by images of an original force and light – Walton
and Victor meet as they are journeying to the source of white light or the
South pole – and by images of electricity, a purely physical force of opposition or contrariety. It is this focus on originating force and light, a striving to reach the point from which all formed life emerges, that precludes
Victor from seeing a meaningful, responsive and humanised world. As
opposed to the responsive Clerval, Victor is only interested in reproducing himself, and remains blind to nature. This primarily 'moral' reading of
the novel focuses on Victor as a negative image of Promethean over-
reaching. Victor has a will that knows no bound or limits, and that cannot
see the properly human place or position within creation. In support of
this reading would be all the references and allusions in Shelley's novel to
Coleridge's 'Rime of the Ancient Mariner,' Wordsworth's *Prelude* and
Shelley's 'Mont Blanc.' Like her Romantic counterparts, Shelley would
both be critical of the scientific reduction of nature to physical force and
affirmative of a human imagination that can recognise an infinite, moral
and spiritual power. Walton insists, recalling 'The Rime of the Ancient
Mariner,' that he 'will kill no albatross' (Shelley 1992, 19). Just as
Coleridge's ballad is narrated by the mariner, who failed to show due reverence for nature, and who is now compelled to retell his fall, so the tale,
as narrated by Victor, can be considered as a caution to Walton. Walton's
raging spirit of inquiry is eventually dampened by the story of Victor's
fall and demise. Victor's transgression of human limits and violent mastery of nature result in his downfall and exclusion. On this reading the
monster displays true humanity, and this is because he desires dialogue
with others and has some yearning for community. The monster's
request that Victor create a female body adds a feminist inflection to the
broader strain of humanism. The monster's desire for inclusion and
community can only be achieved by restoring the (culturally) 'feminine'
elements of experience: nature, the passions, empathy and the body.

Second-wave or radical feminist readings

A more positive or second-wave feminist approach would see Shelley as
more than a feminist supplement to Romanticism, for Victor can also

be read as a negative figure of the male Romantic poet. Not only is the novel about the violence and tyranny of the scientific intellect; it is also about the masculine imaginary exclusion of the feminine. The male Romantic poet can be read as an extension of, rather than departure from, the subject of science. The Romantic imagination still remains narcissistically trapped within itself; the nature and others with whom the male poet feels empathy can only be seen as a mirror of the masculine self. Walton is strangely drawn to Victor as a higher image of himself, and thereby anticipates Victor's desire to re-create his (male) self in the monster. Before Walton encounters Victor he is already striving for a 'man who could sympathise with me; whose eyes would reply to mine' and whose 'tastes are like my own' (17). Not only do Victor and Walton only enjoy nature and others as mirrors of their own selves, the feminine is presented as nothing more than a reflective medium for the male subject. Victor loves Elizabeth, who is both his sister and an echo of his mother, and he also sees her as an object rather than a subject: 'I...looked upon Elizabeth as mine – mine to protect, love and cherish. All praises bestowed on her I received as made to a possession of my own' (35). 'The saintly soul of Elizabeth shone like a shrine-dedicated lamp in our peaceful home. Her sympathy was ours' (37).

Frankenstein can be read as a feminist amendment to Romantic narcissism. The novel demonstrates the continuity between the enlightenment subject of totalising reason and the totalising imagination of the Romantic poet. Just as enlightenment science controls nature through knowledge and manipulation, so the Romantic poet's genius can only imagine nature and others as a reflection of self. On this reading, Shelley's allusions to Coleridge, Wordsworth and P.B. Shelley would be critical and symptomatic. The fact that Walton so often echoes the discourse of Romanticism exposes the gender of Romanticism, its specifically masculine imagination of all that is other than itself in its own image. The positive characters in the novel, such as Elizabeth, Clerval and the monster, would assert those qualities associated with the feminine: other-directedness, empathy, sentiment and respect for nature.

Third-wave feminist readings

On a third-wave reading, which questions the binary between totalising male reason and embodied female care, the novel could be read as a cultural critique of the male–female binary. If we accept Judith

Butler's claim that genders are produced through performance or iteration, then texts do not represent male and female selves; they articulate – and thereby also potentially destabilise – masculine and feminine roles. We only think of a natural femininity that is there to be repressed and represented because of all the discourses, such as Romanticism, that mourn its loss, absence or impossibility. For Butler, the subject is the effect of the discourses that compose it; gender boundaries are produced through texts. *Frankenstein* shows the way in which the discourses of Romanticism and humanism produce a moralistic, punitive and unquestioning subject. Victor's rhetoric is moralistic, dualistic and fatalistic; he imagines himself as the victim of a broader and malevolent destiny (48). His self-identity is produced through the fantasy of a punishing law or Other. Victor's early life is dominated by the presence of his father, a patriarchal figure whose approval produces subjection: 'There was a sense of justice in my father's upright mind, which rendered it necessary that he should approve highly to love strongly' (32).

The gender binary of the tale is produced through both Victor's and Walton's fantasy of innocent female others, who remain outside and beyond the law. Walton writes his tale in letter form to his sister; Victor is haunted by images of his sister (57), his mother and the procreating female monster he cannot bear to create. It is the fantasy of a punishing law that produces the male subject as a subject of judgment, authority and mutual recognition, and the female other as an impossible outside. *Frankenstein*, on this performative reading, would be a critical repetition of the discourse of the subject who can only imagine itself as subjected to law, and who thereby produces the fantasy and horror of a female innocence and chaos beyond the law.

The novel is not a moral tale but is about moral rhetoric and its capacity to produce gender boundaries. Selves are produced through the texts they read. Victor begins his description of self-formation by describing his reading – Paracelsus and natural philosophy – just as the monster describes his humanisation by reading texts such as *Paradise Lost*, Goethe's *Sorrows of Young Werther* and Plutarch's *Lives*. Clerval is steeped in the humanities – tales of chivalry and romance. The text shows the way the discourses of Romanticism, science and empire produce a certain type of (male) subject. The novel itself is nothing but a collection of found texts, of repeated stories; for all its voices are textually located. Shelley is showing the ways in which the borders between the human and the inhuman, the moral and the immoral are textually produced. The self is produced through narration, and the materials of narration are always received from elsewhere. Victor mirrors, variously, Milton's Satan, Milton's Adam and Milton's God. *Frankenstein* therefore shows the ways in which the subject positions set up in *Paradise Lost* – the position of creator/judge and created subject – are not fixed immutably but can be taken up and performed. Power relations are produced through discursive positions. The various speakers of the text produce the feminine as a lost, fantasised and Other object. The novel is therefore critical of the male/female boundary, showing the ways in which the ideology and discourse of sexual difference produces positions and relations of power.

Reading gender

If we were to offer a gendered reading of the novel we would not only look at the way in which the text performs and destabilises gender binaries; the very meaning of gender as a category could be challenged. If Shakespeare's *A Midsummer Night's Dream* and Milton's *Paradise Lost* present genders as forms to which physical matter ought to strive, the modern concept of gender as construction allows for an attention to that sexuality which precedes construction, culture, formation and perceived forms. As we have already noted, Butler's concept of gender as effected through performance precludes the notion of positive sexual difference. Sex is produced as that which gender has always already named and stabilised. Against this attention to the ways in which gender constitutes its outside, *Frankenstein* affirms the positivity of life, difference and sexuality – beyond gender. Just as Milton regards sexuality or physicality as *potential form*, so Butler can only recognise that which is other than formed gender as the destabilisation of gender. Both approaches repeat the privileging of a forming power that produces difference as its dependent or constituted other. More positive theorists of sexual difference, such as Moira Gatens and Elizabeth Grosz, have taken a more empiricist approach where the forces of physical life have a power or potential, which cannot be reduced to or exhausted by the constituted forms of human knowledge.

We have already mentioned the ways in which the novel is dominated by images of contrary forces: the forces of light and dark, positive and negative, life and death. On a moral or humanist reading the human self ought not step beyond its bounds and inquire into the forces of life. Early in the novel Walton articulates a rhetorical question: 'Who can stop the determined heart and resolved will of man?' (21). But both Victor's and Walton's will *is* halted. One could argue that, far from Victor refusing all limits and bounds to the will, he – like the Satan of *Paradise Lost* whom he echoes – falls back into moralising rhetoric. He does so because of his commitment to 'man.' His encounter with the forces of life, with the physical energy from which all forms emerge, is directed only to the recreation of 'man.' And when this man is not a faithful repetition of Victor's own image, Victor can only reject him as a monster, a demon or 'inhuman.' Victor is not a Promethean over-reacher so much as a moralising humanist, who can only think of science and life as issuing in 'man,' and who can only see the failure of his efforts in moral, theological and anthropomorphic terms. Victor sees himself as 'destined,' 'fated,' 'overtaken' by higher forces: 'for when I would recount to myself for the birth of that passion, which afterwards ruled my destiny, I find it arise, like a mountain river, from ignoble and almost forgotten sources' (38). Rather than acknowledging his will, he sees himself as compelled and determined by a power or force he refuses to confront or know.

Victor cannot see elemental forces in other than moralising or fateful terms ('ignoble'), never as a life that might enable other forms and relations: 'Destiny was too potent, and her immutable laws had decreed my utter and terrible destruction' (41). When the monster asks Victor to remedy what he has done by going further and creating a female monster, Victor retreats from the horror of a life and force that would be beyond his all too human control. He claims that such a decision is not his to make: he *cannot* go any further, for he has already transgressed proper human bounds.

> ...yet one of the first results of those sympathies for which the demon thirsted would be children, and a race of devils would be propogated upon the earth, who might make the very existence of the species of man a condition precarious and full of terror.... I shuddered to think that future ages might curse me as their pest, whose selfishness had not hesitated to buy its own peace at the price, perhaps, of the existence of the whole human race (160–161).

The novel is, then, less about over-reaching than it is about a failure of nerve in the face of a rampant life and sexuality beyond human recognition. What dooms Victor's project? His enquiry into the forces of life is channelled into the creation of man. When this man is not Victor's beautiful likeness, he is disowned as monstrous and then presented as the cause of an implacable evil. What stops Walton from his journey towards the light? His captivation by the form of 'man': the figure of Victor who is seductively like himself, a figure who is the image of a will that never quite reaches its potential: 'How can I see so noble a creature destroyed by misery, without feeling the most poignant grief? He is so gentle, yet so wise; his mind is so cultivated, and when he speaks, although his words are culled with the choicest art, yet they flow with rapidity and unparalleled eloquence' (26). And so Walton halts his journey: a journey, which again like Frankenstein's, was driven by an imperialist desire to conquer and be recognised by man, rather than an over-reaching of human limits.

The point is not that Victor and Walton go too far but that both their supposedly boundless wills are already enslaved to the desire of empire and 'man': 'One man's life or death were but a small price to pay for the acquirement of the knowledge which I sought for the dominion I should acquire and transmit over the elemental foes of our race' (27). It is just this retreat from inhuman force, and captivation by the image of modern and imperial 'man' that Shelley's boldly empiricist novel diagnoses. Hers is an empiricism where the forces of difference have no single grounding or governing form, where relations and terms are produced from opposition, life and striving.

The novel is dominated by imagery of light and dark, the pure differences from which all other oppositions emerge – such as master and slave, male and female, human and inhuman, good and evil. Characters constantly retreat or fall from this point of radical difference and appeal to morality, duty, nature or propriety. Far from being a novel that merely criticises constituted genders or the prejudiced norms of male and female, Shelley offers a way of thinking beyond gender to a sexuality, where sexuality is not just the potential to produce already known forms. If empire has been produced through the image of 'man' as the moral animal with a place in the moral order, then *Frankenstein* shows how 'man' has precluded us from thinking a life *without authority*, a life where difference, desire and physicality prompt us to think beyond already conceived forms. In this sense, the novel explores the relation between sexuality and gender. On the one hand, there are the fairly typical and broad-brush gender dichotomies: the scientific, totalising and violently self-projecting spirit of Victor and Walton versus the virtuous, altruistic, unreflective, nature-oriented and desired bodies of Elizabeth and Justine. Underpinning these dichotomies is the rigidly dualist imagination of Victor, who sees the world in terms of good and evil, human and inhuman, master and slave, man and woman. On the other hand, there is the unrealised project of the text: Victor's attempt to uncover the forces of life, Walton's journey towards the forces of life and – most importantly – Shelley's own description of the emergence of good and evil, mastery and slavery, human and inhuman in the narrative of *Frankenstein*.

The novel, in its diagnosis of gender, or in its presentation of the boundaries that produce man can be read as anti-patriarchal. Its genealogy of man takes the form of a diagnosis of our fantasies and desires for submission, the difficulty of confronting a world without an imposed law or form. The text poses the positive possibility of being fatherless or without origin. Recall that Victor sees his father as a high moral authority whose love we should seek: 'There was a sense of justice in my father's upright mind, which rendered it necessary that he should approve highly to love strongly' (32). It is his father's love that allows Victor to see himself as the fulcrum and focus of desire or, in Freud's terms, 'his majesty the baby': 'I was their plaything and their idol, and something better – their child, the innocent and helpless creature bestowed on them by Heaven, whom to bring up to good, and whose future lot it was in their hands to direct to happiness or misery, according as they filled their duties towards me' (33). Parental love – being the desired object of a dutiful and moral father – precludes Victor from seeing a life beyond his destined lot; he will remain 'destined,' if not heaven's 'idol,' for the rest of his recounted narrative. Victor is produced as an ideal object by a father who is described in theological terms as a 'protecting spirit,' who shows 'inexpressible grace' (32). This is the same father who brings Elizabeth home as a possession, and who acts with unremitting 'justice' in the case of Justine, incapable of overlooking her guilt.

Victor's desire for his father's love is the beginning of his megalo-mania – his sense of himself as heaven's plaything – and anticipates the monster's abject subjection to his 'father' Victor. From Victor's patriar-chal point of view his whole destiny might have altered had he remained bound to his father; all that is other than the father's order is, for Victor, evil and destructive. Victor can only see the world in Manichean terms, as morally divided between good and evil. He is incapable of affirming a chance or creativity without an omnipotent power. The only point at which chance can emerge is outside his father's domain: 'Chance – or rather the evil influence, the Angel of

Destruction, which asserted omnipotent sway over me from the moment I turned my reluctant steps from my father's door…' (45). But what if chance were not evil, but freedom? What if destruction allowed for the ruin of empire and patriarchy? What if the monster were to see himself as free and unfathered? Would he be so enslaved to Victor, and is it not this filial enslavement which prompts his reactionary revenge? Like Victor, the monster eventually sees his entire destiny as his 'father's' doing. Shelley does not set the feminine, or even the culturally constructed feminine, in opposition to this patriarchal moralism. Rather, her novel deconstructs the moral binaries of good and evil, male and female, human and inhuman.

We can think of deconstruction as a way of examining a moral opposition, in order to approach the undecidable point from which that opposition emerges. Shelley's novel seems to set up an opposition between a bounded and an unbounded will. The bounded will sees the world from the point of view of man, with what lies beyond man being either expelled as evil, or romanticised as the pure light of femininity (Elizabeth as the beacon of domestic harmony). Recall that just as Walton (like Victor after him) is about to approach the point of light, indifference and pure force, in his journey to the North Pole he retreats because he is seduced by an image of (human and male) power and authority. Walton's perception of Victor echoes Milton's *fallen* Satan:

> He must have been a noble creature in his better days…
> …his full-toned voice swells in my ears; his lustrous eyes dwell on me with all their melancholy sweetness; I see his thin hand raised in animation, while the lineaments of his face are irradiated by the soul within (29–30).

Shelley's novel endeavours to think a will or force before it is seduced by the human and priestly form of authority – the image of judging 'man.' On the one hand, Walton is drawn to Victor's will – his striving to see into the life of things – but on the other hand Walter all too readily gives this will a form of human authority. Rather than pursue force and will himself, Walton submits to Victor's 'soul-subduing' power:

> Sometimes I have endeavoured to discover what quality it is which he possesses, that elevates him so immeasurably above any other person I ever knew. I believe it to be an intuitive discernment; a quick but never failing power of judgment; a penetration into the causes of things, unequalled for clearness and precision; add to this

a facility of expression, and a voice whose varied intonations are soul-subduing music (28).

Walton is, like Victor, driven by knowledge, but (also like Victor, and Victor's father before him) imagines that this knowledge will place him in the position of a creator:

> ...you cannot contest the inestimable benefit which I shall confer on all mankind to the last generation, by discovering a passage near the pole to those countries, to reach which at present so many months are requisite; or by ascertaining the secret of the magnet, which, if at all possible, can only be effected by an undertaking such as mine (14).

Shelley's opposition between the striving towards pure force and the retreat from that striving into moral rhetoric is never strictly maintained in the text. The novel oscillates between the fixed boundaries of kinds – seeming to celebrate the nature, femininity, virtue and justice that Victor destroys – and the utopian destruction of those boundaries, with the very idea of an end to mastery and slavery being fleetingly glimpsed in the early moments of the monster's being. The unbounded will oversteps natural boundaries, loyalties, human nature and reverence, while the bounded will recognises itself (with passivity and calm) as part of the scheme of things, and becomes enslaved or captivated by the image of man. It is *Victor*, who can be read as the image of 'man' (not Shelley), who has a moralistic sense of the will, who sets up the opposition between a good bounded will and an unbounded evil:

> A human being in perfection ought always to preserve a calm and peaceful mind, and never to allow passion or a transitory desire to disturb tranquillity (54).

Whereas Victor has a clear sense of good and evil, human and inhuman, and the proper and improper will, Shelley's novel can be read as undecidably poised between difference and identity. She refuses the idea of a physicality that inevitably produces a formed and moral world; creation can be positively monstrous. But she also rejects the idea that we dutifully and passively remain within the moral rhetoric of a humanism that would see all others only as potentially or ideally identical to the man of reason and empire. We can, therefore, read all the appeals to order, form and authority in *Frankenstein* as received, derivative and imposed – as dependent on a commitment to 'man.' The monster, after all, sees his submission to Victor in remarkably feudal terms. And it is at this point that Shelley diagnoses how stronger forces become enslaved or determined. It is by wanting to be recognised as human, as just like Victor, that the monster produces himself as a slave:

> Remember, thou hast made me more powerful than thyself; my height is superiour to thine, my joints more supple. But I will not be tempted to set myself in opposition to thee. I am thy creature, and I will even be mild and docile to my natural lord and king, if thou wilt also perform thy part, which thou owest me. Oh, Frankenstein, be not equitable to every other and trample upon me alone, to whom thy justice, and even thy clemency and affection, is most due. Remember, that I am thy creature; I ought to be thy Adam, but I am rather the fallen angel, whom thou drivest from joy for no misdeed. Everywhere I see bliss, from which I alone am irrevocably excluded. I was benevolent and good; misery made me a fiend. Make me happy; and I shall again be virtuous (97).

Like Victor, the monster can only imagine being virtuous if he has a father (and a father who will create a female companion *for him*). The monster is produced as less than or potentially 'man' only because he has absorbed the rhetoric of empire from the texts he overhears. Shelley does not just repeat the monster's feudal rhetoric, which positions Victor as a superior because he is a father; she explains the emergence of this discourse. The monster later describes the reading of Volney's *Ruins of Empire* which he has overheard – not read for himself:

> While I listened to the instructions which Felix bestowed upon the Arabian, the strange system of human society was explained to me. I heard of the division of property, of immense wealth and squalid poverty; of rank, descent, and noble blood.... The words induced me to turn towards myself. I learned that the possessions most esteemed by your fellow creatures were, high and unsullied descent united with riches. A man might be respected with only one of these advantages; but without either he was considered, except in very rare instances, as a vagabond and a slave, doomed to waste his powers for the profits of the chosen few! And what was I? Of my creation and creator I was absolutely ignorant, but I knew that I possessed no money, no friends, no kind of property (116).

The monster's later deference to Victor is a retreat from his moment of birth where there are no fixed forms. Like Victor whose inquiry into the force of life can only repeat his own human form, and like Walton whose journey towards the light is halted by his deference to a Victor whom he sees as his own greater self, so the monster will begin with a positive or utopian encounter with pure difference from which he will later retreat. The monster describes the birth of consciousness and difference. He has the privilege of coming to consciousness outside the social form of the family. His 'orphan' status is certainly not a position of loss or abjection. This is pure desire or perception, an encounter with life as difference – before constituted and received hierarchies: a series of polarities that have yet to be interpreted:

> A strange multiplicity of sensations seized me, and I saw, felt, heard, and smelt at the same time; and it was, indeed, a long time before I learned to distinguish between the operations of my various senses. By degrees, I remember, a stronger light pressed on my nerves, so that I was obliged to shut my eyes. Darkness then came over me, and troubled me; but hardly had I felt this when, by opening my eyes, as I now suppose, the light poured in on me again...

> No distinct ideas occupied my mind; all was confused. I felt light, and hunger, and thirst, and darkness ... I began also to observe, with greater accuracy, the forms that surrounded me, and to perceive the boundaries of the radiant roof of light which canopied me.' (99–100)

Victor's search into the origins of life, his irreverence and over-reaching is constantly foreclosed by Victor's fatalistic, moralistic and Manichean rhetoric. There is a suggestion in *Frankenstein* that all the texts of humanism and piety actually underpin empire and servitude. The supposedly human and empathetic Clerval becomes an Orientalist, studying the texts that present the non-Western other as a feminine an object of fascination: 'How different from the manly and heroical poetry of Greece and Rome.' (67)

Against the idea of cultural construction and a law within which we move, Shelley presents monstrosity as a positive possibility. Whereas *A Midsummer Night's Dream* and *Paradise Lost* move from sexuality as potentiality to achieved genders, *Frankenstein* moves from morally and theologically formed 'man' to forces of life, light and creation: a sexuality beyond human intent. Selves and texts are effects of differential movements that precede language, consciousness and textuality. *Frankenstein* exposes the emergence of the rhetoric of good and evil from elemental forces. Characters constantly view these forces in moral terms (good and evil, human and inhuman, natural and unnatural), despite the fact that nature is presented as inhuman and as beyond any of the limited forms the imagination imposes. Far from being anti-Promethean the novel is an attempt to think the very origin and emergence of experience. Victor is undone, not because he overreaches but because he remains within the language of moralism, empire and superstition. It occurs to him that truly radical questioning would lead to the dissolution of empire, to the abandonment of social orders and hierarchies, and it is this monstrous possibility from which he retreats. And it is here also that Shelley diagnoses the way in which moral 'man' is crucial to the 'duty' of empire. Victor regrets his overreaching as typical of the spirit that has brought down empires:

> A human being in perfection ought always to preserve a calm and peaceful mind, and never to allow passion or a transitory desire to disturb tranquillity. I do not think that the pursuit of knowledge is an exception to this rule. If the study to which you apply yourself has a tendency to weaken your affections, and to destroy your taste for those simple pleasures in which no alloy can possibly mix, then that study is certainly unlawful, that is to say, not befitting the human mind. If this rule were always observed; if no man allowed any pursuit whatsoever to interfere with the tranquillity of his domestic affections, Greece had not been enslaved; Caesar would have spared his country; America would have been discovered more gradually; and the empires of Mexico and Peru had not been destroyed. (54)

Shelley describes the monster's emergence into consciousness as the gradual differentiation of light and dark, of positive and negative, of self and other. The novel affirms genesis or sexuality *before* gender, the processes of difference and generation that cannot be reduced to human control, and that go beyond form and rhetoric. The novel has an expanded notion of responsibility, recognising the effect and force of differences beyond human intent. Victor may not have full control of his monster, the monster may not be a perfect copy of his own self, but this does not mean that Victor should exclude and refuse his existence.

The monster begins as free because he is fatherless but becomes more enslaved, more of a *creature*, the more he overhears; he will come to learn that he has a father or creator who disowns him, and that there is a human world that defines him as inhuman. It is with the increasing consumption of Western texts of authority that the monster becomes servile, and fuelled by a bitter sense of exclusion, resentment and servility. Consider the monster talking about Felix and Agatha: 'I looked upon them as superior beings, who would be the arbiters of my future destiny' (111). If he had no story about his origins, no sense of a father who owes him a bond of feudal duty, then he would feel neither exclusion nor envy.

Frankenstein strives to present sensual particulars before moral oppositions, sex before gender. Sex in Shelley's text is more than potential gender; it is a monstrous force in its own right that will enable Shelley to write a tale that will induce terror and fear, rather that awe and respect: 'What terrified me will terrify others' (9). Shelley herself describes the textual process as one of unconscious birth. Unlike Victor who can only see being overtaken by force as demonic, Mary Shelley regards such possession as a gift: 'My imagination, unbidden, possessed and guided me, gifting the successive images that arose in my mind with a vividness far beyond the usual bounds of reverie' (9). She also sees creation as occurring from difference and duality, not from a single author or substance:

> Invention, it must be humbly admitted, does not consist in creating out of void, but out of chaos; the materials must, in the first place, be afforded: it can give form to dark, shapeless substances, but cannot bring into being the substance itself....Invention consists in the capacity of seizing on the capabilities of a subject: and in the power of moulding and fashioning ideas suggested to it (8).

The novel is about positive difference; the sensible and bodily processes from which oppositions emerge. Indeed, the idea that we are located within a textual tradition and that we cannot step outside or overreach constituted values is not only criticised but diagnosed as the myth of 'man.' We seem to have returned to this book's point of creation: the idea of order and form emerging from chaos. But whereas Western thought has been *equivocal* – by seeing one side of the binary as deriving from the other – Shelley's empiricism suggests a *univocity* of sexuality, where both chaos and form have equal reality, where the imagination is not set over against life but is a power within life. Mind and art are responses to powers of life, not constructions or mediations of life. The idea of gender as form set upon matter, gives way to sexuality as force productive of differences.

Annotated Bibliography

Bourdieu, Pierre. *Masculine Domination*. Trans. Richard Nice. Cambridge: Polity, 2001.

Attacks 'postmodern' notions of gender construction by arguing that the persistence of masculine domination is achieved by using a bodily difference to explain and order a series of social and cultural hierarchies.

Beauvoir, Simone de. *The Second Sex*. Trans. and ed. H.M. Parshley. Harmondsworth: Penguin, 1972.

The original text of French feminism. Drawing upon and extending the existentialist philosophy of Jean-Paul Sartre, Beauvoir politicises the existential idea that subjects exist as pure freedom in opposition to an objectivity that simply *is*. Beauvoir established that 'woman' has always been the Other against which man's freedom or transcendence is defined.

Butler, Judith. *Gender Trouble: Feminism and the Subversion of Identity*. London: Routledge, 1990.

Gender Trouble is still probably the most influential book on gender, as it has set the terms of the debate for the relation between sex and gender. In this book Butler challenges the sex/gender distinction by arguing that subjection to the norms of gender produces the fantasy of a body that was there to be subjected. Gender is, for Butler, produced through the acting out or performance of norms. Indeed, the linguistic performative – those forms of speech that produce what they seem to name – becomes Butler's exemplary mode of all speech and interaction.

Butler, Judith. *Bodies that Matter: On the Discursive Limits of 'Sex'*. New York: Routledge, 1993.

In this book Butler answers criticisms directed to *Gender Trouble*. If there is no sex before the norms of gender, what happens to the body or materiality? Butler's argument is that the process of signification and performance is material and that matter and bodies are just those actions which, through repetition, express an identity that then appears to be an identity prior to the action. Butler draws on the work of Irigaray and Kristeva to argue that Western thought has always produced matter as an outside that has being only through secondary acts of formation.

Cealey Harrison, Wendy and John Hood-Williams. *Beyond Sex and Gender*. London: Sage, 2002.

Criticises the social theory of gender by focussing on sexuality. Attacks Butler's reading of psychoanalysis by arguing that the terms of gender – male and female – cannot be used to describe the emergence of the self, for there are sexual orientations, desires and tendencies that establish boundaries between self and other before the norms of gender.

Connell, R.W. *Gender and Power: Sex, the Person and Sexual Politics*. Stanford: Stanford University Press, 1987.

A sociological and political analysis of the concept of gender, with an emphasis on the tradition of 'sex roles' and the politics of gender norms. Mainly concerned with gender as a function of personality formation, and less concerned with philosophical, literary or connotative implications.

Copjec, Joan. *Read My Desire: Lacan Against the Historicists*. Cambridge, Mass.: MIT Press, 1994.

Copjec's final chapter, 'Sex and the Euthanasia of Reason,' provides a brilliant attack on the concept of gender as social construction and argues for the intractable force of sexual difference. Defends a Lacanian approach to film and literary theory against a historicism that would refuse any *a priori* paradigms.

De Lauretis, Teresa. *Technologies of Gender: Essays on Theory, Film and Fiction*. Bloomington: Indiana University Press, 1987.

Prior to Judith Butler's *Gender Trouble*, De Lauretis was one of the most stringent critics of the simple opposition between sex and gender. In the key essay of this volume, 'Technologies of Gender,' she criticises the ways in which represented gender – male and female – is seen as the direct transposition or mirroring of two biological sexes. De Lauretis argues that we need to see the representation of gender as positive, as productive rather than reflective of the male–female binary.

Felski, Rita. *The Gender of Modernity*. Cambridge, Mass.; London: Harvard University Press, 1995.

Felski's first book, *Beyond Feminist Aesthetics* challenged the second-wave feminist ideal of a unique, autonomous and different female subject that might yield an alternative literary tradition, but Felski nevertheless maintained that one could think of a feminist literature formed through a 'counter public sphere': female identity was established through writing and public engagement. In *The Gender of Modernity* Felski looks at the ways in which the ideals of the modern, such as anti-commodification and the critique of passive consumption, are tied up with figures of gender.

Gatens, Moira. *Imaginary Bodies: Ethics, Power and Corporeality*. London: Routledge, 1995.

Not as influential as Butler's *Bodies that Matter* but Gatens provides an early, powerful and lucid critique of the sex/gender distinction. (The volume includes essays published in the 1980s.) Gatens argues that the distinction between biological sex and social gender repeats a Cartesian dualism that separates mind from body – a dualism that has also underpinned the hierarchies of gender in the form of reasoning man and embodied woman.

Glover, David and Cora Kaplan. *Genders*. London: Routledge, 2000.

Provides an overview of the concept and history of gender from the eighteenth century to the present. Explores the concept through literary authors, such as Carlyle, Kafka and Wilde.

Grosz, Elizabeth. *Volatile Bodies*. Sydney: Allen and Unwin, 1994.

Grosz's earlier readings of Lacan and French feminism installed the body in feminism. In *Volatile Bodies* she provides her own theory of sexual difference and insists that the idea of gender as social construction merely repeats a long-standing prejudice against corporeality.

Haraway, Donna J. *Simians, Cyborgs, and Women: The Reinvention of Nature.* New York: Routledge, 1991.

An anti-humanist and polemical manifesto that rejects the return to, or retrieval of, woman and imagines the utopian possibility of a world without gender. Significant for its celebration of technology, the monstrous and the unnatural, and therefore opposed to the nostalgic association of woman with uncorrupted nature.

Irigaray, Luce. *Speculum of the Other Woman.* Trans. Gillian C. Gill. Ithaca: Cornell, 1985.

One of the most influential and contentious texts of post-structuralist feminism. Reads the history of Western philosophy in order to expose the supposedly neutral subject as dependent upon a fantasy (and negation) of woman.

Kristeva, Julia. *Desire in Language: A Semiotic Approach to Literature and Art.* Ed. Leon S. Roudiez. Trans. Thomas Gora, Alice Jardine and Leon S. Roudiez. Oxford: Basil Blackwell, 1981.

Kristeva argues that the distinction between masculine and feminine is metaphysical. In order to have individual subjects who represent and judge the world some distinction needs to be made between the ordering position of law and judgement (the symbolic), which is defined in opposition to the not fully systematised differences of the child–mother dyad (the semiotic).

Laqueur, Thomas. *Making Sex: Body and Gender from the Greeks to Freud.* Cambridge, Mass.: Harvard University Press, 1990.

Provides a historical account of the shift from a pre-modern notion of a one-sex model, where male and female bodies are analogous forms given to one matter, to a modern notion of sexual difference, where male and female genders express distinct material sexes.

Lloyd, Genevieve. *The Man of Reason: 'Male' and 'Female' in Western Philosophy.* London: Methuen, 1984.

Men are not essentially rational and women are not essentially embodied but the history of Western thought has repeatedly produced norms of reason that are aligned with qualities that also define

masculinity. Lloyd gives a breathtaking overview of Western philosophy from Plato to modernity that challenges the supposedly
'gender-neutral' status of reason.

Millett, Kate. *Sexual Politics*. London: Rupert Hart-Davis, 1971.

The central polemical text of second-wave or radical feminism. Famous
for insisting that the 'personal is political,' Millett insists that the
feminism needs to move beyond women's rights and inclusion, and
change the very way in which women are represented and imagined.

Moi, Toril. *Sexual/Textual Politics: Feminist Literary Theory*. London:
Methuen, 1985.

An extremely influential and polemical introduction to French
feminism for literary theorists. Attacks essentialist notions of woman
to insist on the textual construction of masculinity and femininity.

Rubin, Gayle. 'The Traffic in Women: Notes on the "Political Economy"
of Sex.' *Toward an Anthropology of Women*. Ed. Rayna R. Reiter.
New York: Monthly Review Press, 1975.

Despite the fact that Rubin has since tempered her argument of
gender construction with an attention to sexualities, this essay is the
clearest and most influential account of the production of the gender
binary in the transition to culture.

Bibliography

Adams, Parveen. 'A Note on the Distinction between Sexual Division and Sexual Differences,' *m/f* 3, 1979.

Adorno, Theodor. *Metaphysics: Concepts and Problems*. Trans. Edmund Jephcott. Ed. Rolf Tiedemann. Cambridge: Polity, 2000.

Adorno, Theodor and Max Horkheimer. *Dialectic of Enlightenment*. Trans. John Cumming. London: Verso, 1979.

Alcoff, Linda. 'Cultural Feminism vs Post-Structuralism: The Identity Crisis in Feminist Theory,' *Signs* 13.3 (1988).

Althusser, Louis. 'Ideology and Ideological State Apparatuses.' *Lenin and Philosophy and other Essays*. Trans. Ben Brewster. London: New Left Books, 1971.

Aristotle. *The Complete Works of Aristotle*. Ed. Jonathan Barnes. Princeton: Princeton University Press, 1995.

Armstrong, Nancy. *Desire and Domestic Fiction*. Oxford: Oxford University Press, 1987.

Astell, Mary. *The First English Feminist: Reflections upon Marriage and Other Writings*. Ed. Bridget Hill. Aldershot: Gower/Maurice Temple Smith, 1986.

Augustine, Saint. *The City of God Against the Pagans. Vol. 4, Books 11–15*. Trans. P. Levine. London: W. Heinemann, 1966.

Austen, Jane. *Pride and Prejudice*. Ed. Tony Tanner. Harmondsworth: Penguin, 1972.

——. *Pride and Prejudice*. Ed. Kames Kinsley. Oxford: Oxford University Press, 1990.

Barrett, Michèle. *Women's Oppression Today: Problems in Marxist Feminist Analysis*. London: New Left Books, 1980.

Beauvoir, Simone de. *The Second Sex*. Trans. and Ed. H.M. Parshley. Harmondsworth: Penguin, 1972.

Benhabib, Seyla. *Situating the Self: Gender, Community and Postmodernism in Contemporary Ethics*. Cambridge: Polity, 1992.

Berger, Peter L. and Thomas Luckmann. *The Social Construction of Reality: A Treatise in the Sociology of Knowledge*. New York: Doubleday, 1966.

Berkeley, George. 'A Treatise Concerning the Principles of Human Knowledge.' [1710], *Berkeley's Philosophical Writings*. Ed. David Armstrong. London: Collier Macmillan, 1965.

Bersani, Leo. *Homos*. Cambridge, Mass.: Harvard University Press, 1995.

Blake, William. *The Complete Poetry and Prose of William Blake*. Ed. David V. Erdman. Rev. ed. New York: Anchor-Doubleday, 1988.

Bloom, Harold. *The Anxiety of Influence: A Theory of Poetry*. Oxford: Oxford University Press, 1973.

Blumenberg, Hans. *The Genesis of the Copernican World*. Cambridge, Mass.: MIT Press, 1987.

Bordo, Susan. *The Flight to Objectivity: Essays on Cartesianism and Culture*. Albany: State University of New York Press, 1987.

Bostock, David. 'Aristotle on the Principles of Change.' *Language and Logos: Studies in Ancient Greek Philosophy Presented to G.E.L. Owen*. Ed. Malcolm Schofiled and Martha Craven Nussbaum. Cambridge: Cambridge University Press, 1982. 179–196.

Bourdieu, Pierre. *Masculine Domination*. Trans. Richard Nice. Cambridge: Polity, 2001.

Braidotti, Rosi. *Patterns of Dissonance*. Cambridge: Polity, 1991.

Brennan, Teresa. *History after Lacan*, London: Routledge, 1993.

Brownmiller, Susan. *Against our Will: Men, Women and Rape*. London: Secker and Warburg, 1975.

Butler, Judith. *Gender Trouble: Feminism and the Subversion of Identity*. London: Routledge, 1990.

——. *Bodies that Matter: On the Discursive Limits of 'Sex.'* London: Routledge, 1993.

——. 'Against Proper Objects.' *Feminism Meets Queer Theory*. Ed. Elizabeth Weed and Naomi Schor. Bloomington: Indiana University Press, 1997. 1–30.

——. *The Psychic Life of Power: Theories in Subjection*. Stanford: Stanford University Press, 1997.

——. *Gender Trouble: Feminism and the Subversion of Identity*. London: Routledge, 1990. 2nd edn 1999.

——. *Antigone's Claim: Kinship Between Life and Death*. New York: Columbia University Press, 2000.

——. 'Doing Justice to Someone: Sex Reassignment and Allegories of Transexuality.' *GLQ: A Journal of Lesbian and Gay Studies* 7.4 (2001): 621–636.

Cealey Harrison, Wendy and John Hood-Williams. *Beyond Sex and Gender*. London: Sage, 2002.

Cheah, Pheng. 'Mattering.' *Diacritics* 26.1 (1996): 108–139.

Chodorow, Nancy J. *The Reproduction of Mothering: Psychoanalysis and the Sociology of Gender*. Berkeley: University of California Press, 1978.

——. *Femininities, Masculinities, Sexualities: Freud and Beyond*. London: Free Association Books, 1994.

Cixous, Hélène. 'Sorties.' *New French Feminisms: An Anthology*. Ed. Elaine Marks and Isabelle de Courtrivon. Sussex: Harvester, 1981. 90–98.

Collingwood, R.G. *The Idea of Nature*. Oxford: Clarendon Press, 1945.

Cooper, John M. 'Aristotle on Natural Teleology,' in *Language and Logos: Studies in Ancient Greek Philosophy Presented to G.E.L. Owen*. Ed. Malcolm Schofield and Martha Craven Nussbaum. Cambridge: Cambridge University Press, 1982. 197–222.

Copjec, Joan. *Read My Desire: Lacan Against the Historicists*. Cambridge, Mass.: MIT Press, 1994.

——. *Imagine There's No Woman: Ethics and Sublimation*. Cambridge, Mass.: MIT Press, 2002.

Cornell, Drucilla. *Beyond Accommodation: Ethical Feminism, Deconstruction and the Law*. New York: Routledge, 1991.

Coward, Rosalind and John Ellis. *Language and Materialism*. London: Routledge and Kegan Paul, 1977.

Culler, Jonathan. *On Deconstruction: Theory and Criticism after Structuralism*. London: Routledge and Kegan Paul, 1983.

Daly, Mary. *Gyn/ecology: The Metaethics of Radical Feminism*. London: Women's Press, 1979.

Daston, Lorraine. 'The Nature of Nature in Early Modern Europe.' *Configurations* 6.2 (1998): 149–172.

De Lauretis, Teresa. *Technologies of Gender: Essays on Theory, Film and Fiction*. Bloomington: Indiana University Press, 1987.

——. 'The Essence of the Triangle or, Taking the Risk of Essentialism Seriously: Feminist Theory in Italy, the U.S. and Britain.' *The Essential Difference*. Ed. Naomi Schor and Elizabeth Weed. Bloomington: Indiana University Press, 1994. 1–39.

Deleuze, Gilles. *Expressionism in Philosophy: Spinoza*. Trans. Martin Joughin. New York: Zone, 1992.

——. *Negotiations: 1972–1990*. Trans. Martin Joughin. New York: Columbia, 1995.

Deleuze, Gilles and Félix Guattari. *Anti-Oedipus: Capitalism and Schizophrenia*. Trans. Brian Massumi. Minneapolis: University of Minnesota Press, 1983.

——. *A Thousand Plateaus: Capitalism and Schizophrenia*. Trans. Brian Massumi. Minneapolis: University of Minnesota Press, 1987.

Delphy, Christine. 'Rethinking Sex and Gender.' *Women's Studies International Forum* 16.1 (1993): 1–9.

Derrida, Jacques. 'The *Retrait* of Metaphor.' *Enclitic* 2.4 (1978): 5–33.

——. *Writing and Difference*. Trans. Alan Bass. London: Routledge and Kegan Paul, 1981.

——. *Dissemination*. Trans. Barbara Johnson. Chicago: University of Chicago Press, 1981.

——. 'Economimesis.' Trans. R. Klein. *Diacritics* 11.2 (Summer 1981): 3–25.

——. *Margins of Philosophy*. Trans. Alan Bass. Sussex: Harvester, 1982.

——. 'Geschlecht: Sexual Difference and Ontological Difference.' Trans. R. Berezdivin. *Research in Phenomenology* 13 (1983): 65–83.

——. *Glas*. Trans. John P. Leavey, Jr and Richard Rand. Lincoln: University of Nebraska Press, 1986.

——. *Limited Inc*. Ed. Gerald Graff. Evanston: Northwestern University Press, 1988.

——. *Edmund Husserl's Origin of Geometry: An Introduction by Jacques Derrida*. Trans. John P. Leavey. Lincoln: University of Nebraska Press, 1989.

——. 'Choreographies.' Trans. Christie V. McDonald. *Points: Interviews, 1974–1994*. Ed. Elisabeth Weber. Stanford: Stanford University Press, 1995. 89–108.

Descartes, René. *Discourse on Method and the Meditations*. Trans. F.E. Sutcliffe. Harmondsworth: Penguin Books, 1968.

Diprose, Rosalyn. *The Bodies of Women: Ethics, Embodiment and Sexual Difference*. London: Routledge, 1994.

Dumont, Louis. *Essays in Individualism: Modern Ideology in Anthropological Perspective*. Chicago: Chicago University Press, 1977.

Dworkin, Andrea. *Pornography: Men Possessing Women*. London: Women's Press, 1981.

Edelman, Lee. *Homographesis: Essays in Gay Literary and Cultural Theory*. New York: Routledge, 1994.

Eisenstein, Hester. *Contemporary Feminist Thought.* London: Unwin Paperbacks, 1984.

Elaine Showalter. 'Feminist Criticism in the Wilderness.' *The New Feminist Criticism: Essays on Women, Literature and Theory.* Ed. Elaine Showalter. London: Virago, 1986. 243–270.

Elshtain, Jean Bethke. *Public Man, Private Woman: Women in Social and Political Thought.* Princeton: Princeton University Press, 1993.

Engels, Friedrich. *The Origin of the Family: Private Property and the State.* London; New York: International Publishers, 1942.

English, Jane. 'Justice Between Generations.' *Philosophical Studies* 31 (1977): 91–104.

Fausto-Sterling, Anne. *Sexing the Body: Gender Politics and the Construction of Sexuality.* New York: Basic Books, 2000.

Felman, Shoshana. *Jacques Lacan and the Adventure of Insight: Psychoanalysis in Contemporary Culture.* Cambridge, Mass.: Harvard University Press, 1987.

Felski, Rita. *The Gender of Modernity.* Cambridge, Mass.: Harvard University Press, 1995.

——. *Doing Time: Feminist Theory and Postmodern Culture.* New York: New York University Press, 2000.

Findlen, Paula. 'Ideas in the Mind: Gender and Knowledge in the Seventeenth Century.' *Hypatia* 17.1 (2002): 183–196.

Firestone, Shulamith. *The Dialectic of Sex: The Case for Feminist Revolution.* London: Woman's Press, 1979.

Foucault, Michel. *The Order of Things: An Archaeology of the Human Sciences.* London: Tavistock, 1970.

——. *Discipline and Punish: The Birth of the Prison.* Trans. Alan Sheridan. Harmondsworth: Penguin, 1979.

——. *The History of Sexuality, Volume 1: An Introduction.* Trans. Robert Hurley. Harmondsworth: Penguin, 1981.

——. *The History of Sexuality Volume 3: The Care of the Self.* Trans. Robert Hurley. Harmondsworth: Penguin, 1986.

——. *The Use of Pleasure: The History of Sexuality, Volume 2.* Trans. Robert Hurley. Harmondsworth: Penguin, 1988.

Fox Keller, Evelyn. *Secrets of Life: Essays on Language, Gender and Science.* London: Routledge, 1992.

Freud, Sigmund. *On Sexuality.* Ed. Angela Richards. Trans. James Strachey. Harmondsworth: Penguin, 1977.

——. *On Metapsychology: The Theory of Psychoanalysis. Beyond the Pleasure Principle, The Ego and the Id and Other Works.* Ed. Angela Richards. Trans. James Strachey. Harmondsworth: Penguin, 1991.

——. 'Civilisation and its Discontents.' *Civilization, Society and Religion*. Trans. James Strachey. Ed. Albert Dickson. Harmondsworth: Penguin, 1985.

Gatens, Moira. *Imaginary Bodies: Ethics, Power and Corporeality*. London: Routledge, 1996.

——. 'Feminism and "Password": Re-thinking the "Possible" with Spinoza and Deleuze.' *Hypatia* 15.2 (2000): 58–75.

Gatens, Moira and Genevieve Lloyd. *Collective Imaginings: Spinoza, Past and Present*. London: Routledge, 1999.

Gilbert, Sandra M. and Susan Gubar. *The Madwoman in the Attic: The Woman Writer and the Nineteenth-Century Literary Imagination*. New Haven: Yale University Press, 1979.

Gilligan, Carol. *In a Different Voice: Psychological Theory and Women's Development*. Cambridge, Mass.: Harvard University Press, 1982.

Goldmann, Lucien. *Towards a Sociology of the Novel*. Trans. Alan Sheridan. London: Tavistock Publications, 1975.

Grant, Judith. *Fundamental Feminism: Contesting the Core Concepts of Feminist Theory*. London: Routledge, 1993.

Gray, John. *Men are from Mars, Women are from Venus: A Practical Guide for Improving Communication and Getting What You Want in Your Relationships*. New York: HarperCollins, 1992.

Green, Karen. 'Rawls, Women and the Priority of Liberty.' *Australasian Journal of Philosophy* 64, supplement (1986): 26–36.

——. *The Woman of Reason: Feminism, Humanism, and Political Thought*. Cambridge: Polity Press, 1995.

Greenblatt, Stephen J. *Renaissance Self-fashioning: From More to Shakespeare*. Chicago: University of Chicago Press, c1980.

——. 'Fiction and Friction.' *Reconstructing Individualism: Autonomy, Individuality, and the Self in Western Thought*. Ed. Thomas Heller, Morton Sosna, David E. Wellbery, Arnold Davidson, Ann Swidler and Ian Watt. Stanford: Stanford University Press, 1986. 30–52.

Grosz, Elizabeth. 'Notes Towards a Corporeal Feminism.' *Australian Feminist Studies* 5 (1987): 1–15.

——. *Sexual Subversions: Three French Feminists*. Sydney: Allen and Unwin, 1989.

——. *Jacques Lacan: A Feminist Introduction*. Sydney: Allen and Unwin, 1990.

——. 'Sexual Difference and the Problem of Essentialism.' *The Essential Difference*. Ed. Naomi Schor and Elizabeth Weed. Bloomington: Indiana University Press, 1994. 82–87.

——. *Space, Time and Perversion: Essays on the Politics of Bodies.* London: Routledge, 1995.

——. 'Thinking the New: Of Futures yet Unthought.' *Becomings: Explorations in Time, Memory and Futures.* Ed. Elizabeth Grosz. Ithaca: Cornell University Press, 1999.

——. *Architecture from the Outside: Essays on Virtual and Real Space.* Cambridge, Mass.: MIT Press, 2001.

Gubar, Susan. '"The Blank Page" and the Issues of Female Creativity.' *The New Feminist Criticism: Essays on Women, Literature and Theory.* Ed. Elaine Showalter. London: Virago, 1986. 292–313.

Guillaumin, Colette, 'Race and Nature: The System of Marks.' *Feminist Issues* 2.1 (1982).

——. 'The Question of Difference.' *Feminist Issues* 8.2 (1988).

Habermas, Jürgen. *Knowledge and Human Interests.* Trans. Jeremy J. Shapiro. London: Heinemann Educational, 1972.

——. 'Modernity – An Incomplete Project.' Trans. Seyla Benhabib. *Postmodern Culture.* Ed. Hal Foster. London: Pluto Press, 1985. 3–15.

——. *Postmetphysical Thinking: Philosophical Essays.* Trans. William Mark Hohengarten. Cambridge, Mass.: MIT Press, 1992.

Hacking, Ian. *The Social Construction of What?* Cambridge, Mass.: Harvard University Press, 1999.

Halperin, David M. 'How to Do the History of Male Homosexuality.' *GLQ: A Journal of Lesbian and Gay Studies* 6.1 (2000): 87–123.

Hamer, Dean and Peter Copeland. *The Science of Desire: The Search for the Gay Gene and the Biology of Behaviour.* New York: Simon and Schuster, 1994.

Haraway, Donna J. *Simians, Cyborgs, and Women: The Reinvention of Nature.* New York: Routledge, 1991.

Hardt, Michael and Antonio Negri. *Empire.* Cambridge, Mass.: Harvard University Press, 2000.

Hartman, Geoffrey H. *Beyond Formalism: Literary Essays: 1958–1970.* New Haven: Yale University Press, 1970.

Hartmann, Heidi. 'The Unhappy Marriage of Marxism and Feminism: Towards a More Progressive Union,' in *The Unhappy Marriage of Marxism and Feminism.* Ed. Lydia Sargent. London: Pluto Press, 1981.

Hayles, Katherine N. 'The Materiality of Informatics.' *Configurations: A Journal of Literature, Science and Technology* 1 (Winter 1993): 147–170.

Heidegger. *What is a Thing?* Trans. W.B. Barton, Jr and Vera Deutsch. Lanham: University Press of America, 1967.

——. 'On the Essence and Concept of *Physis* in Aristotle's *Physics* B, I.' Trans. Thomas Sheehan. *Pathmarks*. Ed. William McNeill. Cambridge: Cambridge University Press, 1998. 183–230.

Heilbrun, Carolyn G. *Towards Androgyny. Aspects of Male and Female in Literature*. London Gollancz, 1973.

Herdt, Gilbert. *Third Sex/Third Gender: Beyond Sexual Dimorphism in Culture and History*. New York: Zone, 1993.

Hobbes, Thomas. *Leviathan*. Ed. Richard Tuck. Cambridge: Cambridge University Press, 1991.

Hope, Trevor. 'Melancholic Modernity: The Hom(m)osexual Symptom and the Homosocial Corpse.' *Feminism Meets Queer Theory*. Ed. Elizabeth Weed and Naomi Schor. Bloomington: Indiana, 1997.

Hume, David. *Enquires Concerning Human Understanding and Concerning the Principles of Morals*. Ed. L.A. Selby-Bigge. 3rd edn Revised by P.H. Nidditch. Oxford: Oxford University Press, 1975.

——. *A Treatise of Human Nature*. Ed. David Fate Norton and Mary J. Norton. Oxford: Oxford University Press, 2000.

Hundert, E.J. 'Augustine and the Sources of the Divided Self.' *Political Theory* 20.1 (1992): 86–104.

Irigaray, Luce. *Speculum of the Other Woman*. Trans. Gillian C. Gill. Ithaca: Cornell University Press, 1985.

——. *Sexes and Genealogies*. Trans. Gillian C. Gill. New York: Columbia, 1993a.

——. *An Ethics of Sexual Difference*. Trans. Carolyn Burke and Gillian C. Gill. Ithaca: Cornell University Press, 1993b.

——. *Thinking the Difference: For a Peaceful Revolution*. Trans. Karin Montin. London: Athlone, 1994.

——. *I Love to You: Sketch of a Possible Felicity in History*. Trans. Alison Martin. New York: Routledge, 1996.

——. 'The Question of the Other.' Trans. Noak Guynn. *Yale French Studies* 87 (1999): 7–19.

Jacques, Lacan and École, Freudienne. *Feminine Sexuality*. Ed. Juliet Mitchell and Jacqueline Rose. London: Macmillan.

Jaggar, Alison. 'Love and Knowledge: Emotion in Feminist Epistemology.' *Inquiry* 32, 1989.

Jones, Anne Rosalind. 'Writing the Body; Toward an Understanding of *l'Écriture féminine*.' *The New Feminist Criticism: Essays on Women, Literature and Theory*. Ed. Elaine Showalter. London: Virago, 1986.

Kant, Immanuel. 'On a Newly Arisen Superior Tone in Philosophy.' *Raising the Tone of Philosophy: Late Essays by Immanuel Kant, Transformative Critique by Jacques Derrida*. Trans. Peter Fenves. Ed. Peter Fenves. Baltimore: Johns Hopkins, 1993.

——. *Critique of Pure Reason*. Trans. Paul Guyer. Cambridge: Cambridge University Press, 1998.

Ketchum, Sara Ann. 'Liberalism and Marriage Law.' *Feminism and Philosophy*. Ed. Mary Wetterling-Braggin, Frederick A. Elliston and Jane English. Totowa: Rowmans and Allenheld, 1985. 264–276.

King, Helen. 'Sowing the Field.' Ed. Roy Porter and Mikulas Teich. *Sexual Knowledge, Sexual Science: The History of Attitudes to Sexuality*. Cambridge: Cambridge University Press, 1994.

Kirby, Vicki. 'Corpus Delecti: The Body at the Scene of Writing.' *Cartographies: Poststructuralism and the Mappings of Bodies and Spaces*. Ed. Rosalyn Diprose and Robyn Ferrell. Sydney: Allen and Unwin, 1991. 88–102.

——. *Telling Flesh: The Substance of the Corporeal*. New York: Routledge, 1997.

Koyré, Alexandre. *From the Closed World to the Infinite Universe*. Baltimore: Johns Hopkins University Press, 1994.

Kristeva, Julia. *Desire in Language: A Semiotic Approach to Literature and Art*. Ed. Leon S. Roudiez. Trans. Thomas Gora, Alice Jardine and Leon S. Roudiez. Oxford: Basil Blackwell, 1981.

——. *Revolution in Poetic Language*. Trans. Margaret Waller. New York: Columbia University Press, 1984.

——. 'Women's Time.' *The Kristeva Reader*. Ed. Toril Moi. Oxford: Basil Blackwell, 1986. 188–213.

——. *Tales of Love*. Trans. Leon S. Roudiez. New York: Columbia University Press, 1989.

Lacan, Jacques. *Écrits: A Selection*. Trans. Alan Sheridan. New York: Norton, 1977.

——. *The Seminar of Jacques Lacan: Book II, The Ego in Freud's Theory and in the Technique of Psychoanalysis 1954–1955*. Ed. Jacques-Alain Miller. Trans. Sylvana Tomaselli. London: Norton, 1991.

——. *The Ethics of Psychoanalysis: 1959–1960. The Seminar of Jacques Lacan, Book VII*. Ed. Jacques-Alain Miller. Trans. Dennis Porter. London: Routledge, 1992.

——. *The Seminar of Jacques Lacan, Book XX: On Feminine Sexuality, The limits of Love and Knowledge Encore 1972–1973*. Trans. Bruce Fink. London: Norton, 1998.

Laplanche, Jean. *Essays on Otherness*. Ed. John Fletcher. London: Routledge, 1999.

Laplanche, Jean and Serge Leclaire. 'The Unconscious: A Psychoanalytic Study.' Trans. Patrick Coleman. *Yale French Studies*, 48 (1972): 118–175.

Laqueur, Thomas. *Making Sex: Body and Gender from the Greeks to Freud*. Cambridge, Mass.: Harvard University Press, 1990.

LeDoeuff, Michele. *Hipparchia's Choice: An Essay Concerning Women, Philosophy, etc.* Trans. Trista Selous. Oxford: Blackwell, 1989.

Lefort, Claude. *Democracy and Political Theory*. Trans. David Macey. Cambridge: Polity, 1988.

——. *Democracy and Political Theory*. Trans. David Macey. Minneapolis: University of Minnesota Press, 1992.

Levay, Simon. *The Sexual Brain*. Cambridge, Mass.: MIT Press, 1993.

Levin, Susan. *Dorothy Wordsworth and Romanticism*. New Brunswick: Rutgers University Press. 1987.

Levi-Strauss, Claude. *The Elementary Structures of Kinship*. Trans. James Harle Bell, John Richard von Sturber. Ed. Rodney Needham. Boston: Beacon Press, 1969.

Lewis, David and Langton, Rae. 'Defining Intrinsic,' in David Lewis, *Papers in Metaphysics and Epistemology*. Cambridge: Cambridge University Press, 1999.

Lloyd, G.E.R. *Polarity and Analogy: Two Types of Argumentation in Early Greek Thought*. Cambridge: Cambridge University Press, 1966.

Lloyd, Genevieve. *The Man of Reason: 'Male' and 'Female' in Western Philosophy*. London: Methuen, 1984.

——. 'No-One's Land: Australia and the Philosophical Imagination.' *Hypatia* 15.2 (Spring 2000): 26–39.

Locke, John. *An Essay Concerning Human Understanding*. Ed. Peter H. Nidditch. Oxford: Oxford University Press, 1975.

——. *Two Treatises of Government*. Ed. Peter Laslatt. Cambridge. Cambridge University Press, 1988.

Lovejoy, Arthur O. *The Great Chain of Being: A Study of the History of an Idea*. Cambridge, Mass.: Harvard University Press, 1936.

Macdonell, Diane. *Theories of Discourse: An Introduction*. Oxford: Basil Blackwell, 1986.

MacIntyre, Alasdair. *After Virtue: A Study in Moral Theory*. London: Duckworth, 1981.

MacKinnon, Catharine A. *Feminism Unmodified: Discourses on Life and Law*. Cambridge, Mass.: Harvard University Press, 1987.

Macpherson, C.B. *The Political Theory of Possessive Individualism: Hobbes to Locke*. Oxford: Clarendon Press, 1962.

Matthews, Gareth B. 'Aristotelian Essentialism.' *Philosophy and Phenomenological Research* 50, supplement (Autumn 1990): 251–262.

Mellor, Anne. *Romanticism and Gender*. New York: Routledge, 1993.

Millett, Kate. *Sexual Politics*. London: Rupert Hart-Davis Ltd, 1971.

Milton, John. *Paradise Lost*. Ed. Alastair Fowler. London: Longman, 1971.

——. *Complete Prose Works of John Milton*. Ed. Don M. Wolfe *et al.* 8 vols. New Haven: Yale University Press, 1953–1982.

Minow-Pinkney, Makiko. *Virginia Woolf and the Problem of the Subject*. Brighton: Harvester, 1987.

Mitchell, Juliet. *Psychoanalysis and Feminism*. New York: Pantheon Books, 1974.

Moi, Toril. Sexual/Textual Politics: Feminist Literary Theory. London: Methuen, 1985.

Montag, Warren. *The Unthinkable Swift*. London: Verso, 1994.

Montrose, Louis Adrian. '"Shaping Fantasies": Figurations of Gender and Power in Elizabethan Culture.' *Representations* 2 (1983): 61–94.

Oakley, Anne. *Sex, Gender and Society*. Aldershot: Gower, 1985.

Okin, Susan Moller. *Justice, Gender, and the Family*. New York: Basic Books, 1989.

——. 'Political Liberalism, Justice, and Gender,' *Ethics* 105.1 (1994): 23–43.

Olson, Paul A. '*A Midsummer Night's Dream* and the Meaning of Court Marriage.' *ELH*, 1957.

Orgel, Stephen. 'Nobody's Perfect: or Why Did the Renaissance Stage Take Boys For Women.' *South Atlantic Quarterly* 88 (1989): 7–29.

Ortner, Sherry B. 'Is Female to Male as Nature is to Culture?' in *Woman, Culture and Society*. Ed. Michelle Zimbalist Rosaldo and Louise Lamphere. Stanford: Stanford University Press, 1974.

——. *Making Gender: The Politics of Erotics and Culture*. Boston: Beacon Press, 1996.

Owen, G.E.L. *Logic, Science and Dialectic: Collected Papers in Greek Philosophy*. Ed. Martha Nussbaum. London: Duckworth, 1986.

Paglia, Camille. *Sexual Personae: Art and Decadence from Nefertiti to Emily Dickinson*. Cambridge Mass.: Yale University Press, 1990.

Parker, Holt N. 'The Myth of the Heterosexual: Anthropology and Sexuality for Classicists.' *Arethusa* 34 (2001): 313–362.

Pateman, Carole. *The Sexual Contract*. Stanford: Stanford University Press, 1988.

Plato. *The Collected Dialogues of Plato*. Ed. Edith Hamilton and Huntington Cairns. Princeton: Princeton University Press, 1963.

Popper, Karl. *The Open Society and its Enemies: Volume 1, The Spell of Plato*. London: Routledge and Kegan Paul, 1945.

Protevi, John. *Political Physics: Deleuze, Derrida and the Body Politic*. London: Continuum, 2001.

Rawls, John. *A Theory of Justice*. Cambridge, Mass.: Harvard University Press, 1971.

Richards, Janet Radcliffe. *The Sceptical Feminist: A Philosophical Enquiry*. Harmondsworth: Penguin, 1982.

Rorty, Richard. *Consequences of Pragmatism: Essays 1972–1980*. Sussex: Harvester, 1982.

Ross, Marlon B. 'Naturalising Gender: Woman's Place in Wordsworth's Ideological Landscape.' *ELH* 53 (1986): 391–410.

Rubin, Gayle. 'The Traffic in Women: Notes on the "Political Economy" of Sex.' *Toward an Anthropology of Women*. Ed. Rayna R. Reiter. New York: Monthly Review Press, 1975.

Saussure, Ferdinand de. *Course in General Linguistics*. Ed. Charles Bally and Albert Sechehaye in collaboration with Albert Reidlinger. Trans. Wade Baskin. London: P. Owen, 1960.

Saxonhouse, Arlene W. 'The Philosopher and the Female in the Political Thought of Plato.' *Political Theory* 4.2 (1976): 195–212.

Schiebinger, Londo. *Nature's Body: Gender in the Making of Modern Science*. Boston: Beacon Press, 1993.

Schor, Naomi. 'This Essentialism Which is Not One: Coming to Grips with Irigaray.' *The Essential Difference*. Ed. Naomi Schor and Elizabeth Weed. Bloomington: Indiana University Press, 1994. 40–62.

Scott, Joan. *Gender and the Politics of History*. New York: Columbia University Press, 1988.

Sedgwick, Eve Kosofsky. *Epistemology of the Closet*. Berkeley: University of California Press, 1990.

Shelley, Mary. *Frankenstein*. Ed. Maurice Hindle. Harmondsworth: Penguin, 1992.

Showalter, Elaine. 'Feminist Criticism in the Wilderness.' *The New Feminist Criticism: Essays on Women, Literature and Theory*. Ed. Elaine Showalter. London: Virago, 1986. 243–270.

Shulman, Bonnie. 'What if We Change Our Axioms? A Feminist Inquiry into the Foundations of Mathematics.' *Configurations* 4.3 (1996): 427–451.

Solmsen, Friedrich. 'Tissues and the Soul: Philosophical Contributions to Physiology.' *The Philosophical Review* 59.4 (1950): 435–468.

Spelman, Elizabeth V. *Inessential Woman: Problems of Exclusion in Feminist Thought.* London: Women's Press, 1990.

Spender, Dale. *Mothers of the Novel: 100 Good Women Writers Before Jane Austen.* London: Pandora Press, 1986.

Spivak, Gayatri. Interview with Elizabeth Grosz, 'Criticism, Feminism, and the Institution.' *The Post-Colonial Critic. Interviews, Strategies, Dialogues: Gayatri Chakravorty Spivak.* Ed. Sarah Harasym. New York, 1990. 1–16.

Stanton, Donna C. 'Difference on Trial: A Critique of the Maternal Metaphor in Cixous, Irigaray and Kristeva.' *The Poetics of Gender.* Ed. Nancy K. Miller. New York: Columbia University Press, 1986.

Todd, Janet. *Feminist Literary Histories.* New York: Routledge, 1988.

Tompkins, Jane. 'Me and My Shadow.' *Gender and Theory: Dialogues on Feminist Criticism.* Ed. Linda Kauffman. New York: Basil Blackwell, 1989.

Tönnies, Ferdinand. *Community and Civil Society.* Ed. José Harris. Trans. José Harris and Margaret Hollis. Cambridge: Cambridge University Press, 2001.

Vernant, Jean-Pierre. 'Divine Body Dazzling Body' in *Fragments for a History of the Human Body, Part 3.* Ed. Michel Feher. New York: Zone, 1990.

Warren, Karen. Ed. With Barbara Wells Howe. *Ecological Feminism.* London: Routledge, 1994.

Warren, Karen. Ed. *Ecofeminism: Women, Culture, Nature.* Bloomington: Indiana University Press, 1997.

Weed, Elizabeth and Naomi Schor. Eds. *Feminism Meets Queer Theory.* Bloomington: Indiana University Press, 1997.

Whitford, Margaret. *Luce Irigaray: Philosophy in the Feminine.* London: Routledge, 1991.

Williams, Donald C. 'Form and Matter, II.' *The Philosophical Review* 67.4 (1958): 499–521.

Wittgenstein, Ludwig. *Philosophical Investigations.* New York: Macmillian, 1958.

Wittig, Monique. 'Homo Sum.' *Feminist Issues* 10.1 (1990).

——. *The Straight Mind and Other Essays*. Fwd.Louise Turcotte. London: Harvester Wheatsheaf, 1992.

Wittreich, Joseph Anthony. *Feminist Milton*. Ithaca: Cornell University Press, 1987.

Wollstonecraft, Mary. *A Vindication of the Rights of Woman* in *The Works of Mary Wollstonecraft*. Vol. 5: Ed. Janet Todd and Marilyn Butler. London: William Pickering, 1989.

——. *A Vindication of the Rights of Men: with, A Vindication of the Rights of Woman and Hints*. Ed. Sylvana Tomaselli. Cambridge: Cambridge University Press, 1995.

Woolf, Virginia. *A Room of One's Own*. London: Grafton, 1977.

Wordsworth, William. *Poetical Works*. Ed. Thomas Hutchinson. Rev. Ernest de Selincourt. Oxford: Oxford University Press, 1969.

Yeats, W.B. *Collected Poems*. London: Macmillan, 1982.

Young, Kate and Olivia Harris. 'The Subordination of Women in Cross-Cultural Perspective.' *Papers on Patriarchy*. Lewes: Women's Publishing Collective, 1976.

Index

Adams, Parveen 82
Adorno, Theodor 9, 24, 101
Althusser, Louis 118
androgyny 13, 126
anthropology 45, 46, 49, 176, 191, 192–3, 211
Aristotle 5–8, 11, 16, 18, 20–3, 25, 43, 47, 83–4, 95, 97, 98, 160, 235, 236
Armstrong, Nancy 107
Augustine, Saint 19, 71
Austen, Jane (*Pride and Prejudice*) 107–8

Barrett, Michèle 87, 118, 129–30, 135
Beauvoir, Simone, de 3–4, 8, 14, 143–4, 232, 253
Benhabib, Seyla 77, 100
Berger, Peter L. 13
Berkeley, George 8
Bersani, Leo 231–4
binaries 5, 9, 13, 46–8, 51, 54–62, 78, 93, 100, 119, 178–9, 180, 189, 190, 198, 200, 204, 223, 229, 230, 234, 235
biology 2, 4, 6, 9, 10, 15, 17, 27, 31, 33, 38, 43, 50, 52, 57, 80, 85, 87, 88, 101, 110, 116–19, 129–30, 135, 137, 139–40, 142–3, 146, 148, 154, 155, 159, 161, 167, 191, 192–3, 195, 203, 209, 211, 226, 229, 236
Blake, William 2, 74–5
Bloom, Harold 14–41
Blumenberg, Hans 95
Bordo, Susan 100
Bostock, David 6
Bourdieu, Pierre 1, 6, 49–50, 51, 124, 192, 253

Braidotti, Rosi 85–7, 145
Brownmiller, Susan 130
Butler, Judith 52, 92, 109, 152, 169–72, 173, 205, 211–15, 218, 228, 230–5, 242–3, 253–4
Byron, George Gordon (*Don Juan*) 74

Cealey Harrison, Wendy 173, 254
Céline, Louis-Ferdinand 165
chain of being 20
Cheah, Pheng 192
Chodorow, Nancy 137–43, 146, 148
chora 58, 166–7, 169
Christianity 2, 19, 21, 23, 24, 58, 70, 209
Cixous, Hélène 48
Coleridge, S.T. 240, 241
Collingwood, R.G. 96
Cooper, John M. 6
Copeland, Peter 10
Copjec, Joan 156–7, 254
Cornell, Drucilla 57, 84–5, 164, 256
cosmology 2, 6, 20, 23, 94
Culler, Jonathan 54

Daly, Mary 14, 130
Daston, Lorraine 16, 28
deconstruction 54–8, 165, 168, 172–9, 229, 247
Deleuze, Gilles 53, 179–91, 193, 206, 210, 217, 219, 221, 226
Delphy, Christine 9, 13, 135
Derrida, Jacques 8, 41, 45, 47, 52, 53–8, 97, 150, 152–3, 166, 172–9
Descartes, René 15, 99–100, 117, 205, 226, 255

différance   150, 177–8
Diprose, Rosalyn   203
Dumont, Louis   96, 105
Dworkin, Andrea   14, 82

eco-feminism   134, 146
Edelman, Lee   230
Elizabeth I   30–1
Elshtain, Jean Bethke   107
empiricism   89–90, 176, 243, 245
Engels, Friedrich   102–3, 128–9
English, Jane   114
enlightenment   62, 66, 74,
    76–9, 93, 100, 119–21, 126,
    144, 145, 241
equality   78–9, 90, 120–2, 125,
    126, 128, 145, 146, 198
essence, essences   8, 9, 12–15,
    17, 20–4, 36, 57–8, 60, 67,
    74, 76, 82–4, 98, 99, 101,
    103, 110, 114, 115, 122,
    125, 126, 128, 130, 135,
    141, 145, 179, 188, 200–5,
    213, 216, 220, 223, 225,
    230, 234, 235
essentialism   13–14, 43, 50, 82,
    84–8, 127, 146, 168, 200–1,
    227, 229, 236, 257
evil   22–3

Fausto-Sterling, Anne   10, 43
Felman, Shoshana   153
Felski, Rita   45, 86, 255
Filmer, Robert (*Patriarcha*)   104
Findlen, Paula   123
Firestone, Shulamith   81, 129
first-wave feminism   117–19, 145,
    239–40
form   5, 16, 17, 19, 21, 24, 25,
    27, 28, 32, 39, 40, 41, 59,
    69, 73, 74, 76
Foucault, Michel   8, 18, 29, 88, 89,
    206–11, 215–17, 218–20, 233,
    234
Frankenstein   74, 239–52
Freud, Sigmund   1, 55, 111–12,
    120, 137–9, 146–8, 173–4,
    187, 188, 191, 194–6, 197,
    199, 205, 206, 207, 222,
    233, 246

Gatens, Moira   159–60, 224–8,
    234–8, 243, 255
genetics   15
Gilbert, Sandra M.   141
Gilligan, Carol   141, 146
Glover, David   255
Goethe, J.W. von (*Sorrows of Young
    Werther*)   242
Goldmann, Lucien   107
Gray, John   1
Green, Karen   114, 123, 126
Greenblatt, Stephen   26, 29
Grosz, Elizabeth   100, 150–1, 159,
    189, 196–7, 217–24, 228, 235,
    243, 255–6
Guattari, Félix   179–91, 193,
    206, 210, 217, 219, 221
Gubar, Susan   140, 141
Guillaumin, Colete   133, 135

Habermas, Jürgen   77–8
Hacking, Ian   13
Hamer, Dean   10
Haraway, Donna   86–7, 135
Hardt, Michael   95, 96, 226
Harris, Olivia   46
Hartman, Geoffrey   141
Hartmann, Heidi   130, 131
Hayles, N. Katherine   5
Heidegger, Martin   7, 25, 97–9, 205
Heilbrun, Carolyn   13
Hobbes, Thomas   96–7,
    101–2, 103, 104, 109, 110,
    114, 127, 144
homosexuality   10, 17, 228
Hood-Williams, John   173, 254
Hope, Trevor   205
Horkheimer, Max   101
Hume, David   89, 93–4, 111,
    112–13
Hundert, E.J.   23

ideology   118, 124, 130, 132, 135,
    136, 140, 146, 184, 187, 216,
    217, 237–8
imaginary   47, 60, 61, 98, 155–6,
    164, 193, 196–9, 203, 222
incest prohibition   161–2,
    164, 165, 170, 177, 184–5, 187,
    191, 192, 198, 207

Irigaray, Luce 7, 11, 52, 56, 85, 87, 92, 97, 98, 159, 196, 198–205, 217, 221–5, 227, 228, 232, 253, 256

Jaggar, Alison 141
Jones, Anne Rosalind 168
Jouissance 153–6, 168, 193–4, 233
Joyce, James 165
Julius Caesar 32

Kant, Immanuel 77, 94
Kaplan, Cora 255
Keller, Evelyn Fox 100
King, Helen 1
Kirby, Vicki 47, 57, 150, 192
Koyré, Alexandre 95
Kristeva, Julia 52, 88, 145, 147–8, 165–9, 196, 253, 256

Lacan, Jacques 148–50, 152, 161, 165, 167, 168, 179, 181, 185, 191, 192–200, 201, 207, 255
Langton, Rae 25
Laplanche, Jean 154, 155
Laqueur, Thomas 26–8, 41, 52, 256
Lauretis, Teresa de 235, 254–5
law 38, 94–5
Leclaire, Serge 154
LeDoeuff, Michèle 47
Lefort, Claude 94, 95
Levay, Simon 10
Lévi-Strauss, Claude 45–6, 148–9, 160–4, 169–70, 172–7, 179–87, 189, 191, 192, 207, 232
Levin, Susan 140
Lewis, David 25
liberal feminism 78–81, 90, 91, 100, 115, 119–26, 130, 143, 144
Lloyd, G.E.R. 5
Lloyd, Genevieve 59–62, 100, 225, 228, 256–7
Locke, John 83, 88, 89, 102, 103, 104, 109, 110, 236–7
logocentrism 172, 174–6
Lovejoy, Arthur O. 29
Luckmann, Thomas 13

Macbeth 29–32
MacIntyre, Alasdair 95
MacKinnon, Catherine 80–2
MacPherson, C.B. 103
marriage 2, 53, 72, 123–4
Marx, Karl 102
Marxism 108, 120
Marxist feminism 103, 126–36
matter 2, 4, 5, 9, 10, 24, 27, 38–41, 62, 76–80, 88–97, 99, 100–1, 213, 254
matter–form 41–51, 54, 58, 93, 167, 169, 234
Mellor, Anne 140, 141
metaphor 4, 8, 11, 41, 54, 231
metaphysics 3, 6, 46, 82, 88, 98, 104, 147, 168, 172–6, 194, 199, 204, 215, 256
Midsummer Night's Dream 29–39, 40, 44, 243, 250
Millett, Kate 81, 257
Milton, John 94, 107, 141
  Paradise Lost 62–75, 242–4, 247, 250
Minow-Pinkney, Makiko 168
Mitchell, Juliet 135, 137, 160, 198
modernism 53
Moi, Toril 87–8, 145, 168, 200, 257
Montag, Warren 89
Montrose, Louis 30–1, 37
morphology 159–60, 196–7, 198, 218–23, 227, 228

nature 16–20, 28, 29, 31, 33, 35, 36–9, 42–4, 70, 94–6, 99, 101–5, 108, 110, 114, 121, 133–5, 143, 160–4
nature–culture 41, 43–7, 57, 160–4, 170, 176, 180, 198, 203, 225
Negri, Antonio 95, 96, 226
new historicism 29–30
novel 107–9

Oakley, Anne 9
Oedipus complex 136–43, 147, 164, 182–7, 193–8, 206–7, 222, 223
Okin, Susan Moller 78, 119
Olson, Paul A. 29

Orgel, Stephen 26
Ortner, Sherry 6, 45, 46, 124, 164
Owen, G.E.L. 6

Paracelsus 242
Paradise Lost 62–75, 242–4, 247, 250
Parker, Holt N. 192, 208
parody 213–14, 231–4
Pateman, Carole 106–15
patriarchy 82, 84, 86, 87, 104–16, 130–1
performative 109, 211–15, 227, 230, 233, 242, 253
phallogocentrism 97, 174, 178
phallus 148, 158, 164, 165, 174, 186–7, 191, 193, 198, 200, 203, 222, 225, 227, 233
Plato 1, 5–8, 11, 18, 21, 23, 41–3, 46–7, 51, 53, 60, 71, 78, 83, 92, 97, 124, 167, 199, 205
  Symposium 53
  Timaeus 4, 40, 42, 52, 58, 60, 70, 76, 166
Plutarch (*Lives*) 242
Popper, Karl 95–6
postmodernism 53
post-structuralism 85
power 102, 104, 106, 114, 118, 135, 207, 210, 216–17, 219, 230
pragmatism 8
Protevi, John 174
psychoanalysis 49, 135–44, 146–9

queer theory 137, 171, 172, 206–16, 219, 228–34

race, racial difference 60, 180–1
Rawls, John 114–15
reason 16, 18–19, 41, 54–5, 58–62, 63–75, 91, 93–4, 117, 118, 119, 145, 205, 239–40, 256–7
Renaissance drama 28
Richard II 32
Richards, Janet Radcliffe 79–80
rights 3, 78–80, 81, 101, 119, 120, 122, 124, 134, 145, 189, 198, 203

Robinson Crusoe (Daniel Defoe) 107
Romanticism 74–5, 140, 196–7, 239–52
Rorty, Richard 77
Ross, Marlon B. 140
Rousseau, Jean-Jacques 109
Rubin, Gayle 160, 164, 257

Sartre, J.-P. 253
Saussure, Ferdinand de 148–9, 151–2
Saxonhouse, Arlene W. 60
schizoanalysis 188
Schor, Naomi 201, 223
science 5, 7, 41, 61, 80, 83, 89–90, 93–5, 99, 101, 104, 239–40, 244
Scott, Joan 143
second-wave feminism 81–2, 124, 126–135, 142, 144–6, 240–1, 255, 257
Sedgwick, Eve Kosofsky 228–30
sexual difference 51–2, 85, 110, 120, 129, 134, 137, 148, 161, 168, 170, 180, 187, 189, 192–205, 208, 220–1
Shakespeare, William 28
  Julius Caesar 32
  Macbeth 29, 32
  Midsummer Night's Dream 29–39, 40, 44, 243, 250
  Richard II 32
  Tempest 33, 36
Shelley, Mary (*Frankenstein*) 74, 239–52
Shelley, P.B. (*Prometheus Unbound*) 74, 240, 241
Showalter, Elaine 141, 142
Shulman, Bonnie 5, 11, 47
signifier 23–31, 149–55, 163–4, 171, 185–6, 194, 195, 197, 198, 212–14
social construction 8, 9, 10, 12, 31, 38, 43, 50, 77–8, 81, 117–18, 134, 135, 215, 229, 236
social contract 113–14
Solmsen, Friedrich 7
soul (*psyche*) 20, 22–4

Spelman, Elizabeth V.   59
Spender, Dale   142
Spinoza, Baruch de   225–6
Spivak, Gayatri Chakravorty   84–5
Stanton, Donna C.   168
Stoics, Stoicism   207
structuralism   8, 48, 148–50, 152,
    160, 175, 176–8, 216
structure   13
subject, subjectivity   8, 15, 88–93,
    98, 104, 115, 117, 138, 142, 145,
    152–4, 166, 168, 179, 184, 187,
    189, 191, 194, 200–4, 209,
    211–14, 228, 231, 232, 242
substance   11, 24, 58, 76, 97–101,
    105, 117, 120, 174, 188, 206,
    209, 213, 216, 230, 234
symbolic   198
Symposium (Plato)   53

techne/praxis   131–3
Tempest   33, 36
third-wave feminism   82–8,
    145–52, 168, 241–3
Timaeus (Plato)   4, 40, 42, 52, 58,
    60, 70, 76, 166
Todd, Janet   142

Tom Jones (Henry Fielding)   107–8
Tompkins, Jane   141
Tönnies, Ferdinand   95

unconscious   136, 148

Vernant, Jean-Pierre   2, 41
Volney, C.-F. (*Ruins of Empire*)
    249

Warren, Karen   134
Weed, Elizabeth   223
Whitford, Margaret   204
will   22–3
Williams, Donald C.   22
Wittgenstein, Ludwig   77
Wittig, Monique   47–8, 83,
    129, 218
Wittreich, J.A.   63, 64
Wollstonecraft, Mary   79–80,
    90, 91–2, 105, 119, 120,
    122, 123, 124–5, 126
Woolf, Virginia   53, 190
Wordsworth, William   1

Yeats, W.B.   53
Young, Kate   46